SCOTTISH COUNTRY

C. S. Clarke

June 1936

Hills of Knoydart from Loch Hourn
Robert M. Adam

SCOTTISH COUNTRY

Fifteen Essays
by
Scottish Authors

EDITED WITH AN INTRODUCTION
BY
GEORGE SCOTT MONCRIEFF

WISHART BOOKS LTD.
1935

PRINTED IN GREAT BRITAIN BY
WESTERN PRINTING SERVICES LTD., BRISTOL

CONTENTS

		Page
INTRODUCTION	*by G. Scott Moncrieff*	ix
THE NORTH-EAST : THE COLD SHOULDER OF SCOTLAND	*by J. R. Allan*	3
GALLOWAY	*by Bernard Fergusson*	25
A VALLEY IN AYRSHIRE	*by James Fergusson*	45
CAITHNESS AND SUTHERLAND	*by Neil M. Gunn*	59
ORKNEY	*by Eric Linklater*	77
ANGUS AND MEARNS	*by Fionn mac Colla*	99
IN THE SHETLAND ISLANDS	*by Hugh MacDiarmid*	119
THE OUTER ISLES	*by Hector MacIver*	139
LOTHIAN	*by W. Mackay Mackenzie*	159
FISHING FOR TROUT IN THE WEST HIGHLANDS	*by Moray Maclaren*	181
THE CENTRAL HIGHLANDS	*by Ian Macpherson*	199
SKYE	*by G. Scott Moncrieff*	215
PERTHSHIRE	*by Campbell Nairne*	231
THE BORDER	*by Colin Walkinshaw*	249
FIFE	*by J. H. Whyte*	267

LIST OF ILLUSTRATIONS

Hills of Knoydart from Loch Hourn *frontispiece*

Plate

A Fishing Town, Aberdeen 1

The Gairland Burn, Galloway 2

The River Girvan, Ayrshire 3

Ben Stack, Sutherland 4

Near Finstown, Orkney 5

The North Esk, Angus 6

Scalloway, Shetland 7

The Barra Isles 8

Berwick Coast, Lothian 9

Glencoe and Loch Leven, Argyll 10

Glen Affric, Inverness 11

Dunscaith Castle, Isle of Skye 12

The River Tay, Perth 13

Ewes Water, Borders 14

Rathillet, Fife 15

INTRODUCTION

Scottish Country is intended to give the spirit of fifteen divisions of Scotland as felt by fifteen writers who are either natives or intimately acquent with their respective subjects. It is not, therefore, a guide-book, it aims rather at being a second primer for the intelligent foreigner and a selection of studies for the Scotsman himself: and, it is to be hoped, a book that any country-lover may read with pleasure. I, for one, speaking not as editor but as a Scot, have gained a deal of pleasure, and more, from the following essays. It has, of course, been impossible to include the whole of the country in a book of this size. I think it will be found that the land has been well covered; but it is no reflection upon, let us say, Mull or Stirling, Dumfries or Cromarty, that they are not represented. The selection has been largely determined by the *loci* of suitable authors, but attention has been paid to the demands of North, South, East and West. Personally, I am particularly glad that it should have been possible to represent both Orkney, the birthplace of Mr. Eric Linklater, and Shetland, the present home of Mr. MacDiarmid, which, lying at a distance which includes a sea-crossing aptly described by Mr. Linklater, are too frequently overlooked. I should like to see all maps of Scotland delineated with these islands in their proper places instead of in the middle of the Moray Firth (a position that misleads the ignorant, including government departments). In their proper places they provide a strangely new and satisfying cartography.

I was asked to edit *Scottish Country* as a sequel, or perhaps rather as the complement, to *English Country* which was published last year under the distinguished editorship of Mr. H. J. Massingham, and I am tempted to draw comparisons between the two books and from thence between two very different countries. I suppose the most immediately obvious difference is one of contour as is apparent in the photographs; and the camera certainly does Scotland greater justice than it can for England. Conversely, of course, in Scotland the problems presented by hill scenery have contributed to prevent her from receiving her due in terms of paint, since the painter seems inclined to lose himself—as artist—in the hills and his picture in concentration on the physical original. Another divergence in the photographs is the large number of pictures in the present volume that depict, in some guise, the sea. The sea appeared in none of the English photographs. A fact that made me realize how much more intimately the sea concerns the Scot and embraces his land.

Other differences become manifest in the various essays. One, which I had scarcely appreciated before, is the greater persistence of provincial consciousness manifest in some of the following contributions than in any of those in the English volume. To Mr. Allan, for example, Aberdeen, the country, is incomplete if Aberdeen, the town, is not taken into consideration: his essay amply justifies his contention. To the English writers the word 'country' entailed a sharp differentiation from 'town' in any modern form. One is reminded therefore that England has gone further on the road to centralization than we have: that we are still nearer the 'provincial independence' which Mr. Massingham is not alone in regarding as desirable. England, generally speaking, focuses on London. For Scotland there is no single focus: London, as the seat of her government and wealth, shares place with Glasgow, the centre of her population, and Edinburgh, her historical capital with its famous sights and derelict dignity. Scotland has still a proportionately larger rural population, even although her slums and her overcrowding are considerably worse.

In Scotland from the days of the grub-streeter Pinkerton, there has always been much debate and dissension as to racial division and characteristics. Absurd arguments, with foundations at best conjectural, more often merely romantic, have divided her sharply into Celt and Saxon, with a small quota left for the Norseman. I expect many children are still taught, as I was, that the Lowlander is a Saxon and the Highlander a totally different beast, a Celt. But reasoned historical investigation has long since shown that the Highland-Lowland division is, historically speaking, comparatively recent, not even serving to divide the two different Celtic branches: that the country as a whole has the foundation of the mysterious Pict, fused with the Celtic colonization: that the Saxon element is restricted to Lothian, and even there as a minority: that the Norse element, although more considerable than the Saxon, was mainly absorbed by the already constituted racial background. Only in Orkney and Shetland was the Norse overlay made direct upon the Pictish foundation and the Celtic step omitted—except that the Picts were probably Celtic themselves. Racial questions are notoriously controversial and too frequently futile. I only dilate upon them here because the Hanoverian elements in Scotland and England and their spiritual successors of to-day have been at such pains to foist upon us a fictitious parentage; and bastardy—as opposed to racial fusion—is an imputation that demands reply. It is not a racial difference that distinguishes the Gallovidian from the man of Caithness, nor is it a division of importance. The real difference lies, as Dr. Mackay Mackenzie reminds us, at the English Border.

While not giving undue importance to racial matters one likes to think, nevertheless, that there is indeed a resurgence among the Celtic peoples. It does not do to be too sanguine: but in Ireland the process is manifest, and there seems to be a stirring both in Wales and Scotland. Perhaps few in Scotland will yet claim, with Mr. mac Colla, a 'renaissance,' but I think our country shows more symptoms of pregnancy than it has since the birth of the earnest, crippled child of the Reformation. Mr. MacDiarmid is our greatest artist of the time: and it is significant that his poetry has a lyrical quality distinct from that of any written to-day in England, but in definite accord with that of the Irish poets from Yeats to Joyce and the younger men of the present day. This resurgence if it does emerge will be very different from the 'Celtic Twilight:' it will not be defeatist, it will not rest heavily on the past.

Nor will any possible Scottish revival be restricted to the romantic formulæ of the twilight days. The essays of the ensuing authors are different as the countrysides of which they write, and I should imagine that the most circumscribed reader will find something particularly to his liking. Like Mr. Massingham in *English Country*, I reserve the right to my own preferences, but, as editor, am relieved of the task of divulging them. Dr. Mackay Mackenzie, although he comes from further North has made considerable study of the Lothians and dextrously clarifies for us the confused history of the most fertile corner of Scotland, giving at the same time a vivid impression of her scenes of arable and moorland, sea coast and slag heap. Mr. mac Colla gives us of the life of Angus, a province in which the largest town, Dundee, is an intrusion and not, like Montrose or Brechin, a part to the whole. Mr. Bernard Fergusson has the viewpoint of the walker who has gained his intimacy with Galloway from long periods of solitude enlivened by the companionship of the night's lodging. While to Mr. James Fergusson 'a landscape is history . . . a very old parchment on which successive generations have written a record of their doings': to him the loveliness of his Ayrshire valley is wrapped in its continuity with the past. I think he has some affinity with the eighteenth century that he so much admires. Mr. Walkinshaw shows us in the Borders a countryside preserved, despite accessibility, through its lack of mineral resources: a land with its own history and tradition. Mr. Neil Gunn deftly, in his own manner, differentiates for the stranger Caithness from Sutherland. He knows and loves them both, seeing, besides their differences, what they have in common with each other and with the rest of Scotland, making very pregnant comments upon the need for continuity of habitation: comments that are particularly tragic when applied to Sutherland. Mr. Ian Macpherson brilliantly conveys the Central Highlands, past and present, with a grim index to the future, in an essay that lives with the characters who people it. He is acutely conscious of place-love, and its roots that go deeper than reason. Mr. Allan is a province-proud Aberdonian, and he affords us a comprehensive but fine-pencilled view of the land of Aberdeen. Mr. J. H. Whyte shows us in Fife an almost insular county which, unlike the rest of Scotland, is particularly memorable for its villages. Fife's quality is cumulative, not spectacular, and Mr. Whyte indicates how she also has a provincial life welded of farmland, fishing and small industrial townships: composite factors for all their dissimilarities. Mr. Nairne in the neighbouring county runs back to childhood, to the days when one was a passenger on a pushbike. He revels in the variety of Perthshire and follows his recollections to their logical conclusion on the brink of the future. Mr. Eric Linklater's vitality and wit need no introduction; here he employs them to describe his native scene with a vigour appropriate to that most prosperous of Scottish countrysides, the Orkneys. He takes us from island to island, the characters from the sagas animating for him the quiet slopes and the bright blue of inland seas. It is amusing to notice that he gives us a version, different in detail and even in the moral applied, of what appears to be the same legend as one related by Mr. Gunn. Mr. MacIver is a young Lewisman and, I think, the only native Gaelic speaker among the contributors, a factor that marks the style in which he writes of the Outer

SCOTTISH COUNTRY

THE NORTH-EAST
THE COLD SHOULDER OF SCOTLAND

by

J. R. ALLAN

As the traveller goes up the valley of Strathmore on a summer day he sees the blue Grampian Hills standing like a rampart against the north. On this side there are gracious white-walled farmhouses, quiet villages shadowed with ancient trees, and rich red clay of manifold fertility. It is a pleasant land of little streams, set on the warm south of the enfolding hills that close away the north and seem to mark the limit of the known world. Passing from Strathmore into the Howe o' the Mearns, the traveller comes always nearer to the hills. Beyond Laurencekirk the bare bones of the land begin to show, and looking north from the heights above Stonehaven, the traveller may wonder apprehensively what lies across the hills. If he has an imaginative mind, he may people the far side with fearful anthropophagi who bear their heads beneath their shoulders, or with raw red caterans who wear the kilt and feed on thistles. Whatever he expects, every mile beyond Stonehaven bears witness to a changing scene. The rich fields of the Howe have given place to a windy scarp between the hills and the brilliant blue of the cold North Sea. Plenty and easy living are left behind; the bite of the east wind is in the air; and the stony fields betoken a sparse amenity. The quality of the scene has hardened, as if the land, narrowing between the hills and the sea, had taken on the colder qualities of both. This inhospitable, inhuman air increases as the hills run down to the sea, until at Girdleness the traveller stands on eternal rock beaten for ever by the green waves. He may think then that he has reached a point where the ancient enmity of sea and land leaves no place for mortal man. And looking northwards over the bay he may think he has found a new dead world of insentient things. For there, glittering silver and cold as death, are the granite towers of Aberdeen.

This first impression is valuable for, however well Aberdeen conceals its heart, it wears its character on its face. More than any other Scottish town, it is exactly what it looks. Earth and sea have fashioned it —a grudging but not infertile earth and a cold but not unlovely sea. It is hard as they are hard and it has a strong inveterate life, a force of nature fit to maintain its place with either. As Aberdeen is, so is the whole North-East. The country has made the town; the town reflects the spirit of the country; and both together have a character quite unique in Scotland. That character is hard and self-sufficient as the result of a long successful war with circumstance; but these qualities do not deny life, rather they deepen it with stronger passions. So the North-East outwardly cold and spiritually bare, can yet reveal a power of human nature that when roused is brother to the stormy seas.

Aberdeen is provincial in the older sense of the word. Consider the lie of the land. The North-East may be said to extend from Stonehaven in the south to

Moray in the north. It is a varied Lowland country, watered by lovely rivers and cut off from the Central Lowlands by the Grampian Hills. Looking it over, you might say that Nature had done some regional planning on her own. There towards the south-east Aberdeen stands between the Dee and the Don. She is the proper size, neither too big nor too small, but providing most amenities of a civilized existence. Her university, her schools, her theatre; her mills, workshops and warehouses; her harbour, markets and railways fit her to be in everything the capital of the province. Then three lines join her to a number of satellite towns which act as centres for the country districts. Thus we have a province, dependent on the primal industries of agriculture and fishing, and admirably provided with little towns which are closely associated both with the capital and the villages round about them. The city serves the country; the country serves the city; and the fortunes of the one affect the fortunes of the other. Glasgow might flourish by the heavy industries though the Ayrshire farms fell derelict; and Dundee might prosper on jute though never a potato was planted in Angus; but Aberdeen must stand or fall by agriculture and fishing. She can be prosperous only if the province is prosperous. For she is the capital.

So if the traveller wishes a short view of the North-East he may take a walk along the Union Street of Aberdeen on a Friday afternoon at three. Friday is market-day in Aberdeen and country people come in from all over the North-East to buy and sell. During the earlier part of the day they are busy at the various markets but by three they have a leisure hour to promenade the main street of the town. That fashionable hour also brings out the town society, business men leave their offices for coffee, and the students from King's go west for a studious hour at the pictures. In short at three o'clock in Union Street the traveller will meet representatives of the whole provincial world.

It has been claimed that Union Street is one of the finest in the world but it would be difficult to find anything apart from local patriotism to support that claim. Its architecture is undistinguished and its vistas are limited to a Salvation Army Citadel at one end and a Church Training College at the other. The only things remarkable are the cold white granite and, at a winter sunset, the embattled splendour of the west. At three on a Friday afternoon Union Street is just the main street of the North-East, as hard in aspect and as bracing in spirit, the true setting for the crowds who take their pleasure there.

The traveller soon discovers the main types of this society. Business men dressed immaculately after a pattern, step out smartly as if to build their fortunes on the last half-crown of discount. Beautiful ladies from the West end, dressed as immaculately as their husbands and cut as much to a pattern, take the air so graciously that it is unthinkable that their elegance could be founded on a thing so low as trade. University wives go past, less well-dressed than the others perhaps, but trying to show thereby that beauty bought by trade is vulgar. There are other wives who have little to do with elegance and even less with beauty—I mean the bustling ladies from the tenements who walk a mile to save a penny and have a genius in the art of beating down the merchant. They are always in a hurry in case a good thing just eludes them. An occasional country gentleman stalks along, very tall, very thin, very tweedy and very wrinkled about the hose. He has a far-away look in his eyes, as of one who seeks the far horizons or is touched with incipient paranoia. Bands of three and four young students may try to imitate his careless stride but the brightness of their eyes betrays their interest in the world around them. And then the farming people. The traveller might study their variousness for hours. Thin hairy men, with enormous hands and feet and a trapped expression on their faces, carry unwieldy parcels in the wake of round little weather-beaten women whose heads are full of bargains. Others stand on the kerb in twos and threes, immovable, talking and spitting and looking about them with no more sign of excitement than if the street were their twenty-acre fields at home. Bigger men in every way, men who can take an overdraft as if they were doing the Bank a favour, carry their bellies high and engage each other in a grave discourse. They are the representatives of a new order just as the others represent the old. But occasionally the traveller may see one who represents something older still—a man or woman with a ruddy face and white hair, who sees the town in quiet wonder and in whose look there is the innocence of a simpler age.

There is the North-East on market day, a crowd of types though superficially different yet essentially the same. At heart they are all the product of one environment and, if you discount their strange sophistications, a common character remains. Its elements are a good conceit, a keen off-taking wit, a measured though not a mean economy, a due regard for all the public virtues and a private taste for all the pleasant vices. Simple people with a simple faith—that they have inherited the earth and in due time will succeed to the Kingdom of Heaven.

In order to obtain a closer view of the North-East the traveller must follow the crowds to their homes for they are a home-keeping people, and it is the criterion of a sound morality to have a house of one's own. The business men and their wives will go west to the granite terraces of Mannofield and Rubislaw where they will dine at seven, play bridge till eleven and bed at twelve with the consciousness of another day well spent. Next to business, bridge is the justification of their lives; it is more than a game, it is a sign of grace. The radio, the cinema and golf are possible alternatives to bridge. There may even be a little conversation, although that will be confined to the various affairs of the family, and neighbours, for, since all observe the Right Thing, no other aspect of eternal truth can have any existence. In religion, politics and everything else they are conservative; their twin articles of faith are five per cent. and dinner jackets; they are individualists in everything except morality and manners. The Empire is safe in their hands.

If he follows the students and the professors' wives, the traveller will find the greatest glory of the north. Across the hills towards the Don there lies the university town of Old Aberdeen. It is a small, but exquisite place, no more than a street and a few lanes, once surrounded by green fields but now encroached upon by a deplorable housing-scheme. At one end of the High Street King's College stands on a level lawn, a fair memorial of the olden time; at the other end of High Street is the prim, ridiculous and charming Town House, an eighteenth-century discourse in stone; and at the top of the green and ghostly Chanonry beyond, the Cathedral of St. Machar keeps watch above the murmuring Don. There, in less than a mile, is the most complete and perfect part of ancient Scotland; the College, the Town House, the Cathedral and between them old grey houses, fantastically disarrayed, turning their gables to the street and forming quiet lanes beneath the trees. Yet it is not a show-piece. It has a tradition and a life of its own. Not so long ago it was a burgh in its own right with a self-elective council and a reservoir in the Town House loft. It had even a brewery, and that, with its Kirk and College, surely gave the citizens all a reasonable man should ask. But the burgh has been absorbed in the city and the site of the brewery is underneath the College. The temporal glory has departed. The spiritual glory remains. King's College, which with Marischal College in the new town, makes up the University of Aberdeen, was founded by the good Bishop William Elphinstone, Chancellor of Scotland, in 1494. It is beautiful in design; its chapel is indeed a holy place enriched with pious craftsmanship; its library is full of noble works. Yet these are not the whole of King's. Greater and more lovely is its air of peace and wisdom, as if knowledge flowered upon its walls and the love of the Lord were its true foundation. Set in a land where life is a bitter personal thing, the College keeps its witness to calm eternal truth and with its great age corrects the little age of men.

The College, however, is a mute witness and few

people have time to ask its meaning. The North-East is in no way behind the rest of Scotland in the traditional love of learning. Every schoolboy, you might say, carries a matriculation form in his pocket. But the love and the learning, it is to be feared, are only traditional. The reality is a job. For the ambitious a university degree is the passport to a respectable place in society; and to secure that passport in the shortest time is the high ideal of the student. No wonder then that the teachers who have breathed the, presumably, more liberal air of Oxford and Cambridge, become weary of struggling with barbarians and seek what escape they may find in the delicious odour of intrigue that permeates the drawing-rooms of a university town. Marischal College in the new town, a glittering false facade in granite, is more truly part of the grim North-East. It houses the modern side of the University, the science and medical schools, and in spite of its deplorable ventilation, produces a highly efficient type of graduate who does extremely well in the South. Aberdeen is proud of Marischal College, and not without reason, for it symbolizes all the practical successful things that are dear to the people's hearts. The University has thus a unique place in Aberdeen. It is not the whole town as in the case of St. Andrews; nor a relatively unregarded part as in the case of Glasgow; but one of the city's main activities whose products rank along with granite, fish and paper in its exports. The University is a business asset, which is all to the dignity of learning at the present day. But what the good Bishop William would think about it, Heaven alone can tell.

There is yet another part of the town—the miles

and miles of grey granite tenements where the honest working people live. They are well-doing and intensely respectable, as the accounts of the Savings Bank and the Co-operative Society will show. They are Radical on the whole; Socialists of an idealism tempered by the disillusioning east wind. They have nothing of the fire and the fury, the intolerable sense of social injustice which springs from the mixture of races on the Clyde. They themselves are of a relatively pure stock; however various their origins, the type was fixed some centuries ago and no new racial element has affected it in any appreciable degree. They are the folk of the North-East and there are none other like them under the sun. They are good workmen and do their jobs as well as they have to, but work is not their principal interest in life. Cricket for a few, bowls and golf for many, and the football team for all. The fortunes of this team in the Scottish League competition are alternately the joy and the despair of the town. Crowds of ten thousand and upwards attend the matches at Pittodrie; but every man, woman and child takes a personal interest in the result. The team have been successful but never superlatively so, at least since the War, and their failure to achieve the highest honours has inspired many newspaper correspondences of great bitterness besides some rare vituperation from the shilling side. At the same time we must note that the Club have transferred many players at fees reaching into thousands of pounds. Whatever distinctions the team may have missed, the Club has the honour of being one of the few in Scotland to pay a regular dividend on its shares.

The social life of this class is divided between the

Church and the Cinema. The Church offers a great variety of entertainment, from Women's Guilds to Afternoon Whist, and gives almost continuous employment to those who are interested in good works. That being so, it is difficult to account for the even greater popularity of the Cinema, considering its tedious preoccupation with dramas of desire. But it may be that the frivolous passions shadowed on the screen offer the patrons a much-needed escape from their own intense and very practical affections.

It is time to have done with Aberdeen, now that the traveller has seen the life that exists in its shining wilderness of stone. But before we leave it for the country, let us try to comprehend it at a glance. There then is the bay, looking east towards the rising sun. And there are the Dee and Don, twin rivers, with their mouths two miles apart. And there on the rising ground between them is the town, incomparably fair and shining with its granite spires uplifted to the high blue heaven. Here at the mouth of the Dee is the harbour whence the little fishing-boats go dipping bravely into the stormy north. Beyond it the long line of the sands broken by the mouth of the Don then sweeping away to meet the far horizon. Near at hand the houses are closely packed but as we look westward trees appear, and out along the Dee the suburbs of the rich preserve a choice amenity. It is a clean town, a prosperous town and one intensely Scottish. It is Lowland Scots for no Highland brain achieved that bright efficiency. Yet it is Lowland Scots with a difference. The worst horrors of industrialism passed it by. It was allowed to grow slowly as its background's needs demanded. It is the North-East's work in every way.

The land out of which this town has grown is divided into a number of well-defined districts such as Buchan, Formartine, Deeside, Donside, Strathbogie and Banff. These are farming country, though there is a certain amount of manufacture in the satellite towns which are their centres. Then all along the coast there are fishing-villages and towns, communities of a widely different nature from their agricultural neighbours. Together these make up the background of the town.

It is to Buchan that the traveller should turn first, for Buchan is that part where the peculiar qualities of the province are found at their strongest. Nature has made it so. Buchan is the cold shoulder of Scotland, lying north of the Ythan and east of the Deveron, where the coast turns sharply towards the Moray Firth. Though there is some rich land near Fraserburgh and a few good rigs elsewhere, Buchan is a dreary windswept plain, open on two sides to the sea, and broken by only one round hill. Anywhere else this hill would never win a second glance, but, as it breaks the monotony of parsimonious fields, it is loved by the grateful inhabitants of these parts. In their gratitude they have cut the figures of a horse and a deer on its sides, and the White Horse of Mormond has a more than local fame. It is the one touch of wonder from the Ythan to the sea. Going north along the coast road from Aberdeen, the traveller must get the impression of a treeless land, broken up into small farms where hard work and careful management can win a competence but little more. This impression gets stronger when the Ythan is crossed, and in the heart of Buchan it becomes plain that agriculture is a desperate struggle with the inhospitable land. Success is possible only by a fanatical care of the pence and such fanaticism leaves little room for sweetness and light. Here, you might say, the cold granite lies nearest the surface; therefore the people are nearest the granite, and so, more than all others in the North-East, they have its hard unyielding quality. They will succeed where weaker men will fail; they will break but they will not bend; and they have done much to make Aberdeen the hardy town it is.

Buchan, however, has its surprises. At her very heart lies the Abbey of Deer, in whose gracious ruins the traveller may recapture something of the glory of monastic Scotland. And yet further inland, where the Ythan runs along the Bonnie Howe, stands Fyvie Castle, perhaps the finest baronial house in Scotland, equal with if not superior to Glamis. It has its place in Scottish history. Seton, Chancellor of Scotland, owned it; the Gordons followed; and Lord Leith maintained the romantic tradition by making a fortune out of steel in the U.S.A. But Deer and Fyvie are somehow irrelevant to Buchan whose symbols are the windy acres and the seas eternally beating at her rocky shores.

As Buchan is dominated by the featureless Mormond, Central Aberdeenshire is dominated by Bennachie, and the difference between the hills is the difference between the lands around them. Bennachie is a brave blue peak above the valley of the Don, and Central Aberdeenshire is romantic country in comparison with the plain of Buchan. It is better wooded, more diversified and far less grim. Some parts, of course, are dreich enough but others have a quite enchanting beauty. Along the valley of the Don and up by Logie at the foot of Bennachie, the traveller could imagine himself on the road to fairyland, if he goes in early autumn when the woods are full of wild raspberries and the children, themselves burnt ripe as raspberries, go harvesting in the brakes all day. The illusion of fairyland will not bear proximity with the towns. The men who built Inverurie, Turriff and Oldmeldrum have not improved on nature, for those communities have a good conceit of themselves that the outer world is slow to share. They are bare and grey of aspect, unredeemed by architectural beauty or the quaint reliquaries of time. They are just the efficient centres for a practical countryside. There may be fairies on the slopes of Bennachie, but they have no place on the tidy farms below and even less in the dusty village squares. They would be in danger of being put away for loitering with intent to subvert the natives from their sacred rite of gathering gear.

The men of these parts are in all things practical. They are among the cleverest farmers in Scotland and they are unsurpassed in the art of making intelligence repair the poverty of nature. It is no exaggeration to call them artists, for they have a natural taste for quality and many of them would go bankrupt rather than turn to the mass-production of inferior stock. Some have won an international fame as breeders of pedigree cattle. The late William Duthie of Collynie, in many ways a typical Aberdeenshire farmer, had a talent that amounted to genius and his Shorthorn cattle gained him an unrivalled reputation in agriculture, not only in Scotland but throughout the world. During the boom years following the War, his golden calves would average a thousand guineas each. Nothing like

C

that had been seen before; it may be long before anything comparable is seen again; but the Aberdeenshire farmers have the tradition and the stock and time may send another genius.

However, it must not be thought that business is the only concern of Central Aberdeenshire. The bigger farmers at least have a highly developed social life. The War, which brought them more money than they had ever dreamt of, also gave them ambitions of which their fathers would hardly have approved. They thought to set up as gentlemen. They took to dinner-jackets, bridge swept over them like plague, and they have even started a Hunt in a county where foxes are almost unknown if not altogether extinct. Where the fathers bred quality, many of the sons are content to imitate it; and it is possible that the social accomplishments have been bought at the price of nobler virtues.

It is always vain to mourn a change of fashion. Yet I would be sorry if the folk of these parts were to be refined out of all likeness to their fathers. What splendid men those fathers were. Their speech was the index of their nature, using all the resources of the rich vernacular. Their idioms bore the mark of high imagination. When they chose they could speak from the very centre of their thought in phrases, like themselves, intransigeant. As men they were whole and complete, worthies with a magnificent zest for living and a familiar disregard of death. They could get gloriously drunk at market but you would seldom miss them from their pews on Sunday. The peace of the Augustans was upon them. They were at ease in their own world and confident of the world to come. They were the true pagans of the modern time, with all the pagan virtues, love of land and living. They cared little for fashion, but walked by their own light and that light was not wholly darkness. I think the good Bishop William would have understood them for he and they had great loyalties to this life if not to Heaven, quite different from the prim propriety that has taken the place of roistering and honest morals.

I have said that the North-East is cold but, though the granite is all around them, it has not entered into the hearts of the people. They have warm and fertile passions with a religious care for life. That is fortunate. As happens in agricultural districts where a large proportion of unmarried men are employed, the rate of bastardy is very high, but though the children may be unwanted they are seldom uncared for. A cottar may have too many of his own but he will never refuse to shelter his daughter's. The little uncles and nephews play happily together on the floor, to the wonder and confusion of the proper world. It may be thought a pity that the farmers do not apply to their servants those criteria of quality with which they govern the mating of their cattle, but society in these parts still holds firmly by the right divine of reproduction at will, irrespective of every economic law. It is an old custom and is likely to outlive all others.

It is a complete anticlimax to turn to royal Deeside. The river valley is beautiful of course. It has an equable climate, romantic scenery, everything to make it Paradise in summer, and a very successful Paradise it has become. It is a select Paradise for the Best People. The Best People, however, are more at home in the *Bystander* than in Aberdeenshire, and, in trying to make them a perfect setting, Deeside may lose its native character. Perhaps Balmoral has something to do with this. Mr. Scott-Moncrieff in an inspired moment invented the epithet 'Balmorality' to cover the Highland Games, the Lancashire millionaires in kilts and all the parade of this bright but alien season. At Balmorality we may leave it. When the last word has been said, it is foolish to add indifferent footnotes.

Though the North-East is Lowland country, it lies on the eastern fringes of the Highlands and it is sometimes difficult to say where Lowland ends and Highland begins. We may suspect Deeside of being pseudo-Highland now, though it may have been really Highland once; and, as we go up beyond Huntly across Banffshire to Keith and Elgin, the difficulty may arise again. Yet the district should be Highland for it is the great distillery country where some of the finest Highland whisky is made. The scenery too is Highland where the lordly Spey sweeps down between its steeply wooded banks. Here is a gracious majesty that is not truly of the North-East.

Banff, the county town, on the other hand, is Lowland through and through. Its atmosphere is something akin to Old Aberdeen in its quiet yet sufficient life, but while Old Aberdeen has a mediæval air Banff is wholly eighteenth-century. Not all of it is charming; the modern part is rather cheerless; but the centre of the town still wears the aspect of a county burgh of a hundred and fifty years ago. Life then, I imagine, had a provincial elegance in Banff, its polite assemblies were frequented by the County, and it maintained a proper disregard for the foibles of the modish world. Here as in Old Aberdeen the traveller may experience a complete æsthetic pleasure that is little affected by the modern dwellers in the place. Now that, I think, marks both these towns as differing in spirit from their background because it is one of the unique qualities of the North-East that you cannot see it apart from the people who inhabit it. In a still greater degree this puts Elgin quite out with our province, for Elgin, set in the rich Laich o' Moray, lives, as it were, in the broken shadow of its great Cathedral and its spirit has small relation to the very modern life within its streets. Certainly this is not a part of that North-East where, in Aberdeen, in Buchan, in the Garioch and in Strathbogie, the traveller must be so conscious of the will of the living; but in Old Aberdeen and in Elgin he walks among the dreams of the immortal dead.

There remains one more part of the North-East that helped to form the Aberdeen from which we began. I mean the fishing communities around the coast. The principal of these are Peterhead and Fraserburgh in Buchan and Portsoy, Buckie and Cullen in Banffshire. Though they have local differences, they have more important similarities, and they must be taken together in completing our survey of this idiosyncratic land.

These communities are as much of the sea as those are of the land. They are built close to the sea, they make their living by it, and they pay it a yearly tribute from their finest lives. It is a grey sea and the towns have taken on its colour. Indeed they might be waves thrown up on land and frozen into stone. They have no shade, no escape from the sand and the salt wind, and their only music is the drumming of the waves. Not that they are wholly unappealing. Fraserburgh, Macduff and Cullen have charms for those who like a bracing air, and there are a number of quaint small bays that offer a quiet harbourage and an abiding peace. But the coast is lacking in colour and, except in the brilliant height of summer, there is no relief from the monotones of earth and sea. Life is not an easy matter in such communities. It requires a courage and tenacity even greater than anything we have noticed in the hinterland of Buchan. We might find a similarity between the farmers and the fishermen but it would be superficial for there is a fundamental difference in their natures. The fishers are as emotional as the farmers are phlegmatic. This emotionalism is repressed, perhaps for years at a time, for the environment is not one to encourage any facile display of feeling, but it breaks out periodically in waves of evangelical religion. It is not surprising that a fisher community should be religious, for a life spent with only a board between you and eternity makes the love of the Lord a very present comfort. Therefore it is inevitable that repressed emotion should find an evangelical release. During these ecstasies, whole villages go drunk on the Blood of the Lamb. Led by pastors whose eloquence seems inspired by Heaven, crowds enjoy a change of heart, publicly confess their sins and sometimes renew their souls by total immersion of their bodies in the sea. The fleshly lures of the world are cast into bonfires in the street; powder, pipes and novelettes are thrown to the flames as children of the Devil; the crowds, emotionally renewed and spiritually refreshed, join in revival hymns with the sweet sound of angels rather than of men. The ecstasies do not last; the brethren are prone to retrogress; but the fear of the Lord is always with them and they never attain that pagan dour indifference which, in spite of Kirk and

Sunday School, is so remarkable among the farming people. The religious ecstasy is at once the product of and the reaction to the bitter quality of their lives. It is also their most notable difference from their country neighbours since it is so unlike the temper of the landward men whose ecstasies take little heed of Heaven. If that is so the traveller might think that the fishers are not an integral part of the North-East, but I doubt if it is possible to discount them for they have had an important influence on the fortunes of Aberdeen. The city looks to the sea as well as to the land; the fishermen have done their part in building it; and thus it is the complete summation of its various province.

Now that the traveller has seen the parts, I must try to present the whole. Reading over these pages, he may think that I have said a great deal about the people and little about the land. That is true, but I would repeat that it is difficult to see the land apart from the people and that it would not be desirable to see it apart even if we could, so close are the men to the land that bred them. Here then is the North-East of Scotland, a farming county bounded by the mountains and the sea. For the most part it is indifferent tillage redeemed from the waste at great expense of labour, treeless and of a beauty so austere as to be sometimes unintelligible to all but the most determined eye. Along the river valleys and in some strangely diverse patches there is land of great fertility, abundant shade and a sweet domestic beauty. Towards the hills, and particularly on the Spey, there is a natural grandeur that exults the senses. But as a rule we may say—To man the art, to nature the beauty—and the two are seldom found together. We have noticed also the intimate relationship between the men and the land—in the fishing-towns a real esteem for God; in Buchan a dour, a Calvinistic spirit; in the more favoured parts a pagan love of fields and herds with—in the olden days at least—a splendid zest for life; and in the lands most nearly Highland that touch of the unreal—perhaps the pseudo—that marks the borderline of West and East. We have also seen the men of those districts gathered within the microcosm of the city where they have worked upon each other and produced the hardy spirit that is Aberdeen. That spirit is practical for nothing is won except by labour in the north. Aberdeen has no resources but the land and sea—no adventitious aid of mineral wealth or vast colonial markets. Her prosperity has been won from little things which breeds a careful business mind. But, though careful, this spirit is not mean. The people have still the zest of the old pagans in their blood and when it takes command their recklessness is splendid. So we return to a paradox that Aberdeen may seem a glittering city of the dead but yet it breeds a people who at times can show the gorgeous passions of the older world. Only at times, alas; and those times increasing seldom, for an era of gentility has set upon the ancient town. Maybe its blood is growing too refined. Certainly the men who built the fortunes of the town were not in any way genteel. There is a story, grant that it is true, concerning a great citizen whose favourite sport was to go to the fishmarket, catch a fishwife, tie her petticoats above her head, then set her dancing blindly on the causeway. It was a crude sport, perhaps, but strangely enough the fishwives liked it, and the city loved the Bailie for his wit. But the days are gone when a Magistrate would sport with fishwives. How sad that the town should grow respectable—and dull. It is strange how the rich humanity and power of the great Victorians has declined into a proper and a Sabbatarian spirit until the modern town deserves the dreary epithet Victorian. Perhaps it remains eternally behind the times, enjoying under Victoria the glorious humours of the Georgian Age, and only now, a century too late, assuming the moral antimacassar and the shawl. Genteel or not, however, Aberdeen and the North-East are still the most native parts of Scotland. Lowland of course and unregenerately so, with obvious faults and virtues hard to find by strangers; but yet, when every criticism has been spoken, demanding a steadfast loyalty from its children. At the last count it is our own land and there alone we can know ourselves for what we are.

2. The Gairland Burn, Galloway

Robert M. Adam

This delight in Galloway is no disloyalty for a Carrick man. They are the same country, separated only in the thirteenth century, when a lucky lady got Carrick for her dowry. The same rugged sea-coast is theirs, the same pastures and rich soil, the same man-forsaken hill-country. Their people are identical in blood and feature, and peculiar to this corner of Scotland. There are the same white houses, the same keelie patterns on the doorsteps. In the fields, it is true, there are fewer Ayrshire cattle to be seen, and more Galloways; in fact, now that Galloway nags no longer survive as a race apart, the Galloway cow, and in particular, the 'beltie,' is perhaps the thing that most of all is the symbol of the country. A white belt round a black cow's belly may seem a curious thing over which to go into ecstasies; but to the Gallovidian returning from exile it is the first sign of home to be seen from the west-bound train.

And Galloway is home to many types of men. There are hill-shepherds and low-country men, shopkeepers and dairymen, ploughmen and tinklers; and more, perhaps, than in any other part of Scotland they are engaged in the business of their forefathers. The march of progress means little here. Railways have made their appearance, but not very bustling ones—even the Irish mail is less conscious of the importance of its errand when emerging from an English night into a Galloway morning. Motor-cars are on the roads, and petrol stations have sprung up beside them, but even some of these are pretty rustic. There are fewer handlooms about and fewer smithies; more fox-trots (scathingly referred to by an old lady of my acquaintance as 'thae dog-trots') at the village dances; more people go out to see the world, and fewer come back from it. But in spite of all, this corner of Scotland is still a corner of old Scotland, unblackened by factory chimneys and beautified by slow old speech, so that in my boyhood, which is only a few years back, I was able to peep into a life which many people imagine was dead almost before the *Cottar's Saturday Night* was written.

I was lucky indeed in my temporary guardians. I came back from school one holidays having made the acquaintance of S. R. Crockett's *Raiders*, and consequently eager to explore the country of which it tells. I discovered also two other books, Agnew's *Hereditary Sheriffs* and Barbour's poem *The Bruce*, and with these fermenting in my head nothing would satisfy me but to go and walk the country like a gangrel. My wise guardians let me go, and soon I was penetrating the country at the back of the Merrick for the first of many times. Until I left school, hardly a holidays passed without my spending two or three or more days in the hills, scrambling over them by day, and sleeping in shepherds' houses by night; and through all the long terms I would dream of that same country by night and draw untidy maps of it in my school-books by day.

The hills look biggest and most impressive from the west, from which they are seen across a broad and featureless plain. Lamachan, Benyellary, Merrick, Kirriereoch, Tarfessock, Shalloch-on-Minnoch—what a roll-call for a homesick schoolboy!—they spread north and south with hardly a dip between each summit. They look harmless enough, but in their rounded, massive shoulders are hidden many precipitous descents and overhanging crags; and it does not do to take them too much on trust. Between the Merrick range on the west and the Carline's Cairn range towering over the Glenkens on the east, there is a wild area of no such well-defined features. Here instead are a mass of tarns, irregular knolls and sudden mosses, with an occasional proper hill rising out of the jumble. The burns seem to flow out of one lochan when actually they belong to another; they seem to drain in one direction, when actually their courses bend away unnoticed in the other. The whole place is a welter of confusion, where it does not even require a mist to get you into difficulties. One autumn month, I was trying to show off my knowledge of the country to a friend by means of a short cut from the Lumps of Eglin to the Wolf's Slock. After less than a mile, I could see no way on; and in trying to find one my companion fell fifteen feet over the edge on to a boggy ledge among the rocks. Had he missed the ledge, he would have fallen a further twenty feet on to solid jags of rock, and the Cambridge boat the following spring would have had to find another No. 7. That was one of the occasions when I have retraced my steps.

Behind the Merrick, and so close under it that the shadows capture it halfway through the afternoon, lies Loch Enoch, the highest sheet of water in the British Isles. Six miles from the nearest house, it is a stiff climb to make it from any direction except the west, and then it is long and tedious; but the effort is worth while. This was in old days the Mecca, or perhaps the Samarkand, of those whose business it was to sell sand for scythe hones, for here, on certain of its shores, is to be found the finest silvery sand that ever I saw. Its tiny grains are hard and white as ivory, and on a dry day it seems to whisper as you walk on it. There is another curious feature about the loch, and that is the trout that used to be caught in it. Of late years very few have been taken, and I never saw one; but they are said to have no fins on the underside of the body. This is supposed locally to be due to the granite walls and floor of the loch, which have worn them away; but perhaps that is only a tinker's tale, at which a scientist would scoff. At any rate they provide a fair parallel to their cousins in Loch Leven.

From every shore of the loch, long arms of land stretch out to the middle where just out of reach to all of them there lies a small island, and in the middle of the island, most surprisingly, another loch. Once the eerie look of the place lured me to leave my clothes on the shore and swim out to it, and I am glad to have done it; but that is the last time that I shall go over to see Loch-in-Loch, for the water is the coldest imaginable. It was a weird place; the Fang of the Merrick, a huge circular cavity of rock in the cliff above, made a sounding-board for every breath of wind that swept over the wilderness, while the bright sun to the eastward accentuated the uncanny darkness of where we stood. My companion and I were glad to swim back again, and get out into high day.

The Dungeon of Buchan is a valley lying between two ranges of high hills, so deep and unexpected that it almost takes the breath away. After toiling up to the narrow defile called the Wolf's Slock, the farther side of the valley comes slowly into view; but so deep is the floor of it that you have to come right over the brow of the hill before you can see the hither side of it, and the chain of lochs fifteen hundred feet below you. Beyond them, the whole floor of the valley is covered with a vast expanse of water and heather-tussocks. This is the Silver Flow, and constitutes a dangerous obstacle at certain times, when there has been much rain, or when a heavy fall of snow is in process of melting. When a breeze is stirring it, a constant shiver passes over its tufted surface, and it looks like a giant trout lying panting on a river-bank, ready for the creel. Beyond it, on firmer ground, stands the hospitable but-and-ben known as the Back Hill of the Bush; and if you are in luck a column of smoke will be rising from it, to assure you of a welcome in an hour's time at this, the loneliest house in Scotland. (Nine miles from a neighbour it stands, and ten from a road end.) But between you and it lies a wearying descent; many hundred feet of boulders lying precariously on top of each other, on end, sometimes, or with a quarter-inch margin between safety and a crash. Heather grows between them, and if you do not wish to make the Back Hill, you can snuggle deep down in these miniature catacombs and block the crannies with handfuls of it. It is a scratchy sort of bed, though I enjoyed such a one once till the moon rose to light the way to New Galloway. It is best to struggle on while the light holds if you can, and skirting the Silver Flow (unless the weather has long been dry, or hard), knock on Adam's door. But I keep forgetting; they tell me Adam is gone now, over the hills and far away, to the Black Clauchrie. All the same, it was Adam's door when I came knocking on it for the first time, nine years ago, and asked for a bed. His sister answered me, and that night in their kitchen I spent the first of many happy evenings.

The Back Hill of the Bush must surely be what I have claimed for it—the remotest house in Scotland. The shepherd who lives there gets his supplies from the farm that employs him, away over the hill into the Glenkens; twice a month they are brought half-way to him, together with his mail, and left in an iron shelter, from which he has to fetch them. Months often pass without his seeing a soul, unless this modern Elijah's visits to the shelter happen to coincide with those of his ravens, or he foregathers with his colleague of the Glenhead or the Laggan over some strayed beasts. Once a year he goes to the Lanark lamb sales; once a year, perhaps, he may join with other hill shepherds in the early spring in trying to shoot down some of the hundreds of foxes who infest the whole region. The rest of the time his business lies only in and around the Dungeon; so he is not sorry to hear a knock on his door of an evening, and to see a strange if usually dirty face.

The first time I came into the spotless kitchen of the Back Hill of the Bush, Adam was sitting by the fire toasting his toes, a metal-capped pipe in his mouth and a book in his hands. He gave me the usual greeting in these parts—a sidelong duck of the head—without rising from his chair; but he took his pipe out of his mouth and put it back again, by way of making me welcome. Later in the evening I stole a glance at his book: it was the *Vicomte de Bragelonne*.

I have no clear recollection of that evening, but I suppose it must have followed the same course as all the other evenings that I afterwards spent there. Supper, and an excellent one, of scones and bacon and eggs and tea—hottest and strongest imaginable, falling

D

from pot to cup with that inimitable spluttering sound that only the hottest and strongest tea can achieve; gossip, about how many pairs he had had last lambing season, how many Culsharg, how many Buchan, how many Tunskeen; local history and topography, stories of the Murder Hole, of the shepherd drowned a few years before in the Silver Flow, of Billy Marshall, of the Covenanters. I do not think we had any music that night; a fiddle hung, smoke-blackened, beside the fireplace, on one of the hooks intended for bacon or braxy mutton; but it was not till my second or third visit that I prevailed on Adam to play it, and we had an orgy of such tunes as *The Flowers of Edinburgh*, *Cameron's got his Wife Again*, and *Pop Goes the Weasel*. I do not suppose he played it well, but with the atmosphere of that old-fashioned kitchen, the tap of his slipper on the floor and the music that he played, it might have been Neil Gow himself. Thus, and beneath just such black rafters, must he have often played for merry young herds, sprightly at the dancing for all their clumsy boots.

> Gay was it then with us, all the young jovial fellows,—
> Many a dance with the girls in MacGillivray's kitchen!
> Many a creel-full of peats did we burn till the morning
>   Shone through the flowers in the window.

It was always late, by country standards, when we went to bed—a box-bed, of which there were two in the room beyond the door, tired and stiff from the day spent in high winds, while the sister climbed the ladder to an attic. All too soon one would hear Adam heaving himself out of bed while it was still dark, and clumping sleepily across the floor in boots as yet unlaced to lift the latch and go out to the pump. One could lie awhile longer and listen to the burn racing past the window while one wondered whether to turn north to Loch Doon to-day, or south to the Clatteringshaws, or just to dally in the Dungeon. Eventually one would rise and breakfast, with a comfortably stubbly chin—small wonder that Adam wore an ephemeral red beard—declining the baker's bread that one used to bring as a present for Adam and his sister for the excellent home-baked stuff which seemed to them so ordinary, but to us so delicious. It was with regret, and as often as not in a downpour of rain, that one finally set off across the little kail-yard with a 'piece' in the pocket, to carry one to the next stopping-place, wherever it might prove to be.

With the new dam at the Clatteringshaws, and hydro-electric plants at Tongland and Glenlee, such modes of living are perhaps faced with a menace that will eventually kill them. One hopes that with the dam finished, and the great white scar completed across the Dee valley, the hills may regain their solitude, and their inhabitants keep their old ways of life undisturbed. They have survived until now solely because Galloway is on the road to nowhere. All through history this corner of Scotland has been singularly late in coming under the influences of the times, and equally obstinate in retaining them after they have disappeared elsewhere. Thus Galloway remained an independent Province long after Scotland and England had crystallized behind their boundaries; Gaelic lingered on into the seventeenth century, long after it had disappeared from Strathclyde and along the Border; the Covenant retained its full strength after it had waned to a mere flicker in all other of its former strongholds except Fife. So to-day the main trade routes pass it by, just as the drove-roads did two hundred years ago. There have been many efforts to make it the chief route for Irish cattle coming into Great Britain; but they reached their zenith in the middle of last century, and have declined ever since.

The small village of Portpatrick in the Rhins, that curious hammer-head of land in the extreme west, is a lasting memorial of these efforts. It was very tempting, with Ireland to be seen so close across the narrow strip of sea, to make a harbour there, not only to provide a short sea-passage for passengers and cattle, but also in case of sudden military necessity. To this end was built at great expense, about the year 1770, an admirable harbour and a military road running all the way from Dumfries, with a northward branch to Ballantrae. Within a few years the rising township had seen Peter the Great pass through on his way to Ireland, and the veterans of the Black Watch, then the only Highland regiment, arrive home after thirty-two years of foreign service, when they leapt ashore, 'kissing the ground and holding it up in handfuls.' But the only relics that remain of those spectacular days when Portpatrick nearly became a Dover are a small inner harbour, still in use, a derelict lighthouse, some ruined breakwaters, some submerged masonry and a fine old inn. Everything else has vanished in the winter gales, which defied the efforts of the best engineers in the country; and the place has reverted, save for a certain tourist traffic, to a sleepy fishing-village at the end of a laggard railway.

The district of the Rhins, different though it is from

the hill-country, is no less representative of the history, or lack of history, which has touched it. Unlike the hills, which provide many footnotes to some of the most exciting chapters in Scottish history, the Rhins have been little affected by even the most stirring events. Nowadays there are slates where once there was thatch, and threshing-machines where once the women beat out the grain with flails; but the seasons of the year do not change, and it is the seasons that mould the life of the tenant-farmer and the small-holder. The fishermen of Portpatrick, Port Logan and Ardwell have taken to petrol-engines, and only set a ragged mizzen now and then to steady their craft in a bit of a blow; but their nets are still spread on the sea-wall to dry, and their green glass floats bob up and down a couple of cables off-shore where once bobbed the corks that supported the nets of their grandfathers.

Empty along the shore are the caves where those same grandfathers once stacked Valenciennes lace, Hollands and other delicate merchandise. The rock-pigeons build and roost there, undisturbed by the splash of oars bringing the incoming goods, or the creak of carts coming to carry them away. Some of these caves are extraordinarily hard to find. There is one, barely a mile north of Portpatrick, which I have no reason to believe was really a smugglers' cave (though it ought to have been) which is typical of the kind they favoured. It can only be reached by a narrow chimney with an almost invisible entrance, opening high up on the cliff, but a few yards from the footpath that runs along the top. Climbing down it, one reaches a small cove, inaccessible from any other quarter except at the lowest of tides, and also all but invisible from the cliff-path. Not so very many miles away is an old man still living in a lonely bay, all by himself, who ran an illicit still with, I believe, considerable profit until a few years ago. But I must be careful to divulge no more.

Close by the cave already mentioned is the bay from which Portpatrick is presumed to have taken its name. Here there are two caves, standing side by side, each about twenty feet deep and twenty high, for all the world like the footprints of a giant landing from a mighty leap. Indeed, this is exactly what they are supposed to be—the marks of St. Patrick's feet when one day, unable to secure a more conventional form of transport from Ireland, he jumped the twenty miles or so of sea that intervene. One of the caves thus formed has a waterfall in its recesses; and here for a century or more lived a succession of hermits who used this sacred water to cure such diseases as rickets among the pilgrims who came to visit the spot. One Galloway chronicler, with his tongue in his cheek, tells another story of St. Patrick in these parts, how when he was returning to Ireland from his native Dumbarton he was set upon in Glenapp by some of the wild folk who dwelt there; how they cut his head off; how he preferred to wait till he got to Ireland before carrying out the necessary repairs to himself; how reaching Portpatrick he was again unable to find a ship, and how consequently, 'according to the sworn testimony of hundreds of Irishmen,' he swam across the sea carrying his head between his teeth.

The people of the Rhins differ from the people of other parts of Galloway only in so far as they must, by reason of the different nature of the country they inhabit. In blood and feature they remain the same. But it is curious how certain words are used in the Rhins which are found, so far as I know, nowhere east of Stranraer. Having said so much, I find I can remember but one of them: the word 'rattle' for a fox's earth. A keeper (not a native but, in the phrase of the district, an 'incomer') once gave me a list of several such words which he had learnt in the Rhins when first coming to Galloway, and which he had tried to use twenty miles farther east, with the air of one speaking the language of the country, without being understood. Similarly the hill-shepherds have a word 'kent' for the long stick they carry, something like the Highland 'cromag'; and that also is a word which is unrecognized elsewhere. All districts, of course, have dialect words of localized use; but surely not often to the same limited extent as here. This is due to the same causes as I have insisted on before—the little movement that takes place between parish and parish, even in these enlightened days of easier transport. As a general rule, when the Gallovidian does move, he leaves the district altogether; and it is astonishing on the other hand to find how many reach manhood without ever stirring from home. I have a soldier-servant from the Rhins who had only once been in a train before the day he joined the army; and I know also a girl from the same parish who had never been in a train until she entered one to travel to her first place in domestic service near London. Yet with all this close attachment to the soil there was nothing so rare, until recently, as illiteracy or ignorance; it needed the transfer of education to a centralized authority before such a thing came about.

One of Crockett's short stories—one of his worst, yet one of the truest sketches of the country life that he knew as well as anyone—tells of a Minister of Education who came upon a large family in the wilds towards the Merrick, and lamented to their mother the fact that owing to their remote situation they would get no education. To his astonishment she proceeded to demonstrate that their learning far surpassed that provided in his own schools. She and some of her neighbours saved enough money to hire a university student to come and teach their children during his vacations. This is no far-fetched tale, but in former days a common practice enough. On a lonely road in the Rhins there stands at this moment an old school-house, erected more than a hundred years ago by the people of the parish on their own initiative. The well-to-do gave money, the craftsmen of their craft, the farmers of their kind, the labourers of their labour; the thatcher 'theekit' it, the joiner made the desks and doors, the forester fenced it about, and for all I know the saddler (for a saddler there would be in those days) made the tawse. Then when the school was in being some widow with a child to be educated might bring a basket of eggs for the teacher, and a farm-servant would cut and stack peats at the hallan-end to feed his fire in winter. Such was their pride in education that everyone in the parish contributed what he could, whether money from his pocket, or a day's darg from the strength or skill of his hands, to build and maintain a school for their scattered needs. To-day that same school of which I am thinking is the property and responsibility of the State; the highly certificated teacher, appointed by the State, has replaced the dominie, who was in his day the pride of the parish, by whose people he was appointed and maintained, and to whom alone he was responsible. The passing of the parish school and the suppression of the parish council are the two things which have done most to standardize country life, and to destroy the rugged individuality that ought to characterize it.

With the old pride in education there has also vanished some of the old religious feeling; but in Galloway, behind the times as ever, it still retains much of its precious hold. As elsewhere, a road that in old days was black with people on a Sabbath morning now winds over the hill white and empty; for the church-goers assemble by bus, and the old colloquy after service in the graveyard is now cut short by the approach of the big blue S.M.T. But the churches are full, the singing congregational and fervent (and dragged), the sermon long, scholarly and closely followed. The intimations from the pulpit cover the doings of the Mothers' Union and the 'Rural'; the proclamation of somebody's purpose of marriage for the first and only time; the text is given out, and the handkerchief, according to the ancient convention, conceals but does not deny the progress of the 'kirk sweetie' to the mouth. The service, which opened with a psalm, closes with a paraphrase. The old 'gathering note' is used, not because the Revised Psalter prescribes it, but because it has never been abandoned. In fact the Galloway Sunday is much as it always was, but more cheerful without being less dignified.

There is, however, one communion in Galloway which is peculiar to the district. The Reformed

Presbyterian Church, lineal descendant of the old Cameronians, began in the small village of Balmaghie, in the Stewartry, under the leadership of a minister called Macmillan; and almost all its churches and adherents are still to be found in Galloway. They are the last uncompromising upholders of all that the Covenant stood for; and scattered throughout Galloway, in true Galloway fashion they remain faithful to their ancient tenets. The little village where they began their witness, when memories of martyrdoms were still fresh and barely healed, is a quiet corner where one would think that such memories of the Killing Time could hardly live for the peace that hedges it round; but they are kept alive by the martyrs' graves which are to be found, not only in it, but in almost every other parish in Galloway. 'Our fathers worshipped in this mountain' is a powerful text; 'our fathers died for their worship in this mountain' is the reading of it here; so that in some places a martial Covenanting spirit still exists. Less than twenty years ago, a descendant and namesake of one of the bitterest persecutors of those days was staying at a house near Wigtown when he had occasion to send his boots to the mending. The village cobbler took them from the servant and asked whose they were; but on hearing the hated name, he thrust them back into the servant's hands, saying:

'Tak' back thae boots; he's no' get them mended in Whithorn!'

And no more he could, so vile is the memory of the man whose misdeeds were committed two hundred and fifty years ago, and for whom, on his death, the devil is said to have come driving up the waters of Kirkcudbright Bay, 'to fetch his ain bairn.'

The worthiest symbol of the continuity of tradition hereabouts is perhaps the houses in which the people live. Modern housing schemes have their effect on towns and villages alike; and more than one perfect village in a perfect setting suffers from an eruption of modernity. Red roofs where the others are grey is bad enough, and Tudor half-wood walls among harled ones are worse still. But most of the country villages and cottages have kept to the old styles; and where new houses are being built, the owners have usually been wise enough to work in undemonstrative materials which offer little contrast to the old, and which a short passage of years will reconcile to their background. Most houses one sees are genuinely old, and well and solidly built. I have no doubt that in my peregrinations I could have slept under a leaky roof, and lived in insanitary conditions had I a mind to do so; I could have found a dirty housewife instead of ones who kept their houses spotless. But in the ordinary run of things, go where you will, you will find that most of the houses are decently kept by instinct. Their outside walls may be harled or whitewashed; intricate keelie patterns decorate the doorstep, and maybe the kitchen; the peat or coal will be neatly stacked outside; and the garden, for all that it is tended after a long day's work, would not disgrace the local 'big house.'

Most of these country cottages date from the eighteenth century. Built originally with a thatched roof, the modern slates cannot change their character. Even their inhabitants cannot achieve that transformation. Generations have passed through them, and dying have left them the same as the day they were born into them. Generations have trodden down their doorsteps; but the houses have outlived the generations. They have a patient look about them, like an old ewe that has suckled many lambs, and seen them all pass away from her. Harled or whitewashed, sombre or gay, they all have the same air of permanence in a transient world. They are as much part of the country as the hills themselves.

Less enduring, for the most part, seems man's furnishing of the fields, the dykes, hedges and fences, for enclosure came late in this country, and was hotly fought by the inhabitants, led in one district by the famous tinkler chief, Billy Marshall. Barbed wire is uncomfortably common, and wherever one goes, little strands of wool show where some sheep, intent on its own business, has scattered its bounty. Some of the low-country is rather monotonous, as there is nothing to break the view but a wooden feeding-trough, or an abandoned harrow; whereas a thorn hedge or a dyke would give extra values to the astonishingly deep shades of green that one encounters. The variety in these cases has to be sought in the sudden shriek and flash of a snipe as it jinks away from the bog at the bottom of a field, or a hare racing up the hill, or the 'bestial' turning to follow your dog with gloomy head held low. But soon you may come to the top of a rise, and rejoice to see the white farm with its attendant byres and cothouses, or the sea, or the far-away hills; and then the hollow that seemed so dull looks cosy and happily at peace. The moor, too, often has a pleasant trick of coming right down to the field's edge, so that only the breadth of a dyke—for in such places you do find them—separates heather from lush grass. Or the field may run up to a dyke that encircles the broad topmost acres of a hill, wherein are whins alive with rabbits, cropping the avenues of light green, between the turrets of dark green and yellow. In such places, if you listen, besides all the noises of nature, there is one that can always be heard from somewhere—the slow reflective rattle of a farm-cart, the most peaceful and satisfactory of all country sounds.

Here and there in summer one may see the forlorn sight of empty curling ponds—mere wet hollows with thin burns trickling out of them. But in winter they are instead the scene of great animation. There is no more thrilling sound than the rumble of keen stones, and the 'clack' of their coming together, spreading exuberance or dismay among the players. Cries of 'soop, soop!' and 'ye're in the house!' can be heard far down the road where the late-comer is hurrying at risk of limb, the puddle-ice tinkling beneath his feet. Away to the north, between blue sea and sky, Ailsa Craig, from whose granite all the stones are hewn, sits unconcernedly like a hen who neither knows nor cares who is eating her eggs. All work is suspended, bothy and school and field and farm are miraculously empty 'while the frost hauds.' Skaters skim the edge with a furtive air, well knowing they are only there on sufferance; small boys watch the play awhile, then go and slide, but always return to watch the play again; eighteen-stone Craigshalloch button-holes a friend of equal girth, and both go through the ice together. That is one picture I have of happy Galloway days.

Another, of a great wedge of geese coming skriech-ing overhead in the dark of a January morning on the fringes of Luce Bay, shot rattling on their ribs; the sandy whisper of the wind in the bents to the north; the dawn rising over the bay; and last but not least, the piles of ham and eggs to supplement the bread-and-brown-sugar and cocoa of before going out.

Another, the shepherd up the Gloon Burn burying his dog, which had killed itself leaping a dyke, pulling the top stone down to break its back; Mirk and Mist playing with my stockinged toes as I dried them at Adam's fire; the booming of the foghorn on thick days from Killantringan lighthouse; a long caravan of trudging tinkler Marshalls on the Castle–Douglas road; sprays driving on the windows of Dunskey, a mile from the sea, in the westerly gales; Criffel in rain; Anwoth in sun; and the Back Hill of the Bush in both at once.

3. THE RIVER GIRVAN, AYRSHIRE

Raphael Tuck

A VALLEY IN AYRSHIRE

by

JAMES FERGUSSON

THE valley of which I have to tell lies in about the middle of Carrick, one of the three bailliaries into which the shire of Ayr was anciently divided. It forms a basin about five miles long and two wide from hill-crest to hill-crest; and through the middle of it flows a small river. Further north, the river wanders aimlessly, until it bends back into the hills to the east from which it draws, through countless little leaping brown burns, the waters which feed it. But here it runs fairly straight, between calm green meadows where cattle graze, and stately woods of oak, beech, and fir. Its course is roughly from north-east to south-west, and when it passes out of the valley it has only a short distance to flow to reach the sea, or rather the lower part of the Firth of Clyde.

On the south-eastern side the hills rise to grassy moor and go tumbling away for barren miles towards the mountains of central Galloway. On the north-western there runs a long, wooded ridge from the top of which a magnificent view can be had of Arran, Kintyre, and Bute, with Ailsa Craig, that monstrous lump of an island, to the south, and the Argyll mountains to the north. This hill contains a vein of coarse coal and is noted for a legend, which can be traced back beyond the beginning of the eighteenth century, that it is on fire inside.

In any long-civilized country a landscape is like a very old parchment on which successive generations have written a record of their doings. The pumice-stone of time erases each record with varying thoroughness, but the palimpsest always retains something of the original inscription for observant eyes to read. The earliest records may be so faint that only the most skilful archæologist can decipher them; but for the more recent ones quite a small knowledge of the district's history may make its traces astonishingly clear. The more you read or hear of occurrences which have taken place in a country familiar to you, the more plainly the marks of them stand out upon its face. It does not take long to realize that a landscape *is* history; that layer upon layer of its past lives on in its present; that each generation that inhabits the ground enjoys a part of the fruit of its predecessors' labours while it contributes something to the convenience, the comfort, or the pleasure of its successors.

Now the history of this valley and its inhabitants has been for a long time one of my favourite studies; and it is extraordinary how, the more I examine it, the more clearly certain of the earlier inscriptions on the palimpsest stands out, and the more superficial appear those of the last hundred and fifty years or so. The twentieth century has added almost nothing to the record; for the rebuilding of small houses or farm-buildings, or the cutting and re-planting of woods, produces no more than slight and temporary changes in the landscape as a whole. The nineteenth century added only a little: the railway, almost unnoticeable among the deep woods which conceal its passage along the north-western slope of the valley, two or three coal-pits equally well hidden, an extra stone bridge over the river, an enlargement of the area planted with trees, and an extension of hedges and fences. Generally speaking, it did no more than deepen the impressions of the eighteenth century, since which period the character of the valley, then chiefly created, has remained almost entirely unchanged. One important alteration, however, was made in the early part of the nineteenth century—the straightening and embanking of a part of the river's channel, to minimize flooding. This work was done in George IV's time, and it has made parts of the river a good deal less picturesque than, according to a pen-and-wash drawing of 1813, they used to be, though much less damaging to the surrounding pastures. Nowadays, after a few hours' heavy rain, a kind of reminiscence of the river's old course appears in the pools which fill the depressions in the fields where it used to run.

To start, however, with the earliest 'layer' of history's records on the valley, you must come up one of the glens cutting into its south-eastern side. Here stands a fragment of an ancient peel-tower. Seventy years ago it was still nearly a complete building; but to-day there only remains one end-wall, entire from foundation to gable, showing the height of the original structure, and a heap of tumbled masonry, blurred by grass and bracken into a rough green mound. The age of this tower is beyond conjecture. It is supposed to be one of the oldest of its kind in Scotland to be built of hewn stone, and possibly dates back to the middle of the fourteenth century. But immeasurably older as a dwelling-place is a site about half a mile further up the glen, by the side of a burn tributary to that which splashes among the rocks below the tower. This is an oval-shaped mound standing in the hollow between two spurs of the hill sloping down to the burn. It is much shorter and narrower at the top than at the bottom; in other words, its sides slope steeply upwards to a flat top, which is about thirty yards long and ten or twelve wide.

The merest glance at this oddly shaped mound will tell you that it is not a natural structure. Its regularity is too striking to be accidental. Round its foot, moreover, runs a double bank, somewhat broken away here and there by the tunnelling of rabbits, but irresistibly suggesting an old rampart. The whole aspect of the place stamps it as not only an artificial construction, but a place of refuge and defence. It is known locally as 'the Moat Knowe,' and such amateur archæologists as have seen it—I do not think an expert has ever been here—have agreed in calling it a 'pre-historic' stronghold. It is a vague but obvious conclusion: no more can be said about it; the Knowe stands in this lonely glen, aloof, green, and mysterious, the first faint, indecipherable scratch upon our palimpsest.

There is another scratch—of a date perhaps nearly the same as that of the Moat Knowe, perhaps very different, but equally uncertain—up in the hills a few miles beyond this glen. It consists of about a dozen low hummocks, in shape like blunt L's or hatchets, lying in a nearly flat piece of ground about the size of a couple of tennis-courts. A generation ago they were very clear to the eye. To-day the combined depredations of grass, heather, sheep, and draining have made it almost impossible for a stranger to detect them. They are supposed to be the remains of a primitive village of turf dwellings. They are as likely to be ancient places of burial. But, together with the Moat Knowe, they are the only remaining trace of evidence of who inhabited our valley and the surrounding hills before the first dawn of history.

Of the first impression made on this part of Scotland by the early Christian Church the traces are more numerous and more definite. St. Machar and St. Kieran, reputed two of the first Christian missionaries to evangelize Carrick and Galloway, left the district the legacy of their names, attached to more than one consecrated site. Indeed a study of the etymology of Carrick place-names seems to show that at some period the whole of this part of the country must have been studded with chapels, wayside shrines, and the dwellings of priests. Of the first colonization of this neighbourhood by the pioneers of Christianity we have two distinct and tangible memorials. One is the square outline of the foundations of a tiny chapel which once stood on the brink of a narrow and thickly-wooded glen half-way down the valley's south-eastern side. It used to be known by the simple name of 'the Lady Chapel,' and seems to have been a place of pilgrimage in pre-Reformation times. What remained of its walls was pulled down over a century ago, and the stones used, with mistaken piety, to build a kind of small family mausoleum in the village churchyard.

Not far from the old peel-tower, on a high slope which looks down to the sea, and commands a splendid view of the lower part of the valley, stands another memorial of the early missionaries. On this site also there once stood a chapel, known as Machrikill or 'Machar's shrine.' All trace of the chapel walls has long disappeared, but in the little clump of trees which marks the place there still stand two roughly-hewn blocks of stone of quite extraordinary interest. By comparison with similar relics at Iona and elsewhere, they have been identified as the bases of crosses. Each has the deep slot in its top which once held the foot of the cross; and the smaller of the blocks has in addition the outline of a cross rudely incised on one face of it.

After the days of the saints there comes a long gap in our valley's record. The only thing that helps to fill it is its nomenclature. All over Carrick the place-names are predominantly Gaelic. Curiously enough, the Gaelic strain in Ayrshire names weakens as you go northward through Kyle. Its strength in southern Ayrshire testifies to the old kinship of Carrick with Galloway, which, as Lord Hailes wrote in his *Annals of Scotland*, 'anciently comprehended not only the country now known by that name, and the stewartry of Kirkcudbright, but also the greatest part, if not the whole, of Air-shire.' Gaelic was the language widely spoken in Galloway up to the seventeenth century, and there can be no doubt that it survived in Carrick also for a considerable time. The fact that every river, every considerable hill, and every old house and farm bears a name of Gaelic derivation tells us something of the racial characteristics of Carrick's inhabitants during the Middle Ages. It is significant, also, that there seems to be no Norse element in local nomenclature at all, even along the coast.

The next clear writing on the parchment is a part of

the story of Robert Bruce, who began in this neighbourhood his great campaign for the recovery of his kingdom. Turnberry, where he landed after his crossing from Arran, is only a few miles away, and when fresh English forces threatened him after his victory there, it was to the heights overlooking this valley that he retreated before he moved south into Galloway. On the topmost ridge of the long hill rising just south of the glen where the old tower stands, a line of mounds marks the site of Bruce's encampment, where he lay for several weeks. It was an admirable choice for such a refuge. The whole floor of the valley lay open below him, so that no hostile force could approach him unobserved, and behind him was a wild country, practically impassable to strangers, into which he could at any time make his retreat. The traces of the King's entrenchments are very clearly to be seen even to-day; but it is difficult to find the entrance to a small cave in the steep western face of the hill which is traditionally indicated as another of his refuges. It opens on to a narrow ledge concealed by thick-growing stunted hawthorns, and is no larger than a fox's earth. Inside there must once have been comfortable room for several men, but the roof has partially collapsed and the cave is now little more than a passage.

After the days of Robert I the marks of habitation on our valley become more frequent and more enduring. We have reached a kind of miniature Homeric age, when Carrick is full of warring lairds banded together under one or other of the great houses, when the Earls of Cassillis grow to such power as to be known as 'the Kings of Carrick,' and when

'Twixt Wigtoun and the toun of Ayr
And laigh doun by the Cruives of Cree,
Nae man sall get a lodging there
Unless he court with Kennedie.

This period, when every man whose wealth or dignity could support it fortified his dwelling, sprinkled the valley with stone houses or peels. The fragment in the glen is as much as remains to-day of any of them. The rest have either disappeared or become merged into succeeding buildings, sometimes large mansions, sometimes farms; only their names survive. But in the days of James V they were so numerous as to be a very noticeable feature of the scenery. '*Multis amœnis villis cingitur*' was George Buchanan's description of the river four hundred years ago, when he lived not far from it as tutor to Gilbert, Earl of Cassillis; and the description might stand to-day, though there is not one of those pleasant houses which Buchanan would recognize in its present form.

Apart from buildings, it is difficult to decipher what the sixteenth and seventeenth centuries left to us. Under the last of the Stewarts the neighbourhood began to make its reputation for cattle and corn—'*pascuis fecunda*,' says Buchanan, '*non infelix frumento*.' Men began to burrow into the hill-side on the north-west in search of the coal whose outcrops darkened the earth on the lower slopes; they established regular fords over the river, and something of a road was made up the valley towards Ayr. Then came the terrible days of civil war, when men killed each other for the sake of the King or the Covenant. Even in this little corner of Scotland there were sharp divisions. Most of the people were staunch Covenanters. The Maybole copy of the Covenant may be seen in the National Museum of Antiquities at Edinburgh, and many of the names scrawled upon it are still among the commonest in the valley. Many of the inhabitants however were of the Episcopalian persuasion. The owner of the tower in the glen raised a troop of horse for Montrose—and here a line of writing on our parchment comes clear through the marking of later records. In 1827—not so very long ago, historically speaking—there died an old man who remembered seeing in his boyhood the remains of the banks constructed in a field near the river to form the temporary enclosure in which his great-great-great-grandfather kept the horses he gathered for the service of the King's Lieutenant-General in 1649.

The cavalier's son served the same cause in a much less honourable manner. In 1685 he guided a party of dragoons from a farm of his to a cottage a mile or two away where a certain zealous supporter of the Covenant lived. The man heard the approach of his enemies just too late, and was shot while trying to make his escape through a window. The story is recorded in Wodrow's history, and the unfortunate Covenanter's tombstone keeps the memory of his betrayer unenviably green. The churchyard where it stands is a lovely spot, encircled with old trees. The church is now a ruin, but every year a service, known locally as 'the preaching,' is held in the churchyard in memory of the Covenant martyrs, known and unknown, of the parish. It is simple but indescribably impressive, and to see and hear it is to realize how strong, even to-day, is the recollection of 'the killing times.' Other traditions of those days hang about the valley. By the road that leads out of it towards Barr, for instance, stands a great boulder known by the name of 'Peden's Pulpit.' On a hill-top on the other side of the valley, a concealed hollow is pointed out as the place where conventicles used to be held. A few years ago, also, the directions of a bed-ridden old woman of eighty-five led me to discover the grave of two other Covenanters on the moor near the head of the glen where the Lady Chapel used to stand. Her brother, long since dead, 'aye used to gang there to read his Bible on a Sabbath afternoon.' After a good deal of search I found the small tilted stone which marked the spot; it bore four deeply-cut initials and the *memento mori* device of a skull and crossbones common on gravestones of the seventeenth and eighteenth centuries.

And so we come to the eighteenth century and the main inscription, save for a few erasures and insertions, on our parchment.

The great change in the face of Scottish landscapes, due to the advance in knowledge and practice of agriculture which was one of the principal features of Scotland's history in the eighteenth century, began comparatively early in Ayrshire. The peak of the change in our valley came in the 'seventies. The owner of most of the land in it, whose direction of its fortunes lasted from the year before George II died till two years before Waterloo, was a voluminous correspondent and an almost morbidly careful preserver of other people's letters to himself. As a result, it is clearer to us than it could otherwise be that the aspect of the valley on which we look to-day is almost entirely his creation.

This laird completely transformed his estate. He drained, enclosed, and manured his fields, clearing them of stones some of which were so large that they had to be blown up with gunpowder. He opened a lime-quarry to increase the fertility of his fields—the huge caves left by the excavations still survive—established a rotation of crops, and experimented with grass-seeds. He imported English sheep to improve the breed of the native stock. He planted trees indefatigably on both sides of the valley. He laid out roads which to-day have become main highways to the neighbouring towns, and paths through all the most picturesque parts of the policies around his house. He built two really beautiful stone bridges over the river, as well as many smaller ones over burns, and he built a great many small houses and farm-buildings, which were up to the best standards of housing of his day. By the time he died there was little for his successor to do with the estate but maintain it in the condition in which he left it. He had found the valley a half-tamed wilderness and left it a garden. Its beauty of to-day is largely the creation of that eighteenth-century laird. He made his little corner of Scotland neither a rich man's pleasance nor a market-garden, but the perfect mixture of productive utility and natural decoration: wood and field, road and river, blended in the landscape in ideal proportion and arrangement.

It is a green and seductive country, this valley. It has neither the bleakness of the north nor the luxury of the south. It is the loveliest place in Scotland, which is to say, in the world. But to me a large part of its fascination derives from the strong impression it produces on my mind of continuity with the past.

I can hardly walk a mile through it in any direction without coming on some scene or some object that revives that impression. It may be one of the pretty little stone bridges made by that eighteenth-century laird over the burn which goes singing down the glen of the Lady Chapel. Or it may be no more than the old half-decayed pump to which, according to tradition, he used to walk every day to drink a cup of its water, and from which water was brought to him as he lay on his death-bed at the age of eighty-one. His letters, though his epistolary style was more correct than attractive, are most vivid when they speak of projects or improvements made on the estate, as for instance when they trace in detail the course to be taken by a new road, and discuss the adjustments which must be made in the line of a march to enable the road to complete its course without leaving its projector's property. After reading such pleasantly matter-of-fact details, set down in his beautifully formal handwriting, no walk along that road can ever again be dull, however well you may know every turn of it.

Then there was the coin dug up a year or two ago when a drain was being constructed across a field between a recently planted wood and the river. Somewhere in this neighbourhood, we knew, had stood one of the old houses to which Buchanan refers, but of which every trace but its name had vanished. It might have been anywhere within a circle as much as a quarter of a mile wide. But here, a couple of feet below the surface, this coin was turned up—a silver piece about the size of a florin; it was in good preservation, and was identified without much difficulty as a half-merk of James VI's time. We resumed the search for the site of the vanished house with renewed enthusiasm, for there seemed to be no reason except its proximity why that coin should have been dropped just there; and it was not long before we found, at the edge of the wood, the unmistakable outline of the old foundations.

But I think the most astonishingly vivid example I have ever known in this neighbourhood of the past surviving in the present was in a metaphor casually employed by the same old woman who told me of the Covenant martyr's grave. Its strangeness was the more striking in that not only did it obviously derive from the everyday speech of long before the Reformation, but it occurred in the mouth of one living in a district where the spirit of that great change has always been particularly strong. The speaker was discussing a certain house not far from where she lived. It was remarked to her that it was too large a house to be comfortable. 'Ah,' she replied, 'ye can aye sing a mass in each corner.'

4. Ben Stack, Sutherland

Robert M. Adam

CAITHNESS AND SUTHERLAND

by

NEIL M. GUNN

In nearly all the popular guides to Scotland, Caithness is ignored or referred to as a place of little or no interest. I have beside me one of the best of them, *Scotland for Everyman*, where the author in his otherwise excellent and exact survey proceeds to warn the reader, as follows: 'East of Tongue the scenery rapidly decreases in grandeur as one gradually returns to civilization and tarred roads. Caithness is really rather a dull county, not Highland at all but rather Norse, at least near the coast—as the place-names show. Consequently the traveller will not be ill-advised if he decide to cut short this tour by making for Lairg direct. If he does so, he will miss the kudos of having reached John o' Groats, but not very much else.'

This 'return to civilization' (after wandering in Sutherland) may have its points for a Caithness man, as there has always existed a certain rivalry—and raillery—between the two remotest counties of our mainland. But plainly he is not to be comforted by very much else. And as civilization is a vague word and quite different in its implications from that other overworked word, culture, it might be said that the Sutherland man scores—particularly as some of his roads (including the famous old rocky highway to the Ord) have recently been tarred to perfection.

But the inwardness of this matter really centres in the use of that word grandeur. It is a legacy of Sir Walter Scott and all the Highland romanticism to which that noble name must plead guilty. Byron caught the note and sang it 'wild and majestic':

> Oh, for the crags that are wild and majestic!
> The steep-frowning glories of dark Loch na Garr.

To see patriotic Scots roused by this gorgeous stuff is to realize in some measure the religious intensity of the old wife who would not believe that Jerusalem is on this earth. There is a magniloquence about it all, a lack of reality, of exact description, that flatters our vague emotions at the expense of our sight and insight. It is admirably reflected in those pictures for sale in stationers' shops where gigantic crags, their tops swathed in Celtic mist, form a background to smooth purple slopes and the wan water of a loch on whose near shores long-haired Highland cattle for ever stand and dream.

From all this, the curious reader may conclude that I am a Caithness man—preparing the way. He is right. The mind must be prepared for the reception of beauty in its more exquisite forms. The old man of the ceilidh-house realized this, and, before beginning one of the ancient classic poems of the Gael, he tuned the listening minds by telling of the poem itself and of its heroes. But he always followed with the poem. And now I am prepared to follow with two.

But as the Eastern sage has it, 'Haste is an attribute of devils.' Let us see one thing well; let us, then, as we turn east from Tongue, keep our eyes on Sutherland's own mountain—Ben Laoghal. Ben Hope comes before for contrast. And moors and sea-inlets and skylines keep us company. Around is all the grandeur of all the fabled West—with Ben Laoghal added. Watch Ben Laoghal play with its four granite peaks on the legendary stuff of history, or is it of the mind? Sometimes they are the battlemented towers of a distant Mediæval Age; in the smoke-blue drift of the half-light they are the ramparts to the high hills of faery; a turn in the road or in the mood, and they have become perfectly normal again, unobtrusive and strong as the native character. Let me add that once going down towards bleak Kildonan, I unthinkingly glanced over my shoulder and saw them crowned with snow. I have never forgotten the unearthly fright I got then.

From that background, or as it were from that door, you walk out upon Caithness, and at once experience an austerity in the flat clean wind-swept lands that affects the mind almost with a sense of shock. There is something more in it than contrast. It is a movement of the spirit that finds in the austerity, because strength is there also, a final serenity. I know of no other landscape in Scotland that achieves this harmony, that, in the very moment of purging the mind of its dramatic grandeur, leaves it free and ennobled. The Pentland Firth, outreaching on the left, is of a blueness that I, at least, failed to find in the Mediterranean; a living blueness, cold-glittering in the sun and smashed to gleaming snowdrift on the bows of the great rock-battleships of the Orkneys, bare and austere also. The wind of time has searched out even the flaws here and cleansed them.

That is the first picture. Before we come to the

second we follow the road by stone-flagged fences and broad fields to Thurso, a charming old town with a fishing-quarter of rather intricate design and a piling of roofs that, seen from the beach, has a certain attraction. From Thurso, like all good tourists we proceed to John o' Groats, so that we may sing about the end of the road. Picture postcards are here, and an hotel, and the legend of the house with the eight walls, the eight doors, and the eight-sided table, so that the eight men might enter and be seated without raising questions of precedence or prestige. But while listening to this local lore and, with luck, sampling the county's whisky—and Old Pulteney, well matured, does no dishonour to its birthplace—we find our eyes attracted by that long lovely beach of white sand. Not the poet's 'dove-grey sand,' but the crushed shells of whiteness from which all the sticky humours have been withdrawn. It is in its way as typical of this clean-swept county as that first picture I have tried to describe. Hours may be spent on this strand looking for those lovely little shells, the John o' Groat buckies. In the process, too, the native spirit enters and quietens the soul.

But the leisureliness of an older age is gone. A look and a rush and we say we have seen it! The evening is upon us. Yet we have hardly got under way when from the low ridge of the Warth Hill, Caithness suddenly spreads her whole body before us to the blue distant ridges of Morven and the Scarabens.

This, my second picture, is impossible even to suggest, for the effect is entirely one of light. It is not that the quality of this light is magical or glamorous, tenuous or thin. There are few places in Scotland where level light from the sinking sun can come across such a great area; but it is not altogether that. Robert Louis Stevenson, who knew Wick well, may here have first found his 'wine-red moor,' but I have seen it of a paler gold than amontillado. The mind does not debate: it gets caught up into that timelessness where beauty is no longer majestic or grand but something more intimate than life or death. Across the moor, the sun gone, the colour darkening, the far blue turning to deep purple, shadow and more shadow, until the peewits cry in the dark of night.

There is a third picture of Caithness but it is a composite one: the sea-cliffs that form its coast. In a sense, these cliffs are more typical of Caithness than all else for they have entered so much—and so violently—into the life of its people. As sheer rock-scenery, too, they are often magnificent, while the flatness of the coastlands permits of tremendous perspectives. On entering the county from the Ord one may from almost anywhere near the cliffs get a view of the rock-wall all the way to Clyth Head. There are 'flaws' in this structure—fortunately, because they mean so much to the inhabitants, for here they have their harbours or creeks from which they fish with such skill and daring, or, should I say, have fished, for the decline in the sea industry has left an air of sadness and decay along the whole Caithness coast. In small places like Dunbeath or Lybster, where to-day only four or five motor-boats pursue the old calling, little more than a generation ago anything up to two hundred boats fished in the season from each harbour. What activity was there then! Every creek round the coast swarmed with life, while Wick, now going derelict, was a fishing-centre of European importance. Folk worked hard in those days, played hard, and drank hard, too. To live and prosper on such a coast required unusual intrepidity and endurance in the seamen. Few of the mean 'safe' qualities found time to sprout, and as the money came so did it go, with that element of careless generosity that is ever present in the greater games of chance. And sea-fishing is the master game of chance, for not only does a man risk all he possesses, with every grain of skill and strength added, but also he stakes down the hazard with his life. The fish-curers' stations employed as gutters nearly all the available women of the surrounding districts, whose gay tongues were as nimble as their fingers. Shopkeepers prospered. The produce of the land was needed. If there was never great wealth, there was all the living warmth of a healthy communal life.

When we look at the boarded windows of the ruinous curing buildings, we may naturally wonder what cataclysm or what blight descended here. The use of steam, the big drifter, the concentration of the industry in great ports like Wick, were the reasons given. But what of these reasons now? The drifter is in debt to more than a critical extent, and Wick is proportionately as derelict as Lybster.

Politics entered into it, and in a sense with far more drama than is usually found in the interactions of any 'economic law.' The export of cured herrings to the Baltic was lost when Russia began her social experiment. Not that Russia no longer required herrings, but that the British Government kept changing its mind about dealing with her. The herring industry is immensely more important to Scotland than to England. But Scotland could not deal separately in this matter. Norway, however, could and did. The Norwegian Government guaranteed Russian payments to the Norwegian fishermen to the extent of many millions of pounds. The Norwegian Government never lost a penny and the Norwegian fishermen got the market. It is interesting to reflect how the attitude of some politician seven hundred miles away may affect a seaboard and its people. Mr. Winston Churchill, let us say, decides on a little affair in Russia, and our northern coasts come under the grip of a grisly hand that slowly closes. They were such a fine breed of men, too, these Caithness fishermen, daring, self-reliant, rarely hypocritical or sanctimonious, game for whatever life offered in the sea-storm or in the public-house, and God-fearing over all.

Their qualities have been inherited, normal qualities of a healthy stock against an environment demanding courage and faith. Hospitality was the social gift, and the old need for quickness of wits may perhaps to-day find more or less a natural outlet in education. But whether the change from being skipper of a sailing vessel to being a school teacher, minister of the Gospel, clerk, professor, Civil Servant, or what-not, is a change for the better in the human story, may hardly be debated here. Personally, I am inclined to do more than doubt it.

All the coast is studded with castles mostly now in ruins and indicating an older age of tribal rule and self-sufficiency. Sinclairs, Keiths, Gunns; with Mackays, Sutherlands, and the ever land-hungry Campbells, impinging upon them from the outside. The tale of their deeds and depradations is as stormy and bloody and treacherous and heroic as tales from anywhere else in the Highlands. As a good-going example, may I be forgiven for recalling the ancient feud between the Keiths and the Gunns. The chiefs of these two clans agreed to settle their differences by a fight to the death of twelve men against twelve. The Gunn, with his chosen dozen, several of whom were his sons, was first at the lonely moorland rendezvous, and had barely ceased asking the Creator for His blessing, when the horses of the Keiths were seen to be approaching. Twelve horses behind the Keith, yes—but what is this? . . . Each horse carries two riders! . . . The Gunn puts it to his men. There is plenty of time to fly. But the Keigt strategy, for some obscure reason, merely fires them to encounter any odds, and the battle is joined. It was a long and bloody affair, in which the Keiths claimed victory, but in the end three of the Gunns, albeit sorely wounded, were able to leave the field on their own feet.

A certain delicacy of feeling might well make a Gunn hesitate to tell the traditional story, were he not sadly aware that the clan did not know then—and certainly none of them has ever learned since—the technique of acquiring land or indeed notable material wealth of any kind. Nor from this story is any particular moral intended for our age, though I cannot help being conscious of a certain diffused light! We are landless! cried the Macgregors. And not only in the small clan of the Gunns, but in the large clan of the common people of Scotland, the cry has an intimate ring to this day.

These counties of Caithness and Sutherland may be said to have a prehistory of enthralling conjecture.

Those interested in the archæological aspect of things may here dream and dispute to their heart's content. Who built the brochs?—those round dwellings whose walls may still be seen to be from twelve to fifteen feet thick and whose original height must have been anything from fifty to sixty feet. They are structures of unique interest, crammed with novel features. The ruins of a great many of them are to be found in Caithness; rather less in Sutherland; and they diminish in number as we go south, until they become rare in the Lowlands. And perhaps the most remarkable fact about them is that they are to be found only in Scotland. Not a single example in Scandinavia, or Ireland, or England—those countries from which at one time or other Scotland is supposed to have got all she may be said to have! What race built them, then? Was the seat of their power actually in the extreme north? Long ago Columba had to travel to Inverness to meet the high king of our country. Had the governing centre shifted south to Inverness by Columba's time, much as it later shifted to Edinburgh; and still later to London?

It is all a game of questions. But clearly in the courses of time these northern counties have had their day.

No writer can now refer to Caithness without using the word Norse. 'Not Highland at all but rather Norse.' A hundred odd years ago a traveller from the south would have had to penetrate into the county as far as Clyth before he could hear a word of English, no other tongue than Gaelic being spoken. True, you will find Norse coastal names; but you will also find them in the Outer Isles, where the Norse held sway just as long as they held it in Caithness. But they were conquerors, with the conqueror's technique of spoil-getting and land-grabbing. Their exploits are fabulous, and the only adventurers who can be compared with them are the Spanish Conquistadores. They were, however, few in numbers, were not of the soil they held, and in time the native folk of Caithness's hinterland, through their women, largely bred them out. That is not to say that Caithness folk are mostly Gaelic, any more than are other parts of the Highlands. There is an older more predominant strain in the Highlands than either Gaelic or Norse. What folk composed this strain I do not know, just as I do not know who built the brochs; but I have the uneasy idea that they rode one man to a horse.

All of which has brought us a little distance from the rock scenery. Not that the rock scenery is to blame, for it has beauty quite apart from its human associations. The geos and stacks and contorted strata, the colouring of caves and seaweed, the bird life, are elements of ever-varying allure. Memorable days may be passed haunting this world that swings between life and death. Great care should be taken, too, for on a windless sea where no waves are breaking there is always some degree of a swell that may all in a moment lift a small boat on to a sloping ledge and, receding, leave her to turn turtle.

For the rest, Caithness is said to be a flat treeless plain, and perhaps that impression may have been confirmed here; yet like so many general impressions it is only partially true. For Caithness has many shallow straths of delicate beauty, that penetrate inland from the coast and fade into the moor with an air of still, listening surprise. The Strath of Dunbeath is considered to be about the finest example, though I have found Berriedale and Langwell of inexhaustible attraction. There are others, many of them not at all impressive to the casual eye, that yet achieve for the lover an intimacy and charm that may be comparable only to the fragrance of the finer wines.

Possibly I am prejudiced in favour of Caithness, knowing, as I do, that it possesses qualities which, like the qualities of its people, are not readily paraded. Yet let me say immediately that had Caithness denied me, I should have desired, over any other place on the earth's surface (including the vineyard countries), to have been born in Sutherland!

Caithness and Sutherland are, in a way not easily made plain, a mating of the two great elements of sea and land. You can get lost in Sutherland, in its mountain masses, its great glens, its hidden lochs, its peat hags, its woods, its barren moors. It is shaggy and tough and often terrifying. The eye reaches over great vistas where no human being lives or moves. And on the west the traveller finds himself for ever playing a game of hide and seek with the sea. Narrow inlets meet him round corners, sudden flashes of colour drawing his eyes away. The memory of a trip from Scourie northward is curiously jewelled. The greenness of mountains where one had expected to find heather, the land between mountain and sea assuming every shape, fantastic, ancient, grey, brooding in peat black, glistening in loch blue, unexpected in goblin green, dreaming in brown, the wind touching it, passing over it, carrying away its loneliness to some place still more deeply withdrawn. To think of the Caithness coast now is to think of something simple, elemental, masculine. Here is the beauty of ceaseless change, full of a wild charm, alluring, beckoning, heedless, feminine.

Sutherland has always been a pastoral crofting county and the tragedy it suffered in the beginning of last century may best be realized if from Caithness we go 'over the Ord' by the south coast road and come down upon the fishing town of Helmsdale.

Helmsdale, like the Caithness creeks, has fallen on evil times these latter years. But its story is interesting in that it was a direct creation of what is known to history as the 'Sutherland Clearances.' These clearances consisted in the evictions of thousands of crofters from their homes in the glens by a landlord who desired, for his greater profit, to rent his land to sheep farmers. It was the era throughout the whole Highlands of the creation of the large sheep farm, and of the dispossession of the people, frequently by means so ruthless and brutal that they may not bear retelling easily, and always with a sorrow and hopelessness that finally broke the Gaelic spirit. What the disaster of 1745 and the penal enactments of 1747 began, the clearances finished.

We know rather exactly and vividly what happened in the glens of Sutherland because of the accounts of eye-witnesses and the explanations of contemporaries. Donald Macleod, whose wife and family were evicted into a night of storm when he himself was absent, with no neighbour they dare go to without bringing immediate doom to that neighbour's house, described the lurid scenes of burning and destruction in a series of letters to an Edinburgh newspaper, afterwards printed in book form under the title *The Gloomy Memories*. These letters make terrible reading. The Rev. Donald Sage, in his *Memorabilia Domestica*, tells of the hundreds of homes that were burned around him and of how, when he came to preach his last sermon, he broke down and all his people wept with him. For untold generations they and their forebears had inhabited these glens, a courteous people, hospitable, full of the ancient lore and music and ways of life of the Gael and the pre-Gael. No army of invading barbarians ever left behind it desolation so complete as did that ruthless handful of the chief's servants. And Sutherland to this day is haunted by that 'gloomy memory.'

The folk gathered on the seashores, eating shellfish or whatever they could find, while they dug small plots of coastal land and tackled the sea. Helmsdale gradually became a fishing port of consequence. Then Helmsdale declined, as the sheep farms declined, and the great experiment in Progress had its mask torn from it.

From Helmsdale the traveller should take the road that goes up Kildonan strath, over the Heights, and down Strath Halladale to Melvich on the north coast, both for the scenery and to experience, as I think he may, a still lingering intimation of that gloom. For this is the area that, with Strath Naver farther west, suffered most cruelly.

And the first reaction may well be one of surprise that a land so barren and wild could ever have harboured townships of people. How did they manage to live? . . . Until finally he may wonder if the 'clearances' would not have happened sometime anyway.

The further north he goes the bleaker it gets until crossing the high lands he observes little but endless desolation. Then all at once he comes on Dalhalvaig.

In Dalhalvaig there is a public school, a post office, substantial houses on the surrounding crofts, white-washed walls, an air of comfort, of material well-being, of everything, in fact, except that which suggests poverty and misery. Yet half-close the eyes, let the houses disappear, let the heather creep up to the hearth-stones, let all sign of human habitation vanish, and the present Dalhalvaig becomes a place more desolate than any to be found in Kildonan.

How do we account, then, for the Dalhalvaig of to-day? On no other grounds that I can think of than that Strath Halladale was not 'cleared.' It escaped the horrors of 1813–19 because the greater part of it was at that time under the Mackays, and when it did fall into other hands (in 1829, by purchase) public feeling against the evictions had got so inflamed that the new owners found it more advantageous to pursue the intriguing ways of Parliamentary influence than to continue making deserts.

Down the Strath from Forsinard to the sea the descendants of the old crofters remained. Many of them caught the emigration fever as the nineteenth century advanced and went abroad meaning to return, but few of them ever returned to settle, though they sent home money regularly and in other ways exhibited the passion of the Gael for his homeland and his kindred.

In talk and correspondence with the present scholarly parish minister of Kildonan I have been given a glimpse of the kind of men and women Dalhalvaig has produced not only in the past but in living memory. 'Some of the finest types of Northern Highlander, physically and mentally, have come out of this area from Kirkton to Forsinain on both sides of the Halladale river,' Dr. Scott maintains. And he proves his case with fascinating instances of versatility, strong personality, and occasional genius.

I was interested in this contrast between Kildonan and Halladale, and pursued my inquiries quite dispassionately. I think there is here an underlying significance of real importance. A great human stock cannot be planted in a day. What was uprooted so swiftly may not all at once be given root and permanence by a decision of any individual or any Board. But the glens are there. And the final—and representative—opinion was given me in these words: 'All the northern glens might have been like Halladale, if the people had been treated as human beings.'

But this is a depressing subject and for all that may have been written to the contrary, the Highlander loves news and gaiety. As Kenneth Macleod reports of the island schoolmaster, 'My curse on gloom!' Only it is necessary to get some understanding of the forces, human and economic, that have been doing him down in the past in order to appreciate even the scenery amid which he lives now. For not only does environment affect human development, but human development in its turn affects environment. In a happy thriving community the very land, to our senses, takes on a certain pleasant friendliness. Children feel this particularly, and in after life have an enhanced memory of sunlight and of flowering growths. On the other hand, in Kildonan there is to-day a shadow, a chill, of which any sensitive mind would, I am convinced, be vaguely aware, though possessing no knowledge of the clearances. We are affected strangely by any place from which the tide of life has ebbed.

And Sutherland, as I have suggested, is a land of endless variety. There are no big towns, nothing at all like Wick, which in the height of the herring season in the old days used to double its population and present a scene of human interest continuously dramatic. The county town of Dornoch is best known for its golf course. Golspie and Brora also have good golf courses. Here a tourist industry is developing. And as this part of the county is also the seat of landlord power, there is a certain residential feeling in the atmosphere. Surrounding the castle are fields with trees like English parks, while on a high hill dominating all this part of the coast is a tall monument to that Duke of Sutherland under whose reign the clearances took place.

Let us go inland to Lairg, which is the proper centre for the exploration of the real Sutherland. Anything in the nature of motor-car or bus service may be had at the Sutherland Transport garage, where a genial manager, in Gaelic or English, will tell you what you want to know and what you had not thought of. Three main roads radiate from Lairg to the west. The first up the quietly beautiful strath of the Oykel to Lochinver; the second by the long barren stretches of Loch Shin to Scourie; and the third northward across moors, passing the Clibric Hills on the right, to Tongue. All three roads run into the road of the west which winds from Lochinver to Tongue, and is, to me at least, literally the most surprising and magical road in Britain. Not that speedmen would call it a road at all, unless indeed certain parts might be selected for 'observing.'

Through Strath Oykell, by Altnagealgach, and on towards Loch Assynt, where great mountains all at once crowd around: Ben More Assynt (3,273) on our right; Canisp and the remarkable Suilven on our left; Glasven and the Quinag in front. This is the happy hunting-ground of geologists, archæologists, and botanists. Historians, too, will look at the ruins of Ardvreck Castle on the edge of Loch Assynt and think of Montrose and what happened thereof 'deathless shame.'

From Lochinver, a pleasant place, there is a coast road by Clashnessie and Drumbeg to Kylescue Ferry (for Scourie) that no summer traveller should miss. It is not much frequented, but I have always found a great fascination in the wooded inlets that give on Eddrachillis Bay, with its many islands.

Islands, indeed, accompany one along this western seaboard, and exercise their power on the romantic imagination in diverse ways. Some look upon them quiescently, others dreamily with vague thoughts of Tir nan Og, while not a few feel an impulse to own one doubtless out of some innate urge for security and over-lordship. All hopes—or illusions—may be indulged on this road. Life is short, but eternity may be dreamed in a minute.

From Scourie to Laxford Bridge, where the Loch Shin road ends or begins. All this is sporting country. The Laxford River has patrol paths on both sides, and I have heard of young men who strike a match in the dark of night by this lonely water and then wait to see how long it will take keepers to come out of the void upon them! A remarkably short time, I am told. Whether or not it has its point as a game, it certainly illustrates with some irony the whole subject of sporting rights on which I have not touched here. It is really difficult to write of the Highlands without appearing to deal in that accursed gloom. When the sheep did not pay, the deer took their place. I may leave it at that. As for getting a rod on the Laxford, you would first have to buy out the wealthiest duke in England. So you may leave it at that also!

The hotels have, of course, some loch-fishing attached to them. It is the custom, I know, to deplore the heavy charges—six to eight guineas a week—of most of them. But their season is short, their rent and expenses heavy, and they desire profit as naturally as a duke or a grocer. For the rest, they know their business. The Highlands, of course, may yet become a popular tourist playground dependent on tourists and nothing else. After sheep, deer; and after deer, tourists. It is the ascending order of our age of progress. For those who know the deep humanism of a past age, there will be regret at the gradual passing of the human stock that was bred out of it.

But by the time a man has footed the track to Cape Wrath, where there is no habitation other than the lighthouse, and looked down upon the rocks that take the Arctic on their bows, he may feel that men's faiths or creeds, economic or religious, change with the centuries, that his wants and desires change with the days, but that certain deep racial forces persist with extraordinary strength, and that the end of this great country is not yet.

5. Near Finstown, Orkney

Thomas Kent

ORKNEY

by

ERIC LINKLATER

I WENT up to Orkney at the beginning of March this year. At Tain, in the early morning, the smoke was blowing straight out of the chimneys, flat streamers racing before a strong north-west wind. I thought with some foreboding of the Pictland Firth, that boisterous channel into which the Atlantic swell, mounting with the weight of all the western ocean, comes heavily in high ridges, and is broken into eddies, and overfalls, and cross seas, and heaving lumps of sea, by an ebb-tide running westwards to meet it. I remembered the last crossing I had made, a southward crossing that coincided with the first of the winter gales.

That day the Firth was a tremendous spectacle. Our course was diagonal to parallel mountain-ridges of water that lifted the little mail-steamer skyways—she is only a hundred and thirty feet long—and let her slide abysmally from their shoulders. I was on the bridge, and looking downwards the narrow after-part of the ship seemed no bigger than a canoe, and it was exciting to see how violently, under the impact of the sea, she first heeled over, and then was canted up and lifted up, and then fell back, rolling to the other side in the trough. In the middle of the Firth we were swept by a huge wave. There was a hissing roar—a roar in the midst of hissing—and the bridge was blackened by the breaking wave, and we lay far over under its weight. As soon as we returned to an even keel the Captain and the Mate hurried to the weather side of the bridge to see if anything had carried away; but luckily no damage had been done. Thereafter it was a joy to watch the Captain's seamanship, for with the sea growing too heavy to keep a straight course, he had to watch continually, edge this way and that, and run the waves. This he did to perfection; but unhappily his demonstration of how to handle a ship was accompanied by a thick cloud of very strong tobacco-smoke, that filled the little wheel-house and spoiled my attempt to behave in a manly and sailorly way; for presently I had to seek relief outside.

This I remembered, without much happiness, when I saw the strength of the north-west wind at Tain. But the day was so fine, and the country so lovely in the pale hues of the early year, that no thought or memory could long compete with the exhilaration of going northwards and the delight of returning to Orkney. Now as the day grew the sky opened ahead of us like a round window, and the clearest colour was always to the north. The Caithness hills were as red as wine, there were pale green larches, and bracken like an old lion-skin, and tawny brooks, and the Paps of Caithness, under snow, were whiter than any Paris saw on Mount Ida. But there was no colour like that in the window to the north, where the sky was a lambent blue. At midday it was the blue of a thrush's egg, in the afternoon it was green as a duck's egg.

And as though one were a plant, bending to the light or growing to light, it drew one towards it.

Across the Firth the rampart island of Hoy stood like a lilac shadow, clearly drawn. The sea was flecked with white. It ran high, in a leisurely swell that lifted and sank with a pleasant motion, till the ebb tide broke it into roughness. Hoy came nearer and the lilac shadow turned into reddish cliffs, storm-ragged, scarred by the waves. This is the highest land in Orkney, a rampart embossed with a couple of hills, heather-dark, forbidding and majestic. There, where the shore turns a corner and falls from cliff to a shingle beach, is the little township of Rackwick, a dying community that is too good to die: the men are perhaps the most skilful and weatherwise boatmen in all Orkney, and once they had the reputation of being the strongest and most graceful of dancers: but the township exists precariously on a high slope of ground between the hill and the cliffs, and the young people will not stay there. There is a story of a Rackwick man who lost his wife and his cow at one and the same time, for both were blown by a gale of wind off a field that tilted steeply as a roof, and killed on the rocks below. But presently the Rackwick man went to Stromness, and came home from there in unexpected good humour. He met the minister, who said he was glad to see him combating his loss with so manly and Christian a spirit. 'It might have been worse,' said the Rackwick man, 'it might have been much worse. For I've been to Stromness, and I've got me a younger wife and a far, far bonnier coo.'

Round the easterly end of Hoy there is a bay with an older story: it was there, in the year 995, that Olaf

Trygvesson, later King of Norway, converted Earl Sigurd of Orkney to Christianity at the point of the sword. Olaf was a soldier-missionary of the most dogmatic kind: his Norwegian policy was government by baptism, his penal code consisted, quite simply, of capital punishment for heathens. He himself had been converted, by a fortune-teller in the Scillies, not very long before his meeting with Earl Sigurd, which was accidental. Olaf was on his way to Norway with five ships, to fight for his kingdom, and he put into Walls to wait for a tide. Sigurd happened to be there at the time. Olaf, strong in men and his conviction, told Sigurd that he and those with him must be baptized immediately. If Sigurd refused, he would be killed, and Orkney punished with fire and sword. In the circumstances in which the Earl found himself, says the saga, he preferred to become a Christian. Sturdy common sense and an objective intelligence have always been the characteristics of our people.

The Norse period of Orkney's history was very violent, but our temper to-day is entirely peaceful. We are neither envious of others, nor hostile towards them. Foreigners, indeed, whether Scot or Sassenach, are warmly welcomed—so long as they behave themselves—for we are interested in the affairs of the adjacent island of Britain, and we derive much pleasure from observation of the customs and the views of mannerly visitors. Their insularity does not offend us, for we are notably broad-minded, and our comparative prosperity tends to make us rather complacent. This is no place for an economic survey of the islands, but as it is becoming increasingly common to read that Orkney is the happiest county in Scotland, it is worth noting that its economy is based on practice diametrically opposed to modern theory.

Current opinion is strongly in favour of the large farm, the large industrial unit; but Orkney is a land of small farms and small independent commercial enterprise, and the islands have suffered little from the depression that has so seriously affected other parts of the world. There is practically no unemployment in Orkney, there is no tale of bankrupt farmers and ruined shopkeepers. There is, on the contrary, an appearance of quiet and decent well-being. But in other parts of the world, that have followed the fashion in economics, there exist the several varieties of poverty, from financial embarrassment to utter ruin. Can it be that the economists are wrong? Or is the Orkney farmer, because of the accidents of Nature, more fortunately situated than the majority?

He has this advantage, that he is either the owner of his farm, or a solidly established tenant equally immune from the interference and the assistance of his landlord. Pride of ownership is everywhere apparent. Initiative is indigenous—so is a capacity for hard work, and a willingness to work with reasonable assiduity—and friendly competition does the rest. Let one farmer introduce a new variety of seed, and show its value, and within a couple of years all his neighbours are sowing the like—till someone finds a better. Let one farmer breed a prize-winning mare, and within three months three others have bought medal-winners at the Aberdeen Autumn Sales. But this is no cut-throat competition: if your mare founders, and your man falls off his bicycle, and your daughter takes it into her head to go off and get married in a hurry, then your neighbours will turn to and help you. Nobody in Orkney ever lost his harvest for lack of friendly assistance—if it was needed.

The only real poverty is to be found among the inshore fishermen, whose livelihood has been ruined by those magnificent but pestilential thieves, the trawlers, whom a supine, gravel-blind, and perverted government, scarcely fit for lobster-bait, allows to maraud at will. Yet politically we are conservative—on a liberal basis—and the only discernible sign of rebellion is a curious and growing interest in the Douglas Credit system. Its appeal may be that of novelty: we are avid of novelty.

Now with regard to scenery, Orkney can show no more than four varieties: farmland, moor, lake, and the sea-cliffs, which are all at the mercy of the sky. Light is the dominating factor in its scenery, and the town-dweller, on his arrival in Orkney, will screw up his eyes and ask where all the light is coming from. Except Hoy, there are no hills high enough to intercept it. There are no trees to diminish it. There is, on the entire circumference, the sea to reflect it. And beneath a changing sky Orkney can change from ugliness and bleakness to a radiant panorama of lakes more brightly blue than the Mediterranean, a dazzling chequer-board of grass and ploughland, the shadow-and-claret of hills that flow in sweet unbroken lines. It can put on beauty like a song or a dance, so light and airy it is, so brisk, and tender, and gay. And then, in less time than it takes to count the colours, the colours will change again, and the land looks grave and peaceful. Or the sun, gathering the brightness of the sky in one last armful of gold, will step behind the sea, and the long flowing lines of the island will, for no more than a minute or two, take on the swift look of a greyhound, as though it were in fleet pursuit of Phœbus, the micher. One of the islands, indeed, is said to have been a flying island at one time, and to have travelled extensively. That is Eynhallow, in the firth between the mainland and Rousay. But it is stable enough now. Once it was a sanctuary for monks; now it is a bird sanctuary, a pretty green shelf of turf with a tiny white beach.

There are nearly sixty islands altogether, of which twenty-five, I think, are inhabited. If my memory will serve for the round voyage, we might take a sea-circuit of the archipelago, starting from Rackwick and sailing northwards under the tall cliffs, a thousand feet high and more, of that part of Hoy. But do not ask me to describe them, for that is impossible save in the most purple of prose, which is out of fashion nowadays. To sail close in to the foot of them is almost intolerably exciting, and even a long way out, on a summer evening, you may feel, like a tropic breeze, the gathered warmth of the day rebounding from the rock. Hereabout is the Old Man of Hoy, a magnificent pinnacle, four or five hundred feet high, standing in the foam.

Round the corner of Hoy the sea runs like a mill-race into Hoy Sound, and splits about the comfortable green island of Graemsay. North of that island, with its two lighthouses, is the lovely small town of Stromness, where the people have miniature wharfs instead of gardens, and the children learn to row a boat before they can walk. Stromness is a leisurely place, full of retired sailors, and everybody there knows the geography of Cape Horn and the configuration of Borneo as well as they know the shape of their own narrow street. Say nothing about halliards, foot-ropes, or gaskets there, unless you are an expert; for the very infants know the whole rig of a sailing ship, and their seniors are mostly Extra Masters who treat star navigation as one of the lighter pastimes.

Now come out of Hoy Sound again, on the ebb-tide, and go north along the rock wall of the West Mainland. This was good fishing-ground, before the trawlers spoilt it, and the cliffs are full of rock-pigeons and the whole creation of gulls, guillemots, eider duck, puffins, and cormorants. Half-way up there is a fine stack of rock called Yesnaby Castle, of the same fashion as the Old Man of Hoy, but smaller; and a little north of that the cliffs give way and the sea runs in to the rough white sand of Skaill Bay. I remember seeing a sailing ship ashore on a flat rocky shelf here: saving her tattered sails and ravelled gear, she stood as prettily as though she were in harbour: but the next gale broke her up. And in 1916 one of the nest of German mines that sank the *Hampshire*, with Kitchener aboard, came into the bay, and was anchored there. Another was blown ashore, and burst on the beach, and threw pebbles and boulder-splinters far inland. But nowadays Skaill is chiefly famous for its prehistoric village that has newly been uncovered, the village of Skara Brae, about which archæologists have different opinions. But I have only one opinion and that is that it was much pleasanter and more entertaining before they excavated it: for there used to be little more than a couple of grassy cup-like hollows, with little tunnels of masonry running down and away from them, and it was the best picnicking place on the island. We simply called it the Picts' Hoose then, and were quite content with such a description. But now it has become a National Monument, with a keeper and three thousand visitors in the season, and nobody knows how to describe it. Nor can one picnic there any longer. But progress must be served, and the excavation of Picts' Hooses is becoming one of the most important of Orkney's subsidiary industries. There are dozens of them, and whoever the Picts were they must have been an industrious people—if they were Picts, that is, for the archæologists appear to have doubts, and it is difficult to persuade them to make a plain statement.

It was only a few miles north of the Picts' Hoose that the *Hampshire* went down. A lot of mystery has been made about her loss, but the only mystery was why she was sent west-about instead of on the eastward side: for there was such a strong westerly or nor'-westerly gale blowing that her destroyer escort had to turn back, and the sea there had certainly not been cleanly swept, since the nest of mines lay ready off Marwick Head. So down she went, Kitchener and all but a handful of her crew with her, who drove ashore on Carley floats, and with God's grace and bleeding fingers climbed up the cliffs on a cold, dark, stormy night. You may still hear stories about the survivors if you enquire tactfully and in the right quarters. But Orkney was full of strange stories during the War, when the Battle Fleet lay in Scapa, and every sound was blocked and guarded against enemy attack.

North and east, round the corner from Marwick, is the fine farming parish of Birsay, where the crops ripen early in fertile soil, and the red standstone ruins of a palace stand, that was built by Patrick Stewart, a villainous fellow, son of a bastard of James V, and Earl of the Islands. He combined a taste for architecture with a talent for the corvée and falsifying weights; and he and his father Robert very successfully reduced Orkney to famine and bankruptcy in the sixteenth century. Patrick—Black Pate he was called—was finally arrested for treason, and condemned to execution: his sentence was stayed for a week or so that he might prepare himself for a higher Judgment by learning the Lord's Prayer: he was an ignorant man in some ways.

Here, north of the Mainland, you will see a glorious view of the brown hills of Rousay, with the sea lacing the cliffs beneath them, and in the distance the shining cliffs of Westray. On the Mainland side the land rises, in a sinister and forbidding fashion, to Costa Head: Costa looks down at the once vanishing island of Eynhallow, and across to that shore in Rousay where Sweyn Asleifson, the last of the Vikings, once simplified a critical situation in Orkney politics by kidnapping the ruling Earl. There is a fierce roost in the sound between Eynhallow and the Mainland, and in August this is a good place to watch the gannets diving.

But if our circuit of the islands is to continue, we have a long sea-passage to make, to the Noup Head of Westray, and I wish I could remember some of the Westray place-names, which are very agreeable both to the ear and the imagination. Westray is a handsome island, and somewhere in its fine cliffs—it is not easy to find—is the Gentlemen's Cave, where, so they say, half a dozen fugitives from the Forty-Five found shelter. Comfort and romance can both be found in Westray: at the snug harbour of Pierowall, on the other side, is a good inn where they cook well, and a mile from there is the ruined castle of Noltland, that was once spoken of as a refuge for Mary, Queen of Scots, after her escape from Loch Leven. But what I like best in Westray is a small white beach, well enclosed, that you come upon suddenly, with a neat little farm to landward of it, and in the clear calm water—if you have two penn'orth of fancy—a couple of Norse longships, their dragon-prows overhanging the sand, their crews waist-high in the sea as they haul them ashore. It is the finest place imaginable for beaching and tenting a longship: but the farmer near by is as kindly and as gentle as his ancestors were fierce and formidable: I stopped there once, an utter stranger to him, and had my tea, and when I offered to pay, 'That's nothing at all,' he said—or his wife said—'Nothing at all, man. Come back again, and have something you can call a meal.' But that is the way of the islands, where kindness and hospitality are graces as natural as singing to a bird. How often, walking here and there, and stopping to talk, have I been told, 'Come in, man, there's an old hen in the pot. You'll take your tea, and give us your news!' Add to kindliness a rich humour, consider their background of quick sea-loud fields, where spring comes like the peewits, sudden and light-hearted as they, and do you wonder that I choose to live in Orkney?

Now east of Westray is Papa Westray, whither the missionaries of the Celtic Church came, thirteen hundred years ago: and east again from there, over a stretch of sea gaping nakedly to the north, is the curious island of North Ronaldsay. Here the people, who are well-to-do, live girt about by a wall, and outside the wall their sheep graze on seaweed and red ware, and, for all I know, on cockles and limpets. They are little dark-coated sheep, very wild and charming to look at, and they make the sweetest mutton in the world, if you are hard-hearted enough to kill them.

The southward neighbour of North Ronaldsay is the flat, sprawling, fantastically shaped island of Sanday. It is so flat that the houses stand out, on a calm day, like houses in a mirage, for the island beneath them is invisible. A great-uncle or some such kinsman of Stanley Cursiter, the artist, once lived there: a very tall, broad-shouldered man: and the story went that he was the only reliable landmark for ships in all that neighbourhood. On the low shore he stood like a Colossus, visible from miles away. South again from Sanday is Stronsay, well-known to the herring-fleet and to fish-salesmen. The drifters jostle each other there, and lie flank to flank in long rows; the gulls, crying greedily, congregate there; the herring girls gut their fish with rhythmical dexterity; and a couple of Salvation Army officers keep nervous watch over their amusements. There is also rich land in Stronsay, and good farms. But apart from these few facts I know little about the island, except that once, going when a small boy with a parish picnic there, I had to drink tea out of a slop-pail: and this has always affected my feelings about it, so that I think of it less affectionately than of the rest of Orkney.

Now hereabouts the voyage grows complicated, for

the islands are thickly scattered: Westray and Stronsay, Rousay and Sanday, lie something like the arms of St. Andrew's Cross, with Eday at the crossing of the arms, and between them half a dozen smaller isles—Egilsay and Wyre, the Calf of Eday, the Green Holms, where stormy petrels nest in the rabbit burrows, and Fara, and how many more I can't remember. But stay for a little while at Egilsay, which has a bloody history. Here it was that Earl Magnus the Saint was murdered by Earl Hakon's cook, at Hakon's order, with Hakon's fleet in the background. It was a treacherous murder, but popular at the time. The sanctitude of Magnus seems to rest on small foundations: he sang psalms during a battle instead of fighting; he lived with his wife as a virgin, using cold water as an aid to chastity; his statesmanship was eccentric; and he died with a noble mien. But twenty-one years after his death his reputation for holiness was sufficient to give Earl Rognvald, that gay Crusader, an excuse for building the cathedral that now stands to their joint honour, and throws its red shadow over Kirkwall. Not very long ago the skeleton of the Saint was found, buried in one of the huge piers in the nave of the Cathedral. The great cleft in his skull was a tribute to the strength and weapon-skill of Earl Hakon's cook.

Yet another island demands attention, a small place where a great man once lived. This is Gairsay, an island off the Mainland parish of Rendall, with a brown hump of a hill and a green forefoot pointing into the sea. Here lived Sweyn Asleifson, that bold, long-headed, humorous, mighty swordsman and seaman, who beguiled the King of Scotland with his talk, made Earls, pulled down an Earl, harried as far south as the English Channel, took Dublin by storm, and was killed in ambush in the streets of Dublin. The walls of his drinking-hall still stand in Gairsay. Here he kept eighty men throughout the winter, sowed his corn in spring, and then set out a-viking. He was the last of his kind and one of the greatest, but he was rather a survival from earlier times than typical of his own. For when he died, in 1171, the viking age was already long dead.

A school teacher in Gairsay—but there is no school there now—once told me that the ghost of a woman was sometimes to be seen near his hall. She wore a yellow gown, that seemed to hold and reflect a cold light as she walked. Now Sweyn, coming home from raiding in the western seas, brought with him a princess from Man or Ireland, and saffron was the royal colour of Ireland. She may not have liked the rough life in Gairsay, and the noise of eighty men-at-arms. Or when Sweyn went out to Dublin, and his ships came back without him, her grief may have been so bitter that even death could not quieten it. There are other ghosts in Orkney, but none lonelier than the Irish girl in her cold yellow frock. For now when she walks—if walk she does in these later days—there is none to see her, since the island is deserted by all but sheep, save in a month or two of summer.

Sweyn of Gairsay, Thorfinn the Mighty, Rognvald the Crusader, the solid Earl Paul—the Orkneyinga Saga is packed full of such sturdy heroes, of their skilful diplomacy, and their reckless battles. Orkney was then in the main stream of history, but after being mortgaged to Scotland, in 1468, it lay for long ages in a backwater, suffering from the Scottish throne neglect and villainous misrule. The last Orkney battle was fought in 1529, at Summerdale beneath the Ward Hill of Orphir in the West Mainland, between Orkneymen and an invading Caithness army under William Lord Sinclair and the Earl of Caithness. The invading army was utterly routed. Holinshed gives their casualties as five hundred, including the Caithness Earl; and Sinclair himself admitted a loss of more than three hundred. A traditional story says that of the Orkneymen only one was killed, and he in this fashion: being very hot from fighting, and having stumbled into a bog, and knowing the day was won, he went to a farm-house and asked for a drink; but the woman of the house, seeing him so dirty and unkempt, thought he must be one of the Caithness men; so having a stocking handy, into the toe of which she had thoughtfully put a large stone, she hit him on the head so that he died.

From then till 1650 Orkney had no military history. But in that year Montrose, by press-gang methods, raised an army of twelve thousand men and led them, all unwilling, into Scotland. Beside the river Oykel, in Sutherland, they walked into an ambush, and immediately scattered and fled. Now there is a pleasant irony about this disgrace, because it was on the banks of the Oykel that Sigurd, the first Earl of Orkney, being challenged by a Celtic chief called Melbrigd to a battle of forty men a side, prudently mounted two men on each of his horses, and so came into the fight with eighty, and won an easy victory. Melbrigd, rotting to turf on Oykel-side, waited about seven hundred and fifty years to see Orkney suffer for this treachery; and finally got his revenge.

But our voyage must be continued—it was Sweyn who threw us off our course—and from Gairsay it is a pleasant sail to Kirkwall, with Shapinsay on the one side, and the Bay of Firth on the other, with its two islets: Damsay, where the foolish young Earl Erlend got dead drunk and never knew when he was killed; and the Holm of Grimbister, where the present farmer breeds fine heavy cross-cattle, and wades them ashore to win silver cups and medals at the county show. Shapinsay, I believe, is sometimes called the Garden of Orkney: it has indeed a fertile pretty appearance; but its greatest charm is its possession of two incongruities, one a castle, one the record of a birth. Its castle, a large pale structure in the handsome Scots Baronial style, wears an expression of bored aloofness, of supercilious surprise at finding itself in a situation so extremely improbable. And the birth that is strangely recorded is that of Washington Irving's father: so the only begetter of Diedrich Knickerbocker and the *Conquest of Granada* was by half his blood—his mother came from Falmouth—an Orkneyman. I cannot, however, claim that he wrote according to the literary tradition of Orkney, for I fear we have no such thing. There was an Orkney poet, whose name I forget, who lived and wrote during the nineteenth century; but he, I think, was the first since Earl Rognvald, who enlivened his crusade with many spirited verses of his own composition. Our character, when we abandon the tilling of the soil, is perhaps more inclined to be didactic than anything else: we have bred a large number of professors: and for teaching, of course, our excellent bottom of Norse common sense would make us ideally suited, did not our habitual modesty detract from the self-confidence we deserve to enjoy. There was a man from South Ronaldsay, for example, who, when asked where he was born, answered humbly, 'Oh, it's not for me to say that I was born anywhere. I was just foaled in South Ronaldsay.'

But though our cultural past has been for centuries as bare as a board, we are now beginning to take some interest in the arts. On a literary occasion in London, not many weeks ago, I overheard a conversation about the scarcity of good critics to-day. A voice said, 'There's Edwin Muir, of course.' Another voice replied, 'Yes, but he's almost the only one.' Into that perilous debate I shall not enter, except to remark that Muir—poet and novelist as well as critic—was born in the little Island of Wyre, and went to school in Kirkwall; where a schoolfellow, a very backward boy, was that admirable artist and custodian of Scotland's art, Stanley Cursiter. Living at Smoogro in Orphir is Storer Clouston, who, having made a reputation as a humorist—his Lunatic was once as famous as Jeeves—neglected it for pious labours in history and archæology. And throughout the Mainland there is now a furious addiction to drama. Amateur dramatic societies abound, and village halls are filled to see earnest performances of one-act plays. I cannot, as yet, commend either acting or the choice of plays. The acting is generally stiff, unhappily self-conscious; most of the plays are rubbish. But few of us have ever seen a theatre, and lacking a literary background, we have no standards of criticism for the plays themselves. We have made a start, however. We are learning our dramatic alphabet. We have, moreover, at least the promise of a native dramatist, a man whose first play achieved the distinction of being banned by the Lord Chamberlain. But it was a good play, a tragedy on an ancient theme of revenge. . . .

This sin of digression, to which I grow increasingly subject! We were on our way to Kirkwall, and Kirkwall is dominated by the Cathedral of St. Magnus, founded about 1138, cruciform in shape, Romanesque in style, two hundred and twenty-six feet long, with a fine rose window added by Bishop Stewart in 1511, an interior arched roof seventy-one feet high, supported by twenty-eight pillars each fifteen feet in circumference, and four others with a girth of twenty-four feet, being dignified also by a new spire that takes the place of one struck and destroyed by lightning in 1671. So much for the guide book, which may or may not be accurate, and I for one care little. But look at the Cathedral on a fine summer evening, when the low sun adds a bloom to its red stone, and in the little town the great church glows benign. Think then of Rognvald and his father Kol, the artist-craftsman who drew plans for the church, and brought cunning masons into Orkney, and saw in his mind the beauty that you see now. They were great days in Orkney when men, having sailed so far and fought so hard—rhyming as they fought—could turn to building, and build so greatly.

In the winter of 1263 King Hakon of Norway was buried in the choir, and his body lay there till the following spring. The Norwegian power had waned, and Hakon had lost his dominion of the Hebrides. Storms had scattered his vast fleet, part of his forces were defeated at Largs, and Hakon himself, falling ill, had died in Kirkwall. The power also of the Orkney Earls had gone by then. But Rognvald had lived in time, and built his Cathedral to remember them, and now, red in the westering sun, God's minster speaks of the greatness of the Norsemen.

Not for a long time did Orkney see again so numerous a fleet as Hakon's: but in 1914 another came, and made its battle-home in Scapa Flow; and five years later a third arrived, the surrendered Germans. For a little while they lay among the islands, sullen shapes of defeat, and on a morning in June a party of Stromness children were taken by boat, for their annual Sunday school treat, to see the silent and now harmless enemy. But suddenly, to the extreme surprise of the children and everybody else, there were signs of activity in the German ships, which presently began to sink. Their remainder crews had decided to scuttle them, which they did very successfully, at the same time providing the Stromness children with the most memorable and spectacular treat that any Sunday school has ever enjoyed.

Most of the ships have now been salvaged, and it is a good thing they have been, for their ugly protruding funnels and ungainly bottoms, as they lay in shallow water, defiled the shining waters of the Flow. Now, instead of beached destroyers, herons stand by the waterside, and across the dark reflection of Hoy the only boats that pass are those of the lobster fishers.

But I must take you ashore again, to the Orphir shore, I think, and make you climb the Orphir hills—grouse crying 'Go back, go back!' and a hen-harrier stooping in the light—till we see, like a map before us, the West Mainland. There it is, all bravely ploughed and full of little farms, and girt by low brown hills. Two great lochs divide it—and more that you cannot see—and make a brightness equal to the skies. There are fine fat trout beneath that sparkling water, but clever as a Japanese juggler nowadays, though once they were simple as Gotham and would take any fly you liked to throw at them. There used to be such an abundance of them that once, being seized with a kind of sickness or dislike of swimming, they went ashore in the Bay of Howaback, in the Harray Loch, in such quantities that people came down with carts and graips, and shovelled them in. And this is as true as anything I ever said, for I have spoken to men who loaded the carts. But now you must fish with the cunning of the Devil to catch half a dozen, for besides being more educated there are not so many as there used to be: the farmers have drained their fields into the burns where the trout used to spawn, and so, by making their fields better, have spoiled the gravelly beds where the fish dropped their eggs. And also I think it a great pity that the otter has been hunted almost to extinction; for the otter feeds on eels rather than on trout, since they are easier to catch, and the eels are great enemies to trout.

Now looking at this land spread out before you, you will see a grassy tumulus, and, between the lochs, a ring of old grey stones; and I should have told you about these before, for one is Maeshowe and the other is the Standing Stone of Stenness, and they are famous places. I remember on one occasion going to Maeshowe, that royal and ancient burial mound, not more than a week or so after Mr. George Bernard Shaw had visited it. And I asked the guardian of the place if Mr. Shaw had said anything of interest.

'He said plenty,' answered the guardian.

'What did he say?'

'Well,' said the guardian, 'he seemed to have theories of his own about Maeshowe, and when it was built, and what it was used for. But I can't say I thought much of them. They'll maybe do all right in London, but they're not the sort of thing to satisfy us in Orkney.'

Have I said that we are an independent people? It is one of the blessings of a small land. For freedom of opinion, even of action, is still permissible in small places. And when I see the decency of the world progressively menaced by such things as the corporate state, and other such heresies of the ant-hill, I think of the littleness of Orkney, and remember with comfort the Icelandic proverb that says: 'Little things are the last to be found.'

6. The North Esk, Angus

Robert M. Adam

ANGUS AND MEARNS

by

FIONN MAC COLLA

If someone were to ask me which part of Scotland he ought to visit in order to gain in short time and within a limited area what would serve, not too inadequately, for a total impression of the country, I should have no hesitation in recommending him to visit the province of Angus and Mearns. Ideally, of course, one who wished to gain a total impression of Scotland ought to visit all parts of Scotland; but if that is impossible, if it must be only one province, then, I think, it ought to be that one.

That is not to claim that in Angus and Mearns is to be seen the most attractive, most picturesque, or most striking scenery in Scotland, or that the most Scottish type of Scottish people are to be encountered there; for that will always remain, in part at least, a matter of taste and personal preference and opinion. But it is true—and others have remarked it—that in Angus and Mearns will be found together in one area, and in representative proportion, all the features which are recognized as being most characteristic and typical of Scotland as a whole. There are mountains and glens, fertile straths, a loch or two, the sea; there is the shepherd, the crofter, the large farmer, the fisherman. Moreover the province is representative of the chaos of cultures under which it has been the fate of Scotland to suffer during the recent centuries. The national language, it is true, is now practically extinct, only lingering with a few old persons in the glens; although it is not so long, as the life of a nation goes, since it was still in use over a considerable portion of the landward area of the province. The country people continue till this day, however, to use a rich and vivid form of the language which since the sixteenth century has come to be called 'Scots'; that is, the intruding Anglian speech which through centuries of use by a Celtic people and the addition of many Gaelic words and (still more) idioms, came to serve the expression of what remains a Celtic mentality. Then in the towns of Angus in our day, as in Scottish towns everywhere, the Scots speech has gone far towards being extinguished by the modern tendencies, operating chiefly through the schools; the townspeople nowadays make shift with a language which could truly be called neither English nor Scottish, the colourless, flaccid, artificial speech termed 'School-board English,' the language of no culture. For those reasons—because in its people, their language and customs, as well as their works that have remained from other times, can be read the principal features of the more recent cultural history of the whole nation; because it contains within its borders almost all the features recognized as typical of the Scottish scene, but which are not often found elsewhere in so close proximity—Angus and Mearns might not unfittingly be taken as a part representative of the whole, as a kind of Scotland in miniature.

But this representative quality is not the only merit

and attraction of Angus. It has others which are its own peculiar possession, and which mark it off, land and people, from all the rest. In that respect it differs not in the least from every other Scottish province. In the past it has been as frequently commented upon as it must have been strikingly apparent to any observer, how many types there were within the nation, and how individualized, while yet remaining of the national type; how amazingly the scene was diversified, while all was yet recognizably Scottish scenery. This indeed is the first striking fact about the country. In Scotland the scenery is accustomed to change with astonishing frequency and to present at each step unexpected aspects and variations: something not often seen to the same extent, certainly not within so limited an area, and for which the visitor from England or elsewhere abroad is scarcely prepared. And the diversity does not stop at variety of scene, but each marked difference in the physical aspect of the countryside will usually be found as it were reflected among the inhabitants; in a difference of speech, of vocabulary, idiom, intonation, in a variation of habits and customs, even sometimes in a distinctive air and bearing.

Those differences have their roots very deep in the past. Angus and Mearns, like the neighbouring and very different provinces of Fife and Kinross and Marr and Buchan, was anciently a Pictish mormaerdom; and the fact that the old Pictish divisions of the country are found to correspond so closely to a differentiation still apparent in the local populations is only one indication of the great antiquity of the population of Scotland—at any rate of Scotland north of Forth, the old Pictavia. There are families in Angus whose names denote their descent from Scottic settlers known to have arrived considerably more than a millennium ago; and these it seems must be accounted among the comparative newcomers.

But it is one thing to say that Angus and Mearns possesses its particular and distinctive character, even to know and recognize it; it is quite another to describe it and say wherein it consists. An account of unique features or peculiar customs will not suffice to convey an idea of it. Nor will it suffice merely to contrast this province with the other provinces which border upon it, although the differences may be considerable and even striking. It could be said, for instance, that Angus is not *quaint*, like Fife, with picturesque, red-roofed villages clustering on the tops of small hills and eminences; nor, like eastern Aberdeenshire, a country of cold, straight lines, with granite-grey houses, grey-slated, standing on long slopes. But Angus is not merely unlike its neighbours; it is also something in itself. And it is precisely that 'something' which is Angus that is difficult to state or describe, for it is only partly a matter of physical features and the like, and much more a question of a certain 'quality,' elusive of definition, born of the centuries-old interdependence and as it were co-operation of the land and the people. But one thing can be said: there are parts of Scotland that awe and impress at sight, they are dour and sullen, wild or majestic, defiant, wind-swept, storm-shaken, assaulting the mind with colours, startling with bold, aggressive shapes and contours; and there are parts known forever for an accent, a way of speech, never lost and always unmistakable. Angus is not one of them, Angus *dawns*, not bursts with startling scenery or striking speech.

To one approaching from the south, however, having seen so far no part of Scotland but the fertile lands of Lothian and Fife, that statement may well seem to do less than justice to the scenery of Angus. For his first sight of it is bound to be impressive. From the northern Fife shore he sees before him the magnificent expanse of Tay; beyond, a broad stretch of fertile, wooded country; and rising behind it, all along the western and north-western horizon, the blue line of the Grampians. In the evening, at sunset, that scene can be breath-taking. Then the western sky is awash with colours, the Grampians empurpled, the Tay crowded with reflections of the woods and fields. And as dusk gathers, low on the Tay and high over the slopes, the whole eastern bank is quickly alive with lights.

The lights are the countless lights of the city of Dundee. This is one of the oldest of Scottish burghs, as it must also be one of the sites of most ancient settlement in Britain. It is so magnificently placed; for defence—having the steep, isolated Law Hill at its back; and for trade by sea—standing on the safest entry north of the Forth; near one-time excellent fisheries, and surrounded by fertile land; that it seems it must have been continuously inhabited from the most remote times, and traces do in fact remain which testify to its very early fortification and settlement. Moreover, Dundee is a most historic place. Sir William Wallace, the very type of all heroes and liberators, and the nation's noblest son, was a scholar in Dundee. Edward I of England was there in 1296, in the course of his triumphal march through Scotland receiving the submission of the half-Norman barons. Later in the same year Wallace was besieging the castle of Dundee when news was brought to him of the approach of the English army, and went straight from the siege to win the victory of Stirling Brig. Again in 1303 Edward I took the town and threw down the churches and public buildings. In 1313 Edward Bruce retook the castle from the English, and King Robert Bruce renewed and confirmed the charters of the burgh's already ancient rights and privileges, which charters Edward I had carried away or destroyed. The city saw much activity at the time of the religious revolution of the sixteenth century. It was taken by the Marquess of Montrose in 1645. And again in 1651 it was taken, this time by General Monk. That was the most terrible episode in its history. For days the victorious soldiery engaged in a general massacre of the inhabitants, carrying away a booty in plate and money richer than the whole plunder they had obtained 'in the wars throughout all the three nations,' and doing damage to the city in excess of one hundred thousand pounds. On a day in January 1716 James VIII, the 'Old Chevalier,' was welcomed in Dundee and held his court there. And finally in 1745 the town was taken by the Jacobites.

It cannot be said that modern Dundee shows much sign of the burgh's historic past, however—or indeed of anything else that might be accounted in its favour. Nature intended Dundee to be a dignified and gracious city, for the site is one of the most magnificent in Europe. But as men have made it it stands to-day perhaps the completest monument in the entire continent of human folly, avarice, and selfishness; a perfect object-lesson in what results from the divorce of economic life from ethics. Dundee ought to have been the pride of Angus, living with, and within, the life of this old and beautiful and fertile province, the head of a richly individual provincial culture. Instead, Dundee was turned into a shambles of industrialism; and strikes one to-day merely as a tragic accident and a blight on a prepossessing landscape. Strictly speaking, Dundee is not a city; it is merely a monstrously overgrown small town. No total and unified conception governed its disorderly growth. It has scarcely a spacious street, or a dignified building. Its housing is a something monstrous, which can be seen and yet defies belief. Moreover, the conditions governing its chief and vital industry involved a peculiarly horrible circumstance, the preponderance of wretchedly badly-paid female labour. The results are tragically in evidence to-day. It is doubtful if there can be seen anywhere in the world so large a proportion of a population stunted, sickly, and deformed. And now, in Dundee earlier perhaps and more completely than anywhere, the process of capitalist industrialism has worked out to its logical and inevitable end; that which brought Dundee into existence as an industrial city is no longer able to maintain it even at the level of its one-time sordid and poverty-bound prosperity. Dundee is a great industrial derelict.

In the heart of the city, close behind the principal thoroughfares, is an old graveyard granted to Dundee by Mary Queen of Scots. It has long ceased to be used for burials, and the visitor can now see there any day a curious sight: large numbers of the unemployed of Dundee sitting on the graves or wandering about or standing in groups among them, engaged in a surreptitious traffic of petty gambling or more openly in the exchange of grievances and unsocial ideas, the commerce of resentment. This graveyard, 'The Howff,' was the site of the Franciscan convent, founded by Devorgilla, mother of King John Baliol, and destroyed at the Reformation. It was the greatest ecclesiastical edifice in Dundee, and long the burial place of some of the noblest and most historic Scottish families. In this house met the National Assembly of February 1309–10, the members of which declared that, seeing the kingdom betrayed and enslaved, they had assumed The Bruce for their king—an occasion which is central in the national history, for it led on to the final assertion of independence. But nothing of this is known to the men who now inhabit there. The Howff is more than a feature of the particular tragedy of Dundee, it is a tragic symbol of the whole of present-day industrial Scotland: broken, embittered, and hopeless men, the human wreckage of an always inhuman and now decrepit industrialism, stamping over the tombs of the erstwhile great and noble of the land, nourishing resentment and a boundless indifference among ruined and illegible monuments of the nation's liberty and greatness.

Fortunately Dundee is never likely, now, to spread much farther. The pompous 'palaces' of her Jute 'barons'—the offensively pretentious obverse of Dundee's slums—extend for some miles along the road to the north. Then—the country of Angus.

Angus and Mearns, although more roughly than all

Gaul, is divided into three parts. Three physical regions: a broad undulating coastal plain tilting slightly from the sea; a parallel broad fertile strath inland; a highland region of glens and mountains. This first, coastal, region stretching northwards has on the right the North Sea, a broken indented coastline along which the waves are spilling themselves on beaches of fine yellow sand quite as often as they are foaming over rocks or breaking against the foot of cliffs. The northern extremities of the Sidlaws make the horizon inland, a range of heather-topped hills not ten miles distant from the coast. And all, between the Sidlaws and the sea, is cultivated land, fertile and delectable.

Seventeen miles along the coast the red town of Aberbrothoc lies in a semicircular hollow facing the sea. This is, now, the second most populous burgh of Angus, and had ambitions not so long ago to be an industrial town; the people pass in its narrow streets with a slightly purposeful or busy air, as if only a short time since they might have bustled. Its High Street starts at the seashore among plain, small-windowed houses and clouds of seagulls. It bends right, then left, mounting steadily; a rather narrow street of plain-fronted houses of average height, its character and line considerably spoiled and broken, however, in these recent years, by the tawdry fronts of cinemas and cheapjack English multiple shops. At about half a mile from the shore the street reaches its highest point, and there on the right, at the end of a small open space, is suddenly a lofty tower, a great and splendid gateway, and within a vista of majestic ruin. All the finest and noblest things in Scotland to-day are ruins, and the ruins of its magnificent Abbey are the sole glory of Arbroath.

King William the Lion founded this Abbey in 1178, and dedicated it to St. Thomas à Becket, who is supposed to have been his friend. Very soon its revenue and influence exceeded those of all other monastic establishments in Scotland with the sole exception of St. Andrews. From the beginning that influence and those revenues were notably expended in the national cause. Edward I of England came here in the summer of 1296; he had an enemy to his pretensions in Abbot Henry, whose method, it appears, was to hold the English up to ridicule. David Beaton was abbot here, the same great patriot and statesman who was later Cardinal, whom Henry VIII had murdered because he could neither be corrupted nor intimidated. On the 6th of April 1320 the Assembly of the Estates of Scotland met in this Abbey, presided over by King Robert Bruce in person, and it was here and on this occasion that the historic Letter to Pope John XXII was drawn up, which has its own place in the history of human struggle for freedom and justice for its noble and dignified assertion at that early date of the principle of national self-determination. 'As long as a hundred of us remain alive we will never submit to the domination of England. For it is not for honour or riches or glory but for liberty alone that we strive and contend, which no man will give up save with life itself.' Bernard of Linton, Chancellor of Scotland and Abbot of Aberbrothoc, was the writer of it.

Past the Abbey the road rises and runs north, and almost immediately into the country. Here are the broad, tree-bordered fields again. On the left, to westward, the land scarcely rises to a tree-dotted horizon, for the Sidlaws do not extend so far. All this country is a plateau ending abruptly on the east in a line of high red cliffs. Six miles and there is a village, the road dips suddenly, crosses a stream, rises, and the cliffs have given place on the right to Lunan Bay and miles of golden sand. Five miles farther on the plateau is broken. Below, a broad sheet of water comes in sight and a grey town on a strip of land between it and the sea. All at once in the north-west the Grampians have reappeared.

That grey town on a finger of land between two waters, whose towering steeple dominates the whole country about it, was already an important place and of old settlement in the tenth century; in mediæval times it was the second burgh of Angus and one of the most thriving and populous in Scotland. It is named, from its position on a promontory, in the Scottish language Monrois or Munross; since the period of French influence, Montrose. It was a royal residence in former times, and Edward I spent in it five days of July 1296. In 1303 Sir William Wallace came ashore here on his return from the Continent. It is said the Good Sir James Douglas embarked at this port for the Holy Land, carrying with him the heart of The Bruce. And it was from Montrose that James VIII set sail for France after the Rising of '15.

It has often been remarked of the towns of Scotland that all, even those that can make the smallest claim to beauty, possess at least character. This is twice true of the burghs of Angus, which are old as well as Scottish. They have character in the sense in which the word connotes a certain quality of strength or boldness and substantiality, and this they share with all Scottish towns, for it is not, in itself, a pleasant quality. (Even the appalling growths of the industrial era have character in this sense, which consists in being whatever they are with a kind of energy, of intensity. English slums, for instance, may be ugly, sordid, occasionally even grim; a Scottish slum, on the other hand, is like grimness itself, substantial sordidness, ugliness as it were in person.) And they have also, the Angus burghs, character in the second sense, in which it means a quality of uniqueness or difference by virtue of which each is a town by itself and in no danger of being confused with any other.

Character of this second kind Montrose possesses in as great degree as any place in Scotland. It had, of course, an advantage of situation. Surrounded by water on all sides but one it has by nature what another town will have only from foresight and by design, a shape. It has not been able to straggle out and merge into the countryside, and so retains a certain character of self-sufficiency and makes on sight a satisfyingly single or total impression. But the uniqueness of Montrose does not end in its peninsularity. It is by far the prettiest, most orderly, and withal most distinguished-looking town of this part of Scotland, and its unusually broad streets, plentifully interspersed with parks and trees and gardens, give it a very pleasing air of spaciousness. Its High Street runs, straight north, along the low ridge near the western edge of the peninsula; a rather singular street, dignified, very wide, and somehow foreign-looking, as it has been called, its 'foreign-ness' deriving partly from the number of houses built in the old fashion with the gable to the street—from which one-time predominant characteristic of its architecture the inhabitants have their local nickname, 'Gable-endies.' At the Port the street abruptly narrows, and gradually widening sweeps northward in a broad avenue of trees. And the street, and the whole town indeed, dominated to the point of being dwarfed by the great steeple of the Parish Kirk. Below the level of the High Street, on the east a line of parks and gardens runs the length of the town; some of them are planted with the gean, and in spring the young leaves fill their branches with a froth as of pale-green snow. Then on the east more streets and houses; and beyond, the Links extending away northward, edged along their whole length with dunes and golden beach.

Defoe said of the inhabitants of Montrose that they had 'more the air of gentlemen than merchants.' The town still bears itself with a certain air of distinction and assurance—more justified by its place in history than by its present state. It was formerly, however, in some sort a social centre, many families of the local aristocracy had town-houses in it. And it is certainly remarkable how large a number of distinguished persons and prominent in the national history were born in the town or its immediate neighbourhood: most notable among them perhaps the Marquess of Montrose, the greatest military genius of his time, and Andrew Melville, who did more than any other to make a Presbyterian Scotland.

Two miles north the river North Esk marks the boundary of Angus. Beyond lies the Mearns, the sub-province to Angus in ancient Pictish times. To one looking at the county to-day there will seem to have been a certain justice or appropriateness in the position it then occupied; for the Mearns is not unlike a second Angus on a smaller scale. There is the same plain tilting from the sea, but narrower. Inland the Howe o' the Mearns is like a diminished northern extension of the great valley of Strathmore. There are glens, but smaller; trees, but fewer. And the old, stone-built towns, some of scarcely more than a single street, might without straining the imagination be seen like burghs of the larger province shrunken in size and diminished historically.

No description of Angus begins to represent it until particular mention has been made of its trees and woods. They are the glory of the province, and the home-sickness of its exiles. From any random point they are everywhere conspicuous in the view; in long lines bordering the fields, in masses crowning the hill-tops, crowding on the slopes and river banks and in dens and dells of little streams. In spring and summer they make the province one great wooded park, green-cool and leafy; in autumn their colours riot over the countryside in an undulating bright-hued carpet; the cold sky of winter is edged along with a dark tracery of their leafless branches. Had they been pines the province must have had a wild and shaggy look. But the dignified and gracious beech predominates, and Angus is suave in appearance, warm and cultivated and civilized.

From Fettercairn in the inland of the Mearns southward to Edzell in Angus, and so on to Brechin, is almost one continuous avenue of trees. Brechin, on the bank of the South Esk, eight fertile, wooded miles to westward of Montrose, is the toy city of Angus. No one looking to-day at its small size and the leisurely, almost rustic life moving in its steep and narrow streets of old-fashioned houses, would take it to have been the place of note that it was in former times. Yet Brechin was once a rich episcopal see, and continuously till the Reformation a centre of influence and importance. King David I founded the cathedral about halfway through the twelfth century; its beauty and proportions can still be discerned under the post-Reformation 'improvements.' But that was by no means the beginning; Brechin, indeed, is found an important place when history first discovers it. A century and a half before the founding of the cathedral it is already mentioned as a large city and an important ecclesiastical centre. The 'Round Tower' beside the cathedral, which remains entire and architecturally an object of admiration until this day, dates from the Culdees and was built not later, and earlier possibly, than the nine-hundreds.

Angus is so little characterized by peculiarities of speech and accent that if it cannot be told where a man comes from by his speech it is almost safe to put him down as an Angusman. Nevertheless the accustomed ear can detect a difference in the speech of these landward parts. Along the coast the people tend to a narrowing and clipping of their words; inland they speak them with breadth, and throatily. The difference corresponds, it seems, to an unequal distribution of ability or aptitude. Montrose, for instance, on the coast, has become prominent for its connection (by reason of their birth or close association) with a surprising proportion of those outstanding in the modern

'Scottish Renaissance'—in literature, poetry, painting, and sculpture. But Montrose is no place at all for music. Brechin, on the other hand, is musical; and so, away to southward, is Forfar. So too (and, as many say, even more) is Kirriemuir, the farthest inland of the burghs and the true native country of Nellie Mitchell, whom the world knew as Melba.

Otherwise, the people of Angus are fairly of a type, or types. Among the country people especially, who have hardly suffered from immigration and admixture since the nation had its beginning, the two familiar, original types are constantly showing themselves. They may be seen repeated again and again with remarkable fidelity among the groups of ploughmen at fairs and feeing-markets—tall, big-boned, muscular men, with fair or reddish hair; and small, neat-bodied, active men, black-haired and white-complexioned; the Celtic type, and the pre-Celtic.

From Brechin the road runs south by west to Forfar; runs, that is, for thirteen miles through the northern end of the valley of Strathmore, as rich a farming tract as any in Britain. On the left, to eastward, are low hills; on the west, now only a few miles distant, a line of rounded summits, the Grampians. Angus would not be Angus without them. Over the greater part of the province they add both grandeur and variety, dignity and changefulness, to the scene. For the hills are different with every sky-change; let only a cloud pass and they are different. Sometimes, low-looking and leaden-hard, they have receded into distance: and again, growing in bulk, they seem to rise and approach; in winter white with snow and rose-hued in the sunset, in autumn heather-purple.

There are glens among them, winding a half-score miles and more into the mountains—Glen Esk, Glen Lee, Glen Prosen, Glen Clova, Glen Ogil, Glen Isla, and as many more, each one the prettiest of all if only it be the last seen. Two lower hills stand a little in advance of the range, flat-topped and ringed with fortifications since, two thousand years ago, they were twin forts of the Caledonians guarding the passes from the Roman arms; reminding one that it was somewhere along that line of hills that the Romans to their greater caution and respect encountered the Caledonians in the battle of Mons Graupius.

Even in Roman times Forfar is said to have possessed a castle. It was certainly already an old town when a parliament (which restored those whom MacBeth had forfeited) was held there by Calum a' Chinn Mhóir, called Malcolm Canmore now, the life and pious deeds of whose queen, St. Margaret, are also closely linked by tradition with the town and neighbourhood. Unfortunately the ancient past of Forfar can scarcely be discerned any longer except in names and traditions, for the town being strongly royalist and episcopalian the English destroyed its records and charters in 1651. To-day Forfar among its lochs is a straggling, disorderly town, its High Street winding unremarkably among streets of houses of which a great proportion are no higher than a single storey. If the leisurely, almost sleepy, life in those streets is ever touched or disturbed nowadays by any voice or recollection out of a more stirring and important past it is when from the parish kirk the bells ring out, the gift to their native town (in 1656) of two wealthy Stockholm merchants.

Five miles to westward of Forfar, right under the hills, lies the little red town of Kirriemuir, a burgh for the pocket. From its diminutive, three-cornered public square the narrow red streets plunge down giddily or fly away upward; narrow streets that only yesterday were murmurous with the weaver's shuttle. Kirriemuir, too, had its day of pomp and greatness. The Earls of Angus held court there in the day when the Douglas name was all-powerful over half of Scotland, and on the little townhouse in the square the Douglas arms can still be faintly traced. . . .

There is an idea abroad that Scotland is a desperately cold and rainy country, a land of dismal mists where the sun is seldom seen and melancholy rules the elements in perpetual inhospitality. That is not so. There are parts, it is true, that know the mist and the rain too well, for long seasons know them daily; but those are definite areas, and the conditions that affect them are particular. Other parts know no such wild and long inclemency. Some are as familiar with the sun as any equal area in the British Isles, and Angus is one of them. A quite typical day in Angus will be azure slashed with silver—the national colours.

Behind Kirriemuir a beacon-tower stands on a high summit of the Grampians, commanding nearly all the province. From such a vantage point let Angus be viewed on such a day. Behind and just below lies Glen Prosen, a 'fold of sunbeams,' and Glen Clova stretching westward into a region of high hill-masses and mounting summits. Turning, one looks down on the wide valley of Strathmore, the long range of the Sidlaws, a great expanse of delectable country rolling away in every direction into haze and distance. All are there, mountains, glens, rivers, the broad fields, the spreading woods: the dignity of hills, warmth, plenitude.

And everywhere, and over all, the very smell of history.

Lippen on Angus!

7. SCALLOWAY, SHETLAND

J. D. Rattar

IN THE SHETLAND ISLANDS

by

HUGH MACDIARMID

I

Can it be that never more
Men will grow on Islands?
Ithaka and Eriskay,
Iceland and Tahiti!
Must the engines he has forged
Raven so for spaces
That the Islands dwindle down,
Dwindle down!
Pots that shelve the tap-roots' growth?
Must it be that never more
Men will flower on Islands?
Crete and Corsica, Mitylene,
Aran and Iona!

So sings Padraic Colum, the Irish poet, in lines that curiously do not mention any of the Irish islands (unless by Aran he means the Aran Islands) though these have recently come into film fame and, as have the Blasket Islands, yielded literature descriptive of the simple lives of their inhabitants that, written in Irish Gaelic, has nevertheless, translated into English, achieved best-sellerdom both in Great Britain and in the United States. The natural economy of islands may be everywhere declining, save perhaps in the most idyllic latitudes (though this is not due to any real incapacity of the islands even in the coldest regions to support much larger populations than they do, but because 'the very inner logic of the capitalist system under which we live demands concentration, and in times of crises the outlying parts have to surrender their blood for the sake of the central heart'); but it is finding substitutes for itself—*nesophilia* is a great and ever-increasing contemporary cult! As an American writer, Katharine Fullerton Gerould, says: 'When the plight of the planet becomes desperate, people usually begin to babble about islands. I have recently been almost deafened with the word. In the literature and conversation of escape islands have always been more popular than caves or vales or mountain summits. They seem to spell the only secure isolation. Even when authors have merely wished to display some human experiment unhampered by society—Defoe, or Bernardin de Saint Pierre, or Hermann Melville, or H. G. Wells—they have chosen islands for their scene. And, conversely, if authority wishes to be quite free of some human being whom it does not dare to kill, it finds an island for his exile; the Salt Islands—or L'Ile du Diable—or St. Helena—or Trimerus.'

I betook myself to islands—and to islands so little-known and to which so little allure has ever attached itself as the Shetland Islands—for neither of these reasons. I was not surprised to notice early in 1934 when the first issue appeared of the magazine of the Cambridge University Wayfarers Club, that the Arctic Circle had become very popular with the Wayfarers. That was by no means the first indication of a very considerable reorientation of interest. The preceding couple of years had been very markedly Polar Years. Indeed Mr. F. Spencer Chapman in his book, *Watkins' Last Expedition*, the objective of which, as of his previous expedition, was the survey of a suitable base for sea-planes on the East Greenland route, gives, as one reviewer put it, 'a kaleidoscopic picture of the Arctic at a crowded moment of its history. The "Polar Year" had brought French and Dutch ships and scientists to join the normal migratory summer population of Norwegian hunters, Scotch fishermen, and Danish administrators and explorers. The Lindbergs and the "flying family" contributed their quota to the evidence regarding the hazards of the Greenland air route. . . . Mingled with these unusual happenings were the ordinary incidents of Eskimo life. A family of eleven people are shown carrying over stormy seas, in a simple sealskin boat, not only themselves but enough gear to make them completely independent of the world for a year. East Greenland of to-day is a curious *mélange* of the modern and the primitive. Echo-sounding apparatus is used as an aid to halibut-fishing; motor-boats and kayaks navigate the coast; bone-pointed spears and high-velocity rifles are held in readiness at the same seal hole; raw meat and cake with reindeer-hairs and trouser buttons on the one hand contrast with the luxuries of a French Polar Year expedition on the other.'

Why did I come north to live in the Shetlands myself and, finding the eyes of the more intelligent Shetlanders bent on the Faroe Islands, go thither too? The same reviewer's next sentence gives a clue. 'Polar explorers seem to have a natural gift for narrative,' he says. In a volume of essays published last year I dealt with some aspects of this new northern interest and connected it up with the evacuation of St. Kilda and certain developments in the Western Highlands and Islands of Scotland, coming to sinister conclusions with regard to what was afoot in the realms of high policy, but my personal incentive derived from a very different, if not unrelated source. To wit, certain developments in literary tendency. I had always been interested in the great question of North versus South, though the breaking of the old European balance and the titanic emergence of Russia—the East—seemed (and still seems) to me to call for an attempt on the part of the Gaelic elements of the West—Ireland, Scotland, Wales, Cornwall, Brittany—to put forward the Gaelic idea as a complement and corrective to the Russian, making an effective quadrilateral of forces; and in the establishment of Saorstat Eireann and other happenings I hailed what appeared (and appears) to me to be the true 'Defence of the West,' essential to the conservation of European culture. Whatever the general considerations might be, however, my personal concern was not with Gaelic but with Scots and against southern English. I rejoiced in Charles Doughty's poetry and in Gerard Manley Hopkins's return to the sprung rhythm of Langland and Skelton and in the other signs of attempts to get 'back behind the Renaissance,' to break away from the Latin and French influences which had prevailed too long in English literature and return at long last to native rhythms and a deGraecized, deLatinized, and deFrenchified language. The general reasons for the unwonted activities in Greenland and other parts of the North were of less consequence to me than the coincidence that Professor W. A. Craigie was simultaneously publishing a book on the Northern influence in English literature, though I was, of course, very conscious of the relationship of politics and literature. I remembered suggestive things on the possibilities of a more concentrated attention to, and development of, that Northern influence in the writings of W. P. Ker, H. J. C. Grierson, and Edwin Muir. I remembered Elizabeth Elstob's fight for Anglo-Saxon and how long the still dominant (though to-day progressively assailed) tradition excluded Anglo-Saxon from English studies in exactly the same way that English ascendancy has treated Gaelic in Ireland and Scotland, and Scots too in the latter. And, above all, as against the declaration of Dr. G. S. Gordon of Magdalen, Oxford, that Latin 'is the sap of our speech,' I remembered that passage in Professor W. W. Skeat's *Principles of English Etymology* which runs: 'No doubt Latin and Greek form an important element in the English language, but it may be replied that these are least affected by fonetic spelling; that the most important elements of our language are neither Latin nor Greek but English, Scandinavian, and French. The English and Scandinavian elements are very carefully kept out of sight by Archbishop Trench in his *English Past and Present* except in a very few instances; and the French element is treated very briefly and unsatisfactorily.' And finally I recollected, too, how Dr. A. J. Ellis had pointed out that Trench's negligence of the chief elements of English arose through his not having been trained in the Old English at school—a fact which need not excite any surprise when it is remembered that the Chair for

English at Oxford was instituted only between twenty and thirty years ago.

Politics and Literature! Apart from the question of Scottish Nationalism I had also in mind the idea since discussed by Sir Karl Knudson, Sir Norman Angell and others—that the Oslo Convention group, which represents nearly twenty-eight million people, might come within the scope of an 'Economic British Empire.'*

So I took up my residence in one of the little North Isles of the Shetland group.

II

'One must mention the life of the country,' wrote Benjamin Crémieux, apropos his visit to Scotland in connection with the International P.E.N. Conference in 1934. 'That of the Isles surprises one from the very first by its timeless quality. For a Frenchman it is like Brittany ten or fifty or a hundred times intensified. All that man, isolated by mist, wind, and cold at the edge of the ocean, has been able to invent to reassure himself and to calm his fears—magic, legends, superstitions—all are to be found here. It is a vast store of dreams and of nightmares.' But he was writing of the Hebrides. It is a pity that he did not include the Shetlands in his tour as did his compatriot, Louis Cazamian, whose book, *La Grande Bretagne*, renders equal justice to the savage grandeur of Skye and to the

* See also the most interesting discussion of the new role of the Polar regions in diplomacy, the real significance of the dispute between Denmark and Norway over Greenland, and the importance of that region for air communications, in Y. M. Goblet's *Le Crepuscule Des Traites* (Paris, 1935).

changing skies of the Shetlands, the land of the Midnight Sun with its

> summer's night
> When maids could sew by a worm's light

and where, almost if not quite, the sea sends out

> bright hues that like birds flit about
> In solid cages of white ice.

For in the Shetlands the things that M. Crémieux lists as the natural inventions of men isolated by mist, wind and cold at the edge of the ocean are, in contradistinction to what prevails in the Hebrides, conspicuously absent. The Shetlands are 'wropt' in no false glamour, no Celtic twilight; they secrete for eventual finding by the counterparts of Mrs. Kennedy Fraser and the Rev. Dr. Kenneth MacLeod no equivalents of the 'Hebridean Songs'; they are happily very little encumbered with 'memorials of the past' of any kind; they have to all intents and purposes—in the consciousness of the people—no history; they may call themselves 'the Viking Isles' or Ultima Thule, but these are only attempts at imitating the popular appellations of other regions for tourist-attracting purposes—they have really no 'mental climate,' have not entered into the consciousness of the Scottish people even, and are the subject of practically no writing except guide-book stuff and certainly of nothing worth a moment's consideration in poetry or descriptive prose. Nothing has been written of them a tenth part as good as, for example, Compton Mackenzie's pages on the Shiant Isles, on the nursery of Atlantic seals at Gasker, and on Eriskay.

The Shetlands, of course, have a very long and very

interesting, but little known, history. It has never become a clear and collected possession in the minds of the people, however; they have only the vaguest notions and most scattered details of it. And as for superstitions, they have their 'trows' (or trolls), the little underground folk, and all the taboos associated with ships and fishing. They have also their Shetland Reels and the Papa Stour Sword Dance. But they have no developed artistic or literary tradition any more than they have any properly articulated and effective history and their little superstitions and tales of weird happenings are very small beer indeed compared with the colourful and imposing myths of the Gaelic islands. The complete divorce from musical accompaniment which differentiated the verse of the Norsemen from the rest of Teutonic poetry still characterizes the recitations of the old men in the Shetlands, but the poems recited—sea-ballads, often interminably long—are none of them of Shetland origin; they have been gathered from here, there, and everywhere. One other little point occurs to me here. I think the English writer was wrong who, dealing with the late Axel Olrik's book, *Viking Civilization*, wrote: 'His comparison of the "kennings" of the skalds with the distortion of animal figures which characterized the decorative art of the period is suggestive but hardly sufficient to justify the perverse artificiality of a convention which never permitted a poet to call a spade a spade. The Norse poet seems so intent on showing off his verbal ingenuity that he seldom leaves himself room for genuine poetic feeling. Eyvind Skaldaspillir calling arrows "herrings of the bowstring" and herrings "arrows of the sea" is not doing so with any idea of filling a space decoratively; he is merely calling attention to his own cleverness.' This comes ill after the same writer declaring—on the contested question of Irish influence on Northern art and literature before the tenth century—that he agrees with Professor Paasche in his *Norsk Litteratur Historie* in doubting this influence and that 'the fundamental contrast between the fantasy of Celtic legend and the sober realism of Icelandic saga speaks strongly against it.' Waiving the point that a very large proportion of classical Irish literature is realistic enough in all conscience, Eyvind Skaldaspillir's verbal ingenuities sprang far more probably from that practical habit of the fisher-folk which in the Shetland Islands, as in Norway and the Faroes and elsewhere, led and still leads to the use of 'lucky words.' For example, the minister and the church were on no account to be mentioned by their right names at sea; being offensive to the old sea god and sea spirits the church had to be called 'de benihoose' and the minister the 'upstander,' and again, all sorts of figurative terms had to be used instead of the ordinary names for persons, animals and things, like 'de shaavin' for the cat (from the cat's habit of washing itself up round the ears and down over the nose) and 'dratsi' for the otter, from its manner of dragging its tail; together with all the other special words used at the haaf (deep sea) fishing instead of those employed for the same articles or animals at the fireside. Many of these special haaf words are still used by the fishermen at sea, just as the Manx fishermen still use the old Manx language in making up their catch.

The present position of the old Norn or Shetland

language is just as Dr. Jakobsen, the great Faroese philologist described it in 1897. 'The common dialect at the present day in Shetland,' he wrote, 'resembles the Lowland Scotch, but is interspersed with a great many Norn words and phrases and has a distinctly Scandinavian accentuation and pronunciation. It is just now leaving a stage, the prominent feature of which is Scotch, and is entering a stage, the prominent feature of which is English, but still carrying along with it from the first or Norn period, not only a number of words, although this number is rapidly diminishing, but also a pronunciation and accentuation which are distinctly Scandinavian.' Since then the main thing to note is an accentuation of the feeling of Shetlanders that they are Scandinavians and not Scots, and this has been intensified in the last few years by the re-establishment of friendly comings and goings with their kinsmen, the Faroese. The Faroese, unlike the Shetlanders, have fully preserved their old tongue, and it has been the medium of a very active and interesting literary and dramatic renaissance. Before anything similar could be attempted in the Shetlands a full canon of the old language would have to be regained. So far only a little dialect work has been done and this has the limitations of all dialect work—it is mere kailyaird stuff. Again as matters stand the Shetlanders are hopelessly provincialized, while the Faroese are fully European as well as possessed of a political and cultural autonomy which gives them equal status with every other sovereign element in Europe. The cultural and Home Rule movements in the Faroes have gone hand in hand with a notable economic regeneration, and it may well be that in the

Shetlands too none of these three can be achieved without the other two. Eighty years ago the Faroes were reduced to a far worse pass than has yet overtaken the Shetlands, bad as that is. The Faroese then learned from the Shetlanders that cod-fishing industry which has in that brief period—within living memory—enabled them to rise from the slough of despond and make themselves one of the most prosperous, progressive, and independent communities in Europe. It would seem that the Faroes can now repay their debt. What they have so quickly and triumphantly accomplished there is nothing to prevent the Shetlands doing too—given similar determination and enterprise, and a similar realization of the relationship of cultural and economic factors.

It will be a very great pity if they prefer to embark on a mere tourist industry instead, and in lieu of creating a real literature engage in the wholesale churning out of that tenth-rate descriptive stuff, rehashing of old rubbish and silly verse to which the Hebrides have lent themselves on such an appalling scale. Just as it takes a visitor some time to get accustomed to the total absence of trees on these islands and to appreciate that this involves no lack of variety, but that he must seek that in aspects of nature hitherto far less available to him than here—in the shapes and colours of the rocks and their relationships with the sea, so anything will be a sad misfortune which prefers any imitation of what obtains elsewhere to a patient realization of the *differentia* of the Shetlands. Just as the adventures, the dangers, the thrills of work in these dim northern waters are best brought out, not by over-statement, but by a calm regard for fact and an intimate knowledge of the subject—just as the fishermen are engaged in a trade that still demands the qualities of individual judgment, courage and hardihood that tend to disappear both from literature and life—the Shetlands call alike in the arts and in affairs for the true creative spirit. Anything pettier would be sadly out of place in these little-known and lonely regions, encompassed about with the strange beauty of the North, the fluctuation of unearthly colour at different levels of the sun, the luminous air, the gleam of distant ice, and the awful stillness of northern fog. Or transfigured with such marvellous spectacles as when 'the stars are almost dimmed by the shaking curtain of aurora, at first a nebulous radiance but gradually changing to clear-cut ribbons of light quivering and waving like seaweed fixed to a rock in a strong tide.'

As among the Eskimos primitive and modern are found side by side in the Shetlands—and the advantage seldom lies with the modern (save perhaps in the provision of medical services, including different methods than delivering a case of retention of urine with a *haigrie's pen*—a heron's quill—in lieu of a catheter!). It takes the mail steamer, the *Earl of Zetland*, at least an hour and a half to go from Lerwick to the little North isle of Whalsay; the old Shetland fishermen in their 'sixareens' (six-oared boats) with the square-sail could do it in three-quarters of an hour. It seems incredible. What wonderful seamanship they must have had (though it perhaps hardly equals that great, and most necessary, kayak trick, the roll, by which it is possible for the navigator to turn clean over in the water and come up again without upsetting himself or the craft)! Little knowledge of that remains to-day; it is idle to prate of the Vikings when they have forgotten even the strange skills of their grandfathers and great-grandfathers. The halyard-man was of more consequence on one of these sixareens than the helmsman. Working the rope without a block, he had to raise and lower continually as the boat literally flew like a kite on the top of the water—a ticklish business enough in, say, the complicated tideways of Yell Sound. Yet with these boats, only half the size of the little motor-boats the fishermen use to-day for the haddock fishing, they could go to the deep-sea fishing and get as many fish in three days as with all their bigger boats and superior equipment they can get to-day in five. But the fish were far more plentiful. In other words the trawlers had not begun their destructive work. Nor had the ruinous modern organization of the fishing industry complicated their task and begun to make it increasingly difficult to earn a comfortable living. Now a myopic policy is destroying far more than it utilizes, paying no regard to the native economy of areas like the Shetland Islands, and riding rough shod over the traditional way of life of the independent crofter-fisherman. Probably the heyday of the Shetland fishermen was in the eighties of last century. Since then the declension has been rapid.

In 1801 the population of the Shetlands (which is an archipelago of 100 close-lying islands, of which about twenty are inhabited, with, in addition, the distant islands of Foola and Fair Isle, also inhabited) was 22,379, and it continued to increase without interruption, though latterly at a declining rate, up to and including the census of 1861 when a maximum population of 31,670 was reached. Since then its record has been one of persistent decline—specially marked in recent decades. In 1881 the population fell below 30,000; in 1911 below 28,000; in 1931 the total resident population was only 21,341. The average number of persons to each 100 acres is six. Excepting that the average age of males is slightly higher in Sutherlandshire than in Shetland the average ages in the County of Zetland are higher than in any other Scottish county; over twenty per cent. of the inhabitants are sixty years old and upwards. Mr. Thomas M. Y. Manson accurately describes the present economic position in the following passages: 'The standard of life in the Islands is high for a crofting community, and there is no real want or poverty. It has often been said that while the Orcadian is a farmer with a boat, the Shetlander is a fisherman with a croft, and to a large extent this is true; for while Orkney is a fairly low-lying fertile land, the hilly, rocky islands of Shetland permit only small crofts, providing a bare subsistence, and force the people to other occupations. But in past centuries this was more the case than it is to-day, and at the present time there is no great mass of regular fishermen in Shetland as there is in the Faroes. The Shetlanders have chosen rather to follow the sea, to enter all kinds of occupations in the outer world, and to emigrate to the Colonies. As a consequence the Islands are a great nursery of seamen and officers for the Mercantile Marine, and for the population of the county an extraordinary number of natives are scattered over the globe. Those who have remained in the Islands have always suffered from the want of organized industry, even if they have retained a great measure of individual freedom; but so far as industry has developed in the Islands it has now become divided between the men and women in the Herring Fishing Industry and the Hosiery Industry. About forty years ago, when the importance of Shetland for the herring fishing became fully realized in the Islands and in Britain generally, as it had been realized to good advantage for centuries in Holland, that industry seemed likely to become the staple one for the Islands, and hundreds of Shetland sailors came home to participate in it, using the decked sailboat to fish with. But the advent of the expensive steam-drifter, and the auction system of selling herring, effected a very radical change in the industry so far as the native fishermen were concerned. In consequence there arose the present situation under which, while the Shetland waters are still of leading importance for the summer British herring fishing—while, indeed, Lerwick is the Herringopolis for Scotland, assembling annually upwards of 300 herring-drifters and usually curing more herrings than any other Scottish port—the Shetlanders have but a minor share in this industry. If, however, a cheaper type of boat is forced on the trade generally by the pressure of costs, as seems likely to happen, the industry may come more within the grasp of the Shetland crofter-fishermen. . . . It suffices to say that at present the position is one of uncertainty and doubt, which cannot be altogether compensated for by the women's hosiery industry. It has often been urged that progress will not be made till agriculture and fishing are separated. There are signs of increasing attention to agriculture, and the influence is being felt to a considerable degree of successive County Organizers and

Dairy and Poultry instructresses maintained in the Islands by the North of Scotland College of Agriculture. But only in a few parts of Shetland will agriculture provide a decent livelihood. In these times it is a problem to know whether a considerable population could risk throwing themselves altogether on fishing, even if they had capital behind them. It is also a problem to know which or how many fishings should be engaged in.'

This presents the situation very fairly. My own view, in so far as it in any way supplements what Mr. Manson has said, is that there seems to be no good reason why the Shetlands should not recapture a share of the dried white fish market, which they perhaps over-hastily abandoned when the herring industry came to the front. The demand is constant, mainly in Spain and the other Catholic countries. The Faroe Islands subsist prosperously on it, supplying only fifteen per cent. of the demand. If the Shetlands could 'chip in' again in this field (running the whole industry communally and keeping out external financial and other elements—thus ensuring that the total proceeds accrued to the Islands themselves) to the extent of ten per cent. or less of the demand they could reorganize themselves as happily as the Faroese. They could also in this way strengthen, instead of having to surrender as practically any other course open to them implies, that 'great measure of individual freedom' they still retain—and, to give them their due, appropriately prize. The fear of endangering that in any way is behind their political or even local organizational quiescence; that—and a wholesome disbelief in a political system centralized in London.* I do not think there is nowadays much actual antipathy to the Scottish people (an historical hatred dating back to the cruelties and unconscionable exactions of the Feudal days), but the insistence that the Shetlanders are Scandinavians is strong and represents a tendency which I think ought to be encouraged by all possible means, and especially by a recovery of the old Norn tongue, and an effort to build up a vigorous cultural movement on that basis, since that can only help them to preserve and develop a distinctive life which in its insistence on the economic self-sufficiency of every family, and the ability of the adults to discharge the whole range of tasks called for by their requirements, is a very healthy and desirable one in these days of ever-increasing mutual dependence and the division of labour till most individuals are relegated to one repetitive little operation or part of an operation. I have no personal desire to be able to cry like the author of *True North*: 'Every completed object in my house is my own, made with my own two hands. I don't owe anything for it either in skill or time.' Even so there are certain 'chores' that fall to me, and I think it is quite good for me to have to make and 'rest' ('rested' every night it is said there are peat fires in the Shetlands, and in the Hebrides that have never been out for over a hundred years) peat fires in an open hearth, draw water from the well, catch my own fry of fish now and then, and other incidentals of island life.

* A fisherman said to me the other day: "What do you think of the new Herring Board?" I replied that I didn't think it would do much good. He laughed. "There's no question of its doing any good," he said. "All we're concerned about is how much, or how little, harm it's going to do!" This illustrates the general attitude.

Though I have only 'gone native' to such a very small extent, however, I admire the all-round efficiency and adaptability of the men amongst whom I live—cobbling, butchering, farming, fishing, managing their boats, and so on as the rotation of the seasons or the needs of their households may require, and regard their lot as one that at least ninety per cent. of the working-class population of Great Britain might well envy. However that may be, if only because these Islands have proved in the past such a splendid reservoir of men for the Mercantile Marine and for the pioneering life of the Colonies, everything possible ought to be done to see that it does not become enfeebled and unable to continue to yield in the future as heretofore.

III

I have alluded to the peat-fire and the open hearth in my own cottage, but apart from such details Shetland housing has been greatly modernized within the lifetime of the older inhabitants and the old cottages with thatched roofs, mere holes in the ceiling for chimneys, and windows about the size of a hand are all gone. It is difficult to imagine what life must have been in those days not so far distant when communications with the South were exceedingly few and far between, letters and newspapers scarcely ever heard of, and lighting a matter of the old iron 'collies' and fish oil, or out-of-doors on the pitch-black windy Shetland winter nights only a live peat instead of the now ubiquitous electric torches. But it was undoubtedly true of the poor old cottages of those days, as of their counterparts, the old *black houses*, in the Hebrides—that life in them was not only more civilized, in its essentials, than in the average back street of Manchester or the Gorbals of Glasgow, but healthier than in the trig but flimsy cottage erected by the Local Government Board. And the Shetlanders will be well-advised to hold on to or recover whatever they can of their traditional mode of life even if they cannot get back to having cottages in which the passage between two box beds is 'covered over the top with pieces of boat's boards, which form a lame for laying lines, cashies, buddies, skinjups, sea-boots, and other articles requiring to occupy this elevated position, while on the wall and tied with a piece of boucht hangs a rack for the crockery, spoons, etc., and under this rack and close to the wall stands an old oak table, with a very deep drawer, containing the good man's pipe, his seal-skin cash, with some Dutch shag in it, sillock flees, ooin tread, a' auld loopick, a muckle tully, a peerie gipper, a pawm, a sail needle, a tome-spinner made of peat, a yarkin allishen, a Norway ladle, a gruel tree, a cashie-needle, with a variety of smaller articles.'

And although the island quietudes may never again be broken by an old wife railing at her husband in terms like these: 'Gaen stravaigin ower da face o' da eart like a benummed monyment, as if du hed nidder horse or coo ta luik efter. Dere's da puir jures o' kye never haed der stakes muved dis blessed day yet, nor a lempit taen fir gettin' a bone o' fish wi', nor a girspuckle for da beas' meat at nicht, nor da hoes an' skate rumples boiled fir da grice, nor da kail howed dats gaen ower wi' shicken-wirt runshick an' melda, nor da twa lives o' sheep dats fastened i' da ness luiked efter, nor da grain o' dry bare taen ta da mill dats standin' rawin' an' wastin' i' da barn. . . .'

8. The Barra Isles

Robert M. Adam

THE OUTER ISLES

by

HECTOR MacIVER

Our house stood on a high ridge above the sea, on one of the stormiest hills in the Hebrides, so that the first sounds I became familiar with were those of the waves and of the wind. If I describe the life and appearance of this West Lewis village in which I was reared, I shall be dealing with something that is typical of all the islands, for wherever I have gone in the Hebrides I have found only slight variations on the life of that small community into which I was born.

The village was bounded on the east and west by two huge headlands that flung themselves into the Atlantic like two couching beasts cooling their dark bellies in the sea. The wide and shelterless bay that lay below the crofts was cleft by a long skerry at whose outermost end a rounded bastion of rock stood up above the stones. When the tide flowed in over the skerry, this thing looked like the citadel of a drowning city over whose roofs the water was beginning to rise. To the south we were guarded by a ridge of high hills and from the moors behind them the night leapt upon us in the winter time with the suddenness of an animal's leap. The village itself was built for the most part on two rocky ridges that rose gradually from the wide valley which separated them. From the centre of the valley the houses on either ridge could be seen clearly etched against the sky and their huddled forms appeared to stand on the lonely edge of the world. A river came tumbling down through the valley and poured itself into a great fresh-water loch which bordered so closely on the sea that only a few yards of soil kept the peace between them. There were no trees against which the wind could wrestle, to spend its crude strength before it shook the houses. So the winter landscape was bare and desolate, with nothing to hide the outlines of the naked earth; but it had the inexpressible, sad beauty which barrenness has everywhere, in nature and in man. And the barrenness did not last long, for it only required the embrace of the spring to fill the dark earth with new life and new joy. But there was one measure of self-defence taken by the villagers against the colourless winters. Every conceivable piece of wood in the village was painted in bright and striking colours. Red windows peered out from under the golden straw that thatched the houses. Doors of flaming red caught the light of the sun on the top of each ridge and glared at each other across the shivering fields. The boats lay in a cluster at one end of the shore, splashed with shades of blue and white. Sometimes a red petticoat flew from a clothes-line, looking as if it had been dyed in blood, and red ploughs, painted afresh in preparation for the spring, leaned against gables and walls.

The winter was the festive season in the village. If any marriages had been arranged they took place then, and in the celebrations which accompanied them the bitterness of the season was forgotten. When a marriage was about to take place, two messengers were sent out and by calling at the threshold of each house, they invited the whole village to the wedding. The evening began with feasting. Barns were decorated and the guests were seated at long narrow tables lit by oil lamps that hung from the rafters. The young men jested with the girls. Old men leaned backwards and recalled with sly laughter the number of marriages they had ever attended, up and down the island. Someone got up to sing. A girl perhaps. She chose one of her mournful songs. The music of the song possessed her limbs so that her body swayed in answer to the chant upon her lips. Again she sang a *port-a-beul*, a dance tune, and its urgent, lilting rhythm compelled the company to dance. They danced on the clay floor of the barn. At many weddings all the neighbouring barns had to be commissioned for the night. Some of the men folk shouted excitedly as they danced, because the flame of the drink they took had passed into their blood and they felt triumphant and ecstatic. The lamp light threw strange, writhing shadows on the walls as the dancers whirled. The mad laughter of the wind outside mingled with the music of the dance. And above the clumping sound of feet on the clay floor could be heard at times the loud rumour of Atlantic breakers, till the outside world seemed to have joined hands with the dancers in one corybantic revel. But mostly it was bagpipe or accordeon music for the dance, for the singing of *puirt-a-beul* was a strenuous task and could not be sustained for very long. The dancing usually continued till the light of the sunrise fell in white streaks across the floor and the lamplight became a bloodless flame.

The keen desire for dancing among the youth of the

village did not require a wedding to have it satisfied. A barn could be prepared for a dance at any time by piling the barley sheaves into a corner, and, failing a barn, a smooth piece of road was as suitable as anything else on a moonlit night.

Besides that, there was always the dance which followed the *luadh* or waulking of the tweed; for the *luadh* was a piece of ancient labour which had become a social event also in the life of the village. Whenever the weaver had shot the last shuttle through a web, the cloth was taken off the loom and washed in deep tubs. Bare-footed girls went into the tubs and stamped heavily on the cloth till the warm, soapy water released from the threads the oils and grease they had accumulated in the process of manufacture. Then the cloth was rinsed and laid in steaming folds on a low table with an uneven surface, on which the waulking was done. Five or six girls sat at each side of the table and each one coiled a loop of the wet cloth round her bare arms. They pounded the cloth on the rough boards of the table till it had shrunk to the required width. Their movements were at first slow and cautious till they adapted themselves to one another's rhythm and the swing of their bodies as they worked. Then the leading singer among them began a waulking song, and suddenly their work became an exhibition of furious movement and self-expression. The leader supplied the lines of the song; the others replied with a chorus, giving emphasis to each phrase with their arms and bodies. After each separate line of the song the chorus rose in a tumult, like a triumphant wave flooding the rocks. And as the theme of the song moved towards its climax, the singers became more energetic and excited till their arms were moving in semi-circles like those of swimmers in a crawl, and their hair fell in streaming strands into their eyes. Their songs were all traditional and their themes were invariably associated with the mountains and the sea:

On the tide face in the narrows
Youths at their steering now,
Rowing while wind follows,
Foam-spit across their prow.

The youths of the village came in to listen to the song and to hear their names woven into the verses which the singers improvised when the traditional words were all sung. And so the work went on all day, till the lamp-light lit up the flushed and sweating faces of the workers. It was hard and exhausting work but it was done by girls whose bodies were animated with music and who found in the process of waulking a medium for self-expression. After the waulking, till the early hours of the morning, the dance.

When there was no other form of pastime in the village there was always the *céilidh*. *Céilidh* is the Gaelic word for a visit, not for a 'social.' It is not, as is usually supposed, a continual recital of Gaelic songs relieved by interludes of long-winded Fenian sagas. It is much more human than that, because the primary things that interest country people are the events of their daily lives and the attractive gossip that arises therefrom. The islanders have as keen an appetite for gossip and scandal as peasants have in all parts of the world, and it is out of their gossip that their tales are born. For when news is scarce, as it often is in the Hebrides, the most trivial event becomes a sensation and when it has been mouthed by whole villages, it gradually takes on the dimensions of a legend. The result is that many islanders become half legendary characters before they die.

So it was in the village of which I speak. There were songs to be heard at a *céilidh* for the asking, and old men could tell tales of their own experiences that would hold the company spellbound for hours. But quite often the entire evening was given up to the lively gossip and conversation which the different seasons brought round. News travelled round the village like a gust of wind. If a child was born the garrulous midwife called in every house on the way home to announce the event, and in a twinkling it was known at the other end of the village. If any strangers arrived in the village, their identity was quickly known to everybody. If a cow calved or a sheep lambed, the news sent a tremor of excitement through the whole street, for such things were events of importance in the life of the community. If a boat was all but swamped at sea in a sudden storm, as was very often the case, the incident was on everybody's lips. Such were the topics of discussion at a *céilidh*.

But the coming of spring was eagerly awaited, for nowhere in the world does it perform such a miracle as in the Outer Isles. The ferment seemed to begin in the sea, for it cast out of its caves with a moaning like the noise of birth, fresh masses of brown seaweed that lay strewn along the beach. Shoals of haddock and saith appeared on the coast and the sea birds, noticing them, became wild and clamorous. They rose in white flocks from the sunless cliffs, passing in rhythmic flight over the bay, veering against the wind. The gannets dived and shouted, swooping and spinning down from great heights, splashing into the water with clasped wings.

A warmer wind blew in from the moors and produced a mysterious quickening in the dark soil of the crofts. Blood seemed to flow again in the veins of the earth, till it began to throb with the pulse of a new life. It cracked and burst, opening its pores to receive the germs of new crops. The villagers appeared in the fields, seized with the same strange quickening as if the beat of their blood were responding to the earth's pulse. On every hill the forms of workers appeared against the sky. On distant ridges a company of women, bent over their spades, looked like large, grotesque birds pecking at the soil. Their voices as they shouted over the fields were tremulous with eagerness and desire. Everywhere there was a lust for work. Spades were plunged into the moist soil; horses crawled along with their small ploughs, and in their wake a flock of ravenous sea birds snapped up worms and roots and grubs. Clouds of delicate grey mist rose from the moist earth, and in the fields everywhere was the acrid, satisfying smell of soil that had been newly delved. Seed was scattered on the furrows—mostly barley seed because in West Lewis they have great use for barley. They grind it in the village mills into meal for barley-bread, and if the harvest has been a successful one, they brew from the barley seed barrels of rich, creamy beer.

Peat-cutting was the work which followed the tilling of the fields. Then came the summer migration to the sheiling—a custom which only the Island of Lewis preserved. The sheilings were low dwellings of turf and stone, built beside running water in the heart of the moor. They were thatched with heather and streaky rushes cut from the moorland bogs. Inside, little alcoves were let into the wall to hold basins of milk and crocks of cream. The fire burned against the wall at one end of the building, and about two feet away from it was built up a little ridge of turf which served alternately as a table and as a bench. The ground-space behind this ridge was packed with moss and dried grasses to form a bed. There were two doors, so that when the one to windward was closed, entrance and exit could be made on the sheltered side. The doors were very low and one had to bend double before getting inside. The sheiling was the summer headquarters of the cattle. All day long they grazed on the hillsides and among the heather. In the evening they returned to the sheiling to be milked. Every morning a girl from each sheiling returned to the village, carrying with her a day's supply of milk, and sometimes perhaps a crock of cream ready for churning. When she went back in the evening she took with her a creel full of newly cut grass or fresh tangle, to delight the cows at milking time. The moors were covered with fresh-water lochs, in which idling herdboys could fish to their heart's content, and in the evening there was always good company at the sheiling, and the singing of many an old song. There is one exquisite fragment still sung, in which a girl addresses the rowers in a boat, praising the milk of her cattle:

When they've moored her I'll bring them
Milk from my youngest cow,
From the brown one, from the yellow,
Milk that is sweetest now.

Not a drink of brown water
Cold from the moorland spring,
But the milk of my own milking
Fresh from my cows I bring.

Beinn Huitealam stood above the village. Its name was Norse, like most of the place names of Lewis for when the Northmen came to the islands in prowling hordes, to plunder and rape, they left behind them something more beautiful than the traces of their slaughter—the names of lochs and headlands and streams. From the top of Huitealam on a summer's day I could see the greater part of Lewis rising drowsily from the sea, its limbs thrown out like those of a tired animal stretching itself and shaking off weariness. The blue fields of the sea were smooth at last, no longer a mass of running crests, throwing white curls of spray behind them. On the beach the small waves tumbled and raced upwards to embrace the warm sand and shellgrit. The boats swung at anchor in the bay, waiting for the men from the fields and the looms. Under them the sea was shallow and its water a light green that merged into blue beyond the rocks.

The village itself (called by the Norse *Siabost* or Steading by the Sea) sat on its warm ridges, all thoughts of its blotchy winter landscape forgotten. The green crops swayed lifelessly, waiting for the swish of summer rain. Down to the Butt, the villages of West Lewis were all visible, their windows reflecting the rays of the sun. Dimly the Butt lighthouse rose from its rocky perch, looking impotent and silly in the fierce light. Muirneag hill on the moors of Ness brooded over her widowhood. The four peaks of the Barvas hills threw their long shadows over the sheilings below them. Below Huitealam was Loch Raoinabhat, a straggling sheet of water from whose face the floating clouds in the sky were reflected like white flames. Beside the loch, in a circular hollow among the hills, was the lovely village of Dalbeg, with its few scattered houses. To the west lay the finest sea loch in the Hebrides, the mighty Loch Roag whose tides swirled round countless islands. The little island of Bernera lay in its mouth, a place that breeds the most dare-devil fishermen in the Hebrides. Outside Bernera the desolate rock of Bereasaidh appeared like the back of some huge whale. On this rock Neil MacLeod, the illustrious warrior of Lewis, spent three years during the clan warfare of the sixteenth century. Above Loch Roag rose the dark blue towers and pinnacles of the Uig mountains, the highest range in Lewis. Mealasbhal and Suainabhal loomed above their neighbours, Mealasbhal's frowning precipices and mountain chasms floodlit with strong light. The sands of Valtos Bay gleamed yellow in the distance. To the south the sky-line was chequered with the vivid outlines of the Harris hills. And stretching towards them were the broad folds of Lewis moors, that seemed to burn and quiver and shake in the summer heat, like a landscape seen through the mad mind of Van Gogh. The purple and red blooms of heather lit up the moors, giving them the colour of *fion na Spaine*, the rich Spanish wine so often mentioned in waulking songs. Far across these purple fields was the hill of Roinabhal. It stood at the head of Loch Erisort, a serpentine sea loch that eats into the east of the island, shooting out long tongues among the quiet hills of Lochs. There is a whole parish called Lochs, and for good reason. The land is half covered with water. There are innumerable fresh-water lochs and so many arms of the sea that a man with a boat scarcely knows which one to use. The village of Maravig on Loch Erisort can be approached from the sea through five different channels. Loch Eriscort has a company of splendid neighbours; in the same parish are Loch Sealg, Loch Claidh and Loch Seaforth, all of them associated with poaching adventures. For the Forest of Eisginn, into which they run, is the best deer forest in Scotland.

The Isle of Harris is a place of wild and barbaric scenery, a riotous country in which new hills seem to grow up every year, like an army of conscripted warriors. Clisham is the highest peak in the Forest of Harris. It stands like a haggard outlaw, baring its sinews and looking down in scorn upon the plains. Among these mountains—most of them over two thousand feet—can be found many days of excited climbing. The road that leads into this contorted land climbs stiffly over the outlying ridge of the forest and then dips down towards the light green waters of West Loch Tarbert. But not the mountains alone give the island its interesting character. A crazy road runs from Tarbert to Rodel, passing along the Bays of Harris on the east of the island. Here the sea has torn the coast into rags and tatters, and so many crooked bays stretch inland that the road has to follow a drunken course round each of them, winding and looping, until it almost ties itself into knots. The rocks here are in low grey shelves, unlike the tall jagged spears of the Lewis coast, and a hungry sea has licked and eaten away every scrap of earth upon the ledges, so that even a sea-flower cannot take root among them.

Yet there are houses here in plenty, built like sea-birds' nests in the most daring places on rock edges, and looking as if a light wind might topple them over. It is difficult to see them unless a blue spiral of peat smoke points to their presence: the straw that thatches them is so like the colours of the tangle that lies on the skerries, and their stone walls so like their surroundings. It is possible to fish from the doors of some of these houses, or to tie to a peg at the gable head the painter of a skiff that swings in the water below. On the rock-faces fleeces of wool can be seen drying in the sun, dyed with lichen or vegetable roots or the tips of heather; for Harris is an island of tweed makers whose cunning in the blending of colours cannot anywhere be surpassed. The village of Rodel lies below the hills in the south of Harris. Here in the churchyard of St. Clement lies Mary MacLeod, the seventeenth century poetess of the Isles, whose Gaelic songs are the best in the language. Compared to the Bays, the south and west coasts of Harris are practically unbroken. At the south-west end the great Toe headland puts its long body out to sea, as if it wanted to have a glimpse of Lewis round the corner. Miles of delightful sands lie along these coasts, so white when the sun strikes them that the fringe of foam from the breaking waves seems to be part of themselves.

Uist has a reputation in the Outer Islands for yellow barley fields and noble horses. The island has been a famous mart for horses ever since the seventeenth century, when Allan of Clan Ranald brought home Spanish steeds to breed on his wide machairs. Allan's own stables were the wonder of many parishes. When he went on holiday to the Continent, it is said that his cavalcade clattered through the streets of Paris, each horse shod with shoes of gold stamped with the proud name of Clan Ranald. All this splendour is now dead, but the names of the Clan Ranald chieftains and the nobility of their deeds are rooted forever in the stories and legends of the islands. And in the Isle of Uist a child may still be rocked to sleep with the lullaby of Clan Ranald, which the bard MacCodrum composed while he walked with the infant chieftain in his arms twice round the garden of the child's home. Borve Castle, where for a time the chieftains lived, is now a toppling ruin on a machair in Benbecula. It is some hundreds of yards from the sea. Yet at one time, according to tradition, the waves of the Atlantic swilled round its rocky base, and a stately sailing ship with three white sails, moored herself below its walls. Since then the flood tides have thrown up banks of sand, the machair has surrounded the castle, and the gay waves have left off their flirting with its stones.

In all the Hebrides, Benbecula is the sea's dearest child. That is why the returning tide races so quickly over the sand, hurrying with pouted lips to kiss its shore. And when the night's embraces are over, the sea leaves Benbecula again, like a mother bird going to forage for its young. When the sea goes out, Benbecula is no longer an island. It is a patch of green earth in a desert of white sand: the North Ford and the South Ford are dry, and the crossings to the Uists are open to horses and carts. I saw the North Ford on an autumn evening from the village of Uachdar in Benbecula. It looked like a huge field of snow into which the thaw had set. For the dazzling whiteness was interrupted here and there with warmer colours. Wisps and strands of russet tangle were patterned upon it. Brown and red skerries rose up here and there, with little pools of foam floating about them. In the large sand furrows little green streams ran towards the sea, carrying along with them the slaver of brown spume that the tide had left behind it. Suddenly I heard the crack of whips, and from the headland on my right three gipsy gigs rushed across the ford, like hurrying thieves. The horses ran at a merry gallop but their hooves made no murmur on the sands. Their dark manes flowed into the wind. The laughter of the gipsies rang out in the silence of the ford. In a moment their shapes became dim as they drew near the coast of Uist. Scarcely had they crossed when their tracks were covered up by the flowing tide. The sea was returning to Benbecula to protect its child.

South Lee and Eaval are the only high hills in North Uist; the rest of the island is an extensive machair cut up into shreds and fragments by scores of fresh-water lochs. South Uist has three tall guardsmen on the east—Hecla, Beinn Mhor and Buail a' Choill—but the sweeping machairs of the west are open to all the frantic winds that dance upon them in winter with frozen feet. So that according to MacCodrum, 'Swift is the bad wife's husband on the plain of Uist.'* But the summer wind blowing over the machair is full of the rich smells of clover and bog grasses, and the host of red poppies that open their delicate leaves in the shelter of the barley fields. Hundreds of cattle roam about in the Uist machairs in wandering herds. Once a week a brisk and exciting cattle sale is held in the

*The poor fellow being scantily clad.

village of Milton, and the Polachar Inn sees later the settlement of many bargains. One of the delightful characteristics of Uist is the freedom and fine style with which men drink. Even at their funerals great observance is given to this ancient ritual. Martin Martin, coming upon the custom in Harris, gave it a gentlemanly explanation in his book, saying that 'the air is temperately cold and the natives endeavour to qualify it by taking a dose of aquavitæ, or brandy.' From Polachar in South Uist it is but a rock-bird's flight to the magic island of Eriskay, a place round which the seals swim in silent companies, looking with homesick eyes at the land. It is an isle of legends and old tales, where Gaelic is spoken with the pure and rippling sound of running water.

Across the water from Eriskay is the Isle of Barra, known in Gaelic legend as '*Barraidh Ghorm NanLong*' —Blue Barra of the Ships. Its rounded breasts lie on the surface of a dim tide. Little boats with tawny sails steal out of its long creeks, manned by the cunning fishermen of Barra. The shadows of Kishmul's grey walls rise and fall in the Castle Bay, like the swaying blades of tangle below them. But Kishmul is no longer a centre for piracy. The MacNeills' sea-reiving is at an end. South of Barra, the lonely islands of Mingulay and Berneray mark the limits of the Hebrides.

As far as tourists are concerned, the Hebrides are still virgin soil. Few visitors have explored the fantastic caves that lie around the coast of Lewis, or seen the sunset sprinkling drops of blood on the doors of South Uist. Fewer still have seen the miracle that the spring works in the earth, or the sorcery of the sea when it snatches the Flannan Islands from sight on a summer's day. The home of the Clan Ranald and the birthplace of Flora Macdonald are known only to the Islesmen themselves.

The Blue Men of the Minch, according to Hebridean legend, sprang up from the sea in the Sound of Shiant and put to the skipper of every passing ship two lines of Gaelic poetry. Unless he could quote the next two lines of the text, they light-heartedly sank his ship. It meant that he was not of the blood. The Blue Men were artists who did not want the island culture to be contaminated, and perhaps it was their pranks that held off for such a long time the influence of the outside world.

But the splendid culture of the Hebrides is now exposed to the forces of decay within its own shores, because the people themselves, who were once a self-supporting community, and who even exported to the Continent barrels of beef and fish, are now having a hard struggle to find a livelihood. The sea fishings, on which half their existence used to depend, have been ruined by piratical trawling which has been going on for years without interference from quarters competent to put an end to it. The fishing-banks on the west of Lewis have been swept clean, so that in villages where thousands of white fish were landed every season, the boats are now lying in dry staves upon the beach. The failure of a Stornoway fishing season means not only lack of employment for scores of fishing-girls, whose homes largely depend on their earnings, but it means actual poverty in the fishing villages of Lochs, where the men folk of the whole community are engaged in the fishing. The lands used to provide the other half of an Islesman's resources but, since the breakdown of the old economic system. whereby rents could be paid in kind, it became an increasing struggle to find the necessary ready money for the purpose of the rent. The tendency grew to neglect the land and turn to some occupation which would yield enough money for the landlord and for the ordinary commodities of life that could no longer be obtained without it. The tendency led ultimately to emigration and hundreds of Islesmen had to look for a living in other countries. And nowadays, every small-holder and crofter from Barra Head to the Butt of Lewis, is paying an exorbitant rent which is out of all proportion to the produce of his soil. Unless these people are soon made rent-free altogether, agriculture in the islands will become a forgotten art.

The people have still a deep and resolute faith in the possibilities of the crofting system, and in the traditional policy of exploiting the resources of land and sea side by side. They are conscious that it was such a system that gave them the life of idealistic communism from which their culture and their character have sprung. That is why the people of Lewis stubbornly refused to sell their birthright to Lord Leverhulme, who offered them an industrialized and commercialized island in its place. Fortunately, Leverhulme's schemes had no greater success than those of the Fife Adventurers whose plans for the development of Lewis came to grief in 1601. Had Leverhulme succeeded, the culture and individuality of the island would have rotted under his factories, and the language of the people would have been already dead.

Writers who in their dreams behold the Hebrides, have a misleading habit of suggesting that dreaming is as fashionable in the islands as it is among themselves. But the sweating labour of spring and autumn, and the continual fight with the sea does not leave much time for the weaving of dreams. Living is not an easy matter in the Hebrides. It is an exhausting struggle, but a struggle that is cheerfully accepted because it is familiar and has always been the way of life. There is neither pessimism nor melancholy anywhere, but a live spirit of gaiety that even the holy waters of the Church have not managed to quench. And strangely enough, the second menace to the culture of the Hebrides—a menace even greater than the economic one—is the Church, and the sterilizing religion which it preaches. As interpreted by the Presbyterian ministers of the Hebrides, life is identified with asceticism and repression. The crucifixion of the body is the monotonous theme of all their discourses. Drinking, dancing, music and recreation are officially condemned. But these gentlemen in their fanatical and destructive campaign forget that such taboos cannot be imposed on country people, whose nature it is to set more store on human values than on ascetic ones. And the more their human wants are denied them, the more they tend to excess. So that in the Isles the arts of drinking and dancing are still in a very healthy condition, for when they have to be pursued in secret, they become an exciting adventure. To this extent the people have managed to resist the self-mortifying demands of the Church—and the fact that fresh songs are brought forth yearly from the Western Isles would seem to indicate that there is no deterioration in the art of music. But these are not new songs; they are traditional things that have managed to survive in spite of difficulties. The creative impulse in the arts has been successfully stifled by the Church—except in the Catholic islands where the gospel of humanism receives more of its due. If anybody were now to produce a chant of such pagan and sensual beauty as the Dawn Prayer of Clan Ranald, which Dr. Alexander Carmichael found in the Hebrides, he would probably be brought to account by the Church. Yet the hymns and incantations of *Carmina Gadelica* reveal a philosophy of much greater beauty and spiritual depth than anything now known within the Protestant Church of the Isles.

Owing to their geographical position the Hebrides are destined to be the last outpost of Gaelic in Scotland, It will be a pity if the arts which are conceived in that language are dead in the islands before the language itself. If the movement towards a resurrection of Celtic culture in Scotland is ever to take more than a surface root, the islands must be saved.

9. Berwick Coast, Lothian

Robert M. Adam

solitary and uninviting, or broken into twisting lumpy hills, and then at any vantage point on the height he suddenly overlooks the Merse, spreading before him almost at his feet, a vision of tilled, undulating plain, divided by hedgerows, and showing in a pleasing irregularity woods and park-lands, mansions, hamlets, and farmhouses, with the vague grey, smoky patches that are the few small towns. So viewed it is perhaps the most surprising piece of landscape in Scotland, all the more because it seems uncharacteristic, the sort of prospect one associates with the softer setting of southern England. At all times, even in its unkempt, undrained, and untimbered days, it has stirred this emotion of surprise. 'Little thought to find so fair a country in Scotland as the Mershe and Tyvydale,' was the comment of the Earl of Hertford, when in the forties of the sixteenth century he arrived with a horde of foreign mercenaries on one of his errands of destruction; after which he could exult in the numbers of villages and houses he had burned and the cattle or corn he had destroyed or carried away. 'Plentiful of corn' is another comment of the time on this countryside, and is echoed by Cromwell's soldiery two hundred years later. But trees were scarce, and the people for their fuel had to burn the crops of reeds on the bog-lands that are now luscious meadows and, in Falstaff's language, 'convey' from across the border the timber for their houses. The agricultural enthusiasm of the late eighteenth century was to change all that. Planting became the hobby of the Scottish laird, as lairdship became the hobby of the new-rich of the time, and now there is no part of Scotland where trees flourish more happily along the many roads, on the green sward of the park, or in appropriate copses. And not the stiff, common-place, quick-profiting fir that shadows so much of the north country, but the more sociable and dignified oak, beech, ash, and chestnut, or lime, with the homelier hawthorn instead of stone walls bordering the fields, an equipment which the old-time Scottish farmer regarded as uneconomic because providing shelter for birds who would feed on the corn. Only on the more exposed upper slopes do firs find a place.

But when we pass to Greenlaw we leave the richer soils of the Merse proper and reach the conditions that have helped to put the 'stalk o'carl-hemp' in the Scottish character. For west of it on to Lauderdale, which was accounted to be in the Middle March, the arable land has largely been won from the reluctant moor, as is also the case eastwards to Polwarth and Duns and the Whiteadder, behind all which as we rise in height we leave the fruitful Merse levels and range to the Lammermuirs and its sheep-lands. Great fields in this intermediate stretch, with stone dikes instead of hedges, form a margin in a colder, restrained tone to the colourful picture below.

Along this zone, between plain and hilltop, are to be found the few larger towns of the Merse—and small places at that—linked together by the single railroad that traverses the country east and west. The Merse is not a land of towns, nor therefore of large-scale manufactories, nor of any industry much more than what ministers to the cultivation of the soil. Towns are scarcely to be expected along the bank of the Tweed, for in old days a river as such was not a very desirable neighbour where flooding was possible, and settlement was frowned upon by the great, high-set castles of Norham and Wark on the English side. Tweed had many fords but also a most unpleasant practice of drowning them with sudden, surprising, short-lived spates, even in fair weather. Many fugitives from Flodden found that weeks of rain had made the crossings death-traps, a condition which a foolish Italian correspondent wrote of as a miracle. Coldstream grew up at the lowest reliable ford, but for the Border it is not a very ancient place, being a substitute for the older Lennel half a mile eastwards. Just across the bridge is Cornhill, but there the Northumbrian burr tells you that you are in England; it is not heard in the true Scottish speech on the north side. So sharp still is the line of demarcation. The main roads which do not converge on the crossing at Coldstream make for Berwick, which is English with many a Scottish difference. Three direct highways go lengthwise through the Merse, two from Greenlaw on the north, one from Kelso in Roxburghshire, and all terminate at Berwick. Along them and especially, as already stated, on the most northerly one, lie the little places that break the cultivated continuity of the region. And even on the higher levels they once preferred an eminent site, above undrained land and with a commanding outlook in the direction of danger. Greenlaw, in a loop of the Blackadder, indicates by its name its older situation on the Law, and its early organization by the scattered holdings of its small farmers in the common 'acres.' The prominent and disproportionate tower of its church was built as a prison, but the church was lengthened to absorb it, and the den of thieves became part of the house of prayer. A place of not much more than one long street, Greenlaw achieves what Blake would have called a twofold quiet. For, even as Kipling's private soldier could boast that he had been 'a corporal wanst,' it can claim that for a brief interlude it had been the county town. As evidence of the dignity there are still the unexpectedly imposing buildings that once were the county headquarters; so that to the native peacefulness of an agricultural community is added the subtle sense of having fallen from a high estate, which the material survivals never allow one to forget. Yet that short spell of local pre-eminence was only an interregnum, for Duns recovered the status it had possessed before, and again 'Dunse dings a',' its ample clattering market-place dominated by a town hall in revival Gothic. On the eastern edge of the Merse, beyond the gorge of the Whiteadder, beautiful in all its varied course from a stripling of the hills to a pastoral stream, is the loftiest of its villages, Chirnside, upstanding bare against the sky-line. Eastwards spreads a landscape that has much the character of that behind Greenlaw—bleak, exacting country rolling towards the rugged barrier of the coast. Northwards the ever-roughening gorge of the Whiteadder opens the way for the single road that climbs and winds through the Lammermuirs, past deserted Ellem and Cranshaws, with its five-storeyed tower, amid fir plantations in a sheep country just inside the boundary between Berwickshire and East Lothian; then under the shadow of the great hill-fort on Friar's Nose, a prehistoric village within triple ramparts, and so down the stiff bald slope of Priestlaw to Garvald in one direction and forking to Gifford in the other, the latter being the unaccustomed route by which Scott brought Marmion on his hapless mission:

> Oft on the trampling band, from crown
> Of some tall cliff, the deer look'd down;
> On wing of jet, from his repose
> In the deep heath, the black-cock rose;
> Sprung from the gorse the timid roe,
> Nor waited for the bending bow;
> And when the stony path began,
> By which the naked peak they wan,
> Up flew the snowy ptarmigan.

Desolation is and must be the note of the upper Lammermuirs, which are not so much a range of hills as a gigantic rampart between two of the most fertile regions of Scotland. For some twenty-five miles they stretch from Lauderdale to St. Abb's Head, their crest an almost continuous moorland of rough grass and heath. On the Berwickshire side, indeed, man has fought his way upwards in reclaimed land, in sheltering fir-woods, and sheep-runs. And behind Duns and between Longformacus and Abbey St. Bathans, in the region of the upper Whiteadder is a complexity of wooded dales and heathery heights, a confused conflict of hill and plain ere one or the other establishes its dominance. On their northern face the Lammermuirs drop more suddenly and are broken in their length by the steep banks of wooded ravines, but even here the plough has in many quarters forced its way upwards, so that turnips or oats occupy the place of whin and juniper and fringe the fastnesses of the sheep. Between the foothills and the broad valley of the Tyne intervene a series of irregular dells or hollows, strangely parallel and not transverse to the Lammermuirs, for they are the work of ice not of water, and in these nestle picturesque little hamlets or villages, like Humbie, Gifford, Garvald, Stenton and Spott, masked by their immediate trees amid their fields and pastures. Each of these names is of special interest. Humbie was once Keith-Humbie till it was united with Keith Marischal. But combinations of the name Keith are still scattered over the district to show that its original designation was this old British word, which here as often elsewhere—Dalkeith is another example—appears to have the meaning of 'wood.' In feudal days the lands were attached to the office of Marischal and Robert de Keith, one of the heroes of Bannockburn, was the first of his family to hold both the territory and the office, though their later and more familiar associations are with Aberdeenshire. Gifford, again, was once Bothans, another Celtic name usually but erroneously connected with the saint responsible for Abbey St. Bathans on the Berwickshire side of the Lammermuirs, but really an anglicized adaptation of the Gaelic plural *bothain*, 'shielings,' common enough in its English singular equivalent 'shiel' all over Lothian, as at Stobshiel, Penshiel, etc. The fifteenth-century 'collegiate church of St. Cuthbert of the Bothanis' still stands, a silent shell. Gifford was the designation of the family that built the neighbouring castle of Yester, which afterwards passed to the Hays, but is now a ruin, in which, however, remains the unique underground 'Goblin Ha'' of a character only to be explained as the work of magic. In these two villages, then, the ancient name is discernible under the modern one, as in a palimpsest, but in Garvald the Gaelic is still extant—*garbh allt*, 'rough stream.' Stenton is a substitute for the older parish name of Pitcox, which embodies the prefix of Pit or Pet so familiar all over Pictland for a 'portion' or 'share.' Such items are the fossils of history.

But the villages, too, have happily undergone the local transformation of the later eighteenth century. From that time onwards they, like the other villages and small towns of Scotland, were being rebuilt. What attraction they may now have, apart from their setting, is one of period, and even that is encroached upon by the hybrid intrusions of villadom. The roof of red tiles is characteristic of East Lothian, and on a white-washed cottage, that 'looks yellow when the snow comes,' shows like an open flower. Houses are usually lined up, Scottish fashion, along the highway, ribbon-wise, or at cross-roads, and if not irregularly picturesque have at least something native in their economic treatment, and severity, confronting the secular enemies of winter and rough weather. Here and there, as at Ormiston and Pencaitland, an ancient market-cross recalls a localization of business that has passed with the older system of things, with the bonnet laird and the small farmer. Gifford between an unbeautiful kirk and a tree-shaded stream from the woods of Yester offers an appearance of restful seclusion remote even from its historic memories.

Rise from these foot-hills to a commanding position, such as may be found almost anywhere along the northern escarpment, and the eye can take a wide sweep, which recalls the Merse. Here, too, is flat or rolling land, displaying every feature of laboured and responsive soil. But there are superficial differences. This is a more dramatic landscape. Northwards is the great hollowing curve of the shore with Berwick Law a sentinel to the Firth at one end and Arthur's Seat o'ertopping the metropolis at the other. Between them field elbows field; the woodland generally more compact and some of it, as at Keith and Ormiston, of quite ancient origin. The Tyne cannot rival the Tweed, but nevertheless is what the poet Cowper called the river Ouse, an 'agreeable circumstance.' Like the Merse, however, East Lothian is eloquent of the untiring industry of men, their skill and persistence in tillage under all conditions, even over the hard heart of the county between Garvald and Pencaitland. The traveller Pennant was paying a high compliment when, in the late eighteenth century, he wrote that 'East Lothian is the Northamptonshire of North Britain.' Over the next hundred years this countryside experienced, on the whole, a high degree of prosperity, with some intermissions, and could continue to nourish the great mansions in their ample park-lands, many of which now wilt in decay or abandonment or are given over to some communal use. Newbattle was once a great abbey; now its supplanter as a lordly mansion is at the end of its noble days. Dalhousie Castle is a school. But, under present conditions, this form of dilapidation is common to the United Kingdom. In East Lothian agriculture somewhat speedily jumped into being a sort of large-scale business, its farm-yards, as Cobbett put it, merely "factories for making corn and meat." As in the case of the Merse, it had been namely for corn long ago; its crops, too, were a source of wonder to Cromwellian soldiers. It had seen the earliest cultivated grasses; at

Ormiston turnips were first sown in drill, though it was a farmer in the Merse who had raised the pioneer crops; and 'Saltoun barley meal' became a household word after a mill introduced from Holland had begun to displace the old 'knockin' stane.' The potato was a welcome stranger, and anyone discriminating in his potatoes knows the 'red soil' of Dunbar. Thus every square yard of fertile soil was perseveringly brought under the plough, and only what was unusable left as pasture or waste. It was not really different on the Merse, yet there the result deceivingly seems but a flowering of natural resources; it is hard to think of that region otherwise. On this coastal plain, however, particularly in its eastern quarter, the toil is laid bare, as it were, before our eyes in the large regularly disposed fields, the stark, stone dikes or less numerous close-clipped hedges of thorn, the general sense of deliberate systematic effort to subdue the land wholly to the necessities of human life. If the Merse looks the garden of Scotland, East Lothian is its model farm.

And though the long, low ridge rising eastwards in the Garleton Hills flanks to the south the shallow valley of the Tyne, and that again rises to the foot-hills of the Lammermuirs, the coastal plain is really all one, and this roll and rise southwards a feature of the greater part of it. It appears with local variations in the other administrative divisions of Midlothian and West Lothian, with the Moorfoot Hills and the Pent-lands taking the place of the Lammermuirs, but striking south, and their lesser though, in the upper courses, more picturesque streams flowing north not eastwards like the Tyne. These western divisions share in the stretches of fertile cultivated level and good hill pasture. Here, however, are urban and industrial intrusions that break the homogeneity of Lothian. At Tranent and westwards in the valley of the Esk and then in West Lothian, the coal measures, that lurk in the Merse too far down for exploitation, heave upwards even to the surface, a fact discovered and traded upon at least some seven hundred years ago, when the white monks of Newbattle Abbey were setting men to work the seams that could be got at a few feet below ground, accessible from banks and scaurs where the ancient horizontal shafts can still be seen. Coal was being increasingly demanded not only for domestic use, where it took long to establish itself, the odour being considered unpleasant, but in the production of salt, for centuries a staple industry on both sides of the Firth. The source of this essential article was sea-water boiled in 'pans,' and the smoke of the burning along these miles of shore was a perpetual spectacle; Prestonpans is one combination that registers the fact to this day. But even the many natural woods in the neighbourhood could scarcely continue to meet the claim for fuel, all the less as it was required for the household hearth, and it might be for the house itself: ancient Edinburgh was built as well as heated from the oaks of the Boroughmuir. As the woods wasted, coal came into its own. But so unpleasant were the occupations of salt-making and coal-mining that men and women were 'thirled' to the job, slaves in all save that they could not be sold individually in the open market, though disposable along with the pans or collieries to which they were bound. A collier or salter was such for life and his children after him to all generations. There is a story of a great coalowner, who visiting the colliery of another, thought the accent of one of the workers similar to that of his own district, and inquired, in the Scottish fashion, whether he had not come from it. 'Oh,' said the collier in some surprise, 'd'ye no ken me? Do ye no ken that your father sold me for a pony?' That was some time in the first half of the nineteenth century, for the enslaving acts had been repealed completely only in the closing year of the preceding one, having begun their baleful career in the early seventeenth century and continued throughout the various religious reformations into the century of enlightenment. Coal was an increasingly necessary product; as a seventeenth-century Scottish poet in Latin put it, 'without you our winters would be insufferable.' Pity 'tis that the winning of it should entail the conditions implicit in the term 'miners' raws,' rows of what are proverbially nondescript lodgings.

In West Lothian are the added disfiguring growths thrown up from the shale-mines drained of their oil. These rubbish hillocks are no acquisition to a landscape diversified in a way pleasant enough at its best but never markedly picturesque, and somewhat dreary towards the south-west. The county is tucked in between two rivers flowing to the Firth of Forth, the Almond and the Avon, both good Celtic names, but the cardinal feature is the dry valley or broad depression traversing it from east to west, through which go road, river and canal. Near the far end of this valley is Linlithgow, and that position at the gates of the west generated the mile-long street that was the old town. But rapid communications have robbed it of this significance: it is now too near the capital. It shares the fate of county towns generally. Haddington, its eastern counterpart, is another case. The smaller town goes the way of the countryside. Its self-contained local industries die down. The old crafts shrink or disappear. Professional organizations lose vitality. Once the county town supported a social and cultural life of its own. In it the big country lairds had their town-houses, and their share in its dignity and self-sufficiency. In a sorry relic crudely called 'Bothwell Castle' in Haddington one can see all that is left of such an urban mansion. At Linlithgow is a special and more imposing residence that long ministered to the town's importance:

> Of all the palaces so fair
> Built for the royal dwelling
> In Scotland, far beyond compare
> Linlithgow is excelling.

But now its walls are desolate.

Edinburgh, of course, is in a niche by itself, largely independent of merely local vicissitudes and drawing from all quarters, as a capital city should. The serried aspect of its ancient and more elevated part has set the ink flowing from a thousand pens, and the original planning of the New Town was a noble accomplishment, the pleasing features of which later generations have laboured to disfigure and distort. From a very early time its reputedly impregnable fortress on a lofty crag gave it prestige, which lessened as the knightly years passed. These characteristics, however, would not of themselves have brought it to high estate. Stirling, for example, could boast as much. It was Holyrood Abbey not the castle that confirmed Edinburgh as a place of royal residence. But no less important in the really slow rise of Edinburgh to pre-eminence among Scottish towns was the commercial development of the burgh. And that success was, in a sense, parasitic, being rooted in the neighbouring port of Leith, where the outlet of a comparatively small stream provided the only practicable port in the lower reaches of the Firth. Elsewhere was but open beach, at its best imperfectly sheltered. Cromwell found this to be the case at Musselburgh, where his food-ships could not face the oncoming of stormy weather. But the royal burgh of Edinburgh held control of the Leith harbour, so that all goods entering or leaving that port should pass through the hands of its merchants. Leith in respect of traffic was but a landing stage; the profits went to Edinburgh. And should any new port be established near, its term of freedom was short. King James IV thus instituted the New-haven at the place still so named, but he had not been long dead when Edinburgh bought up the possible rival to its own harbour at Leith. This type of monopoly was all in the economic manner of the time.

The southern shore of the firth, indeed, was not so well furnished as that on the Fife side with inlets that could be utilized as harbours. The whole sea front of Lothian, east and north, is inhospitable, though in different ways. From the mouth of the Tweed, which made Berwick of old so valuable, to the mouth of the firth, it is a rocky, precipitous, and jagged coast line, with a few fishing-villages huddled here and there in recesses of the coast, at places the names of some of which witness to a breaching from the landward, such as Burnmouth and Eyemouth. The little harbour of Pettowick nestles boldly at the base of St. Abb's Head. These villages with their modern piers thrusting stiffly seawards cannot but look picturesque in such a position, however commonplace their constituents. Their inhabitants have little in common with the people of the flat, sheltered, and fruitful lands behind. Fishermen are a folk apart: occupation overrides race. Mankind is uselessly classified into long-heads and short heads; the operant divisions are landsmen and seamen; tillers of the soil, herdsmen, and dwellers in towns. Inwards from the cliff edge are breezy uplands brought under the plough or in pasture, where Ayton near parklands with noble timber and overlooking the wooded dale of the Eye; Coldingham, a compacted not a ribbon village which grew up beside the abbey that was an outlier of Durham; and old-world Cockburnspath beyond the wooded gorge of the Pease Burn, are all places of individual quality, with as much history in their humble annals as Fast Castle on its almost isolated skerry, a place 'fitter to lodge prisoners than folk at liberty,' but in keeping with the troublesome and dubious records of the Homes; or Tantallon near North Berwick, even as a ruin dominating and defiant like the Douglases who built it; or the weird station of the Bass; or even Dunbar redolent in memory of battle and siege.

But once round the corner the ruling element changes. It is no longer rock but sand, and contrary to proverbial wisdom sand has proved a firmer foundation for modern interests. At an earlier stage it was long an unpleasant intrusion by the mouth of the Tyne till in 1706 Lord Haddington, with an enthusiasm that to sage heads seemed akin to folly, began to plant the waste with the trees that now are an enchanting feature. He had already subjected the moorland round Binning to the same embellishment, thus with foliage and its shelter at once beautifying and enriching a seemingly barren countryside. He was generous with oak, the tree he loved, but beeches supply noble avenues. On the opposite side of the peninsula, however, on the firth itself, sand showed itself an even worse enemy. Early in the seventeenth century the wind was eident with it to cover both kirkyard and kirk at Gullane, so that the building had to be abandoned for a new one farther inland at Dirleton. The sand which in those days was an infliction has since settled down under a fine, short turf to provide an unequalled succession of golf-courses from North Berwick to the neighbourhood of Edinburgh. But the historic golf on Leith Links had to be transferred to Musselburgh, as also the horse-races that so long had distinguished Leith Sands, and are commemorated in Robert Fergusson's poem.

Lothian was a varied country and its destiny was to be as varied in its population. The Romans found in it a Celtic-speaking people akin to those south of the Cheviots but appear to have left it in great part alone. Roman dispositions were directed to maintaining of the Vallum with its forts and road between Forth and Clyde and that began at Bridgeness in West Lothian—a task which occupied and finally exhausted their energies. The northern peoples within two generations broke through and rolled up these elaborate defences and in later times would seem to have established some sort of hold upon Lothian itself, leaving a witness of their presence in the massive 'broch,' an intruder from the far north, whose characteristic remains are to be seen above the Whiteadder at Edinshall. Old British footprints survive, also, in such place-names as Forth and Tweed, Peffer and Tranent. But neither river nor shore attracted the Celtic people as sites for habitation. They were neither fish-eaters nor traders by sea. Their settlements were on the tops of bare hills, where there was pasture for their herds and naturally drained land that could be worked with the hoe for their patches of crops. Dunpender, now the hill of Traprain, in East Lothian is a prominent example; Kaimes Hill in Midlothian is another. The low lands obstructed with natural forest and frequent marsh they could not occupy. As late as the seventh century St. Cuthbert was making these mountain villages a feature of his missionary journeys. It was apparently the intruding Angles or English, a forest-bred people, who first made clearings in the woods for their 'hams' and 'tons.' They, in turn, were overrun by another Celtic-speaking folk, the Gaels of Scotia, who infused their own names for places. Catcune in Midlothian is Gaelic for 'common-land.' The Cistercian nunnery at North Berwick was erected on a site known as 'Gillecalum's-ton,' showing a Gaelic lord of an Anglian settlement. Where the Knights Templar settled in the parish of Temple in southern Midlothian, is still known as Balintrodach, Gaelic for the 'stead of the warriors' of the Temple who had established themselves among a Gaelic-speaking people. The victory at Carham on Tweed in 1018 ended a couple of centuries of Gaelic penetration, and definitely made Lothian a part of Scotland.

It was about the close of the same century and in the course of the next that a fresh wave of immigration from south of the Tweed intensified what, in a loose sense, may be called the English aspect of Lothian, though its vanguard was Norman in character. But predecessors even of this company were the Northumbrian fugitive Cospatrick who was made Earl of Dunbar, and Thor Longus, also from northern England, who settled and erected a church at Ednam in Berwickshire. Thereafter not solitary incomers but a battalion—de Morevilles in Lauderdale and Salton, de Vaux at Dirleton, where a noble range of their castle still stands, de Vipont at Bolton, de Quincey at Tranent, and so on. The traces of the lordship and influence of these "little bullet-headed men, vivacious and splendidly brave," as Mr. Belloc describes the Normans, are to be seen at many places in the relics of churches in the Norman-Romanesque style, of which the most complete example is at Dalmeny in West Lothian; as also in the establishment of religious houses like Coldingham for black monks, nunneries at Coldstream and North Berwick, and Dryburgh of the white canons, all now

> only dead walls or vaulted graves
> That, ruined, yield no echo.

It was these immigrants who, with their tail of English and Flemings, beat out that high road into Scotland which in due time was to become the lure for Scotsmen into England so aggravatingly vaunted by Dr. Johnson.

But in truth Lothian was long to play the part of a gateway to Scotland, for which 'beyond the Tweed' was to become a synonym. Once over the river, the long-drawn barrier of the Lammermuirs had to be skirted at either the east or the west extremity. A glance at the map suggests the former route and certainly the railway expresses now thunder down it. But in the days before road engineering it was not to be followed without good reason. Ere Dunbar could be reached there was what Pennant called 'the black joyless heathy moor of Coldingham,' hard going for man and beast, after which one struck the sheer ravine of the Pease Burn, a natural profound trench hated and feared by invading columns, down the one side of which and up the other travellers had to go by zig-zag paths with 'much puffing and pain,' as Hertford's men found in the sixteenth century. The railway avoids its challenge, finding a way round farther inland, but the highroad is carried over on what was once accounted and possibly was then the highest bridge in the world, a hundred and thirty feet above the stream, but is now a small thing in comparison with the Forth Bridge at the other end of the province. Beyond Dunbar the Tyne must be crossed at Linton, where there was always a bridge that makes it a familiar name in history, but whose determining feature now is a fine reach of the river up to Hailes Castle, that draws to it both anglers and artists. There was a way up the Tyne to Haddington, a prosperous burgh where long ago stood the friars' church known for its beauty as the 'Lamp of Lothian,' and where still stands most of the ancient parish church, its tower walls pitted with the English bullets in the sixteenth-century siege. Northwards over the hills goes the road to Aberlady, once a port of a kind, and joins up with the highway that has come round the Garleton Hills and followed the coast, to strike the next natural barrier on the Esk, making this stream of old the outermost defence of the capital. The battlefields of Pinkie Cleuch and Prestonpans are both in the neighbourhood.

In face of these difficulties, it is no wonder that the preferable ancient route was by Lauderdale, entering the valley of the Leader beyond Earlston and going northwards till by easy, winding gradients it reached Soutra and overlooked the whole of the low lands from Arthur's Seat to North Berwick Law. By this highway the resplendent English army marched confidently to overwhelming disaster at Bannockburn, and James IV with a matchless train of artillery to similar disaster at Flodden, and Hertford back from the slaughter at Pinkie Cleugh. To-day it no longer wears its old importance; the railway going south passes it by on the other side by the Gala Water, or between the Moorfoots and the Pentlands, after which all roads tend westwards.

More than any part of Scotland Lothian lies in the track of ancient wars, but, that fitful fever past, its natural fruitfulness could be increased manifold. The eighteenth-century fondness for landscape-gardening and a personal taste for trees softened the hard lines of the agricultural pattern. For all its length of coast the sea, save in the case of Leith, has not been a proportionate factor, and mineral workings must, soon or late, give out. But a good land it will remain, one offering, too, a rich variety of prospect, tarnished to only a limited extent by the less attractive accompaniments of an industrialism that has over long stood for civilization.

10. Glencoe & Loch Leven, Argyll

Robert M. Adam

FISHING FOR TROUT IN THE WEST HIGHLANDS

by

MORAY McLAREN

When the Editor asked me to contribute to his book, he told me that I must choose one part of Scotland to write about, and was kind enough, with a few exceptions, to give me what is almost literally a *carte blanche*. At first, my task seemed easy, but as soon as I began to think about it, I realized that my difficulty was that I knew at once too much and too little about Scotland. During the last four years my job has led me into every shire in Scotland, and long before that I had memories, vague in detail, but strong in general, of the various parts of Scotland into which my childhood holidays led me. I found myself subject to a conflict of loyalties. I remembered a voyage to the North-East: I asked myself whether I could not write about that part. The North-East, however, a few minutes later seemed poor in comparison with the Western Islands. Then the Far North, I told myself, was a part of Scotland ill appreciated in general, but well loved by those who knew it. The Borders I had studiously learned to know, and so on. There was no one part of Scotland to which I could honestly say I had an especial claim; I had enjoyed too much, and had concentrated too little.

And then, turning back upon the past, I surprised myself once again in vague memories of Scotland that were so intensely enjoyable that I was certain that if I could pin them down I would have the key to deciding what was to be the subject of my essay. I found that these memories, though they might vary in the scene which was their background, had always one common element, and that was the fishing-rod. Undoubtedly, the happiest experiences of my life in rural Scotland have been associated with angling for trout. Some of my earliest pleasures have been watching fish, some of my latest have been that of catching them. When I tried to precipitate these memories into some definite result, I found that I always associated them with mountains, small hill lochs, peaty burns, the Atlantic Ocean, and long drenching mists—in a word, the West of Scotland.

And so I sought permission to write about angling for trout in the West Highlands of Scotland. I could not, I explained, confine myself to one portion of the West, for my memories ranged up and down the entire coast, from the Firth of Clyde to Wester Ross. Permission was granted, and with this wide horizon within which I was allowed to range, I set myself the task of writing about fishing in Western Scotland.

I hope I may be allowed by the reader, therefore, the same indulgence which was granted me by the Editor, and break the topographical exactitude of this book by describing the impressions of a certain part of Scotland on a certain type of person—the angler. While it is true that your real angling purist will be as much excited by stalking (if you can imagine such a thing) a fat trout with a dry fly in a stagnant canal in the back streets of Leeds, as he would be by hooking that same fish in a clear stream in the most beautiful scenery in the world, all anglers are not purists. Indeed, most of them are human beings, and if there is one particularly human or natural quality in the angler, it is his facility for absorbing and being absorbed by the countryside in which he practises his craft. Unless you are born and bred in the remoter parts of the Western Highlands of Scotland, there is no one, I make bold to say, who can more wholly enjoy and sympathize with the Western Highlands than the angler; the silence, the loneliness, the patience, the observation, and the long heedlessness of time—all these essential qualities prepare in him a peculiar appreciation of his peculiar circumstances.

Despite the huge publicity which the grouse has managed to achieve for itself, I cannot help thinking that in some way shooting is foreign to the West Highlands of Scotland. Shooting in many people's minds is associated with long warm autumn days in the South, stubble fields alive with partridges, huge stone jars of cider, and with all the other agreeable appurtenances of English country life. There shooting is a natural adjunct to the arable scene. In the West of Scotland the intrusion of shooting parties on to the moors in the autumn seems almost like an impertinence; and anyone who knows his history of Scotland in the last two centuries must be oppressed by the thought of the evictions and the driving forth of human life which has gone to make this lonely scene habitable by the grouse.

Not so the angler. He is quiet, unobtrusive and natural to his surroundings, wind, water, rain, must all these come pleasantly to him. He takes everything in the West as it comes and is the heir of countless generations who as quietly and as patiently as he have fished for trout long before anyone dreamed of shooting grouse.

Angling for trout is the most democratic pastime in Scotland. I do not use democratic in the ordinary newspaper sense; in other words, I do not mean that it is solely the sport of the poorer classes. I mean that it is enjoyed by representatives of every kind, class, and age of each sex in Scotland. If anyone doubts this, let him get into a suit of country clothes, take a fishing-rod in its case in his hand, wear a fishing-basket on his back, and walk through the streets of any town or village in Scotland. The odds are that before he has gone very far, he will have been stopped by someone who will wish to exchange fishing gossip with him. Should he interrupt his walk to stop for a drink, or wait on the platform of a railway station, the probability that he will be spoken to will become a certainty, and the remarkable thing is that there will be no particular type of person who will speak to him. It may be a business man, with a bowler hat and striped trousers; it may be a navvy who is mending the road, a country gentleman, or a minister. No display of golf-clubs, tennis-racquets, hiking-shorts, climbing-boots, nor indeed any other obvious implements of outdoor sport will have this same effect.

It is true that the greatest of all angling-books was written by an Englishman—Isaak Walton—but the bibliography of Scottish angling is enormous. It has been written by all classes and kinds of people, and the style of writing ranges from the incoherent to the flowery, from plain statements of catches to first-class prose. Angling is right in the Scottish blood, and though you may angle for trout in any part of Scotland, from the Mull of Galloway to John o' Groats, from East Lothian to Cape Wrath, it is perhaps in the West Highlands of Scotland that this delicious pursuit is most delicious.

The eastern parts of Scotland have beauty all their own, a hard, austere kind of beauty, but it is not one to tempt the angler away from his craft. If you are out after trout in Eastern Scotland, it is the trout alone that will occupy your attention. I for one can never get away from the suspicion that the streams and lochs in the East are somehow muddier, dirtier, more full of the dregs of town life. And so, if, on a fishing expedition in the East, the sun comes out, the wind drops, and the water sinks, one is only annoyed, and cannot lay down one's rod, and to the same extent enjoy the compensations, the superb scenery of the West. Somehow, angling in the West is more natural; you cannot walk more than a mile without coming across some tempestuous or trickling burn. Lochs that are clear, or stained with peat to the colour of strong tea, are hidden over the shoulder of each hill; and the long arms of the sea that insinuate themselves into the hills are not only promises of the sea trout that may run with the first rain, but are also continual reminders of the great fishy waste of the Atlantic, on which every angler must, at some time or another, meditate with awe.

Any angler who has fished for trout in the West of Scotland must have his mind stored with a number of vivid and intensely personal memories. There are often seconds that stand out so clearly in one's mind that one feels that they will not be forgotten if one lives to be a hundred. There are days, of which the details may be forgotten, but which leave behind them a tremendous sense of enjoyment which is far more important than any detail. Anyone, therefore, who writes about such a subject can hardly be expected to resist the temptation of a few personal reminiscences. For myself, there are two fishing memories which stand out more clearly than any others.

The first was many years ago, when I was a schoolboy on holiday in Argyll. I had bought a rod for five shillings from the local village grocer's store, a yard or so of coarse gut, a reel and brown line, and some heavy hooks; all this because I had seen a few small trout darting in and out from under the banks of a pool in the burn beside the village. For two weeks, however, we had had a succession of those endless fine days which sometimes come to the West, days in which the sun never seems to tire, and which dry up the burns till they are no more than little trickles connecting a succession of dessicated pools. I had flogged that wretched stream with my rod, using flies and worms, and even bare hooks, but as soon as I touched the water the trout would dart away under the stones, and it seemed to me that it would require a lifetime of skill and cunning even to get within fishing distance of these darting little creatures which disappeared whenever I looked at them. I was bitterly disappointed, but I merely went on fishing—because, well, there really was not much else to do. Then one day someone in the village told me that there was a good burn about six miles up the glen on the other side of the hills. I got up early one morning, and made the journey on my bicycle. When I was half-way there, a heavy rain began to come on, and I nearly turned back. However, some instinct prompted me to carry on, and when I arrived at the burn I found a place where I could shelter from the rain and eat some of my sandwiches. When the rain stopped, the burn had already begun to rise, and though I felt thoroughly miserable and depressed by the weather (not realizing how much the weather was my friend), I thought I might as well have a shot at the stream, considering how far I had come to find it. I threaded a worm on to my hook, and threw it into the peaty and foaming little burn. The line was carried quickly down over a run, and then into a pool, where it drifted slowly down. Suddenly it stopped, and I began, for the first time in a fortnight, to hope. I knew that I had to leave time for the fish, if it was a fish, to get hold of my bait before I struck, but there are instincts stronger than knowledge, and I lifted the rod slowly into the air. There was a kicking, struggling feeling at the end of it, the water broke at the top of the pool, and a little trout, six inches long, was swung, wriggling and struggling on to the heathery bank. I threw down my rod, and rushed at it. It fell off the hook, and I held it in both my hands and carried it a full twenty yards from the bank of the stream. I had never suspected that trout had such yellow sides, nor such red spots; I had only seen them from above, as I looked over the bridge, their dark grey backs darting in and out amongst the stones. I think the colour of the sides of that trout was one of the greatest astonishments and pleasures which I had that day; it was even more exciting to see it than to feel the struggles of the little fish as he first took my hook.

Luckily, I had come away with a full tin of worms, and throughout that day I fished that stream, going upwards towards the little loch from which it emerged. More rain came in from the Atlantic, and following it a white mist made the scene dreary in only the way that certain West Highland scenes can be dreary. Patches of mist floated across the little glen, now hiding, now discovering the heather and the bracken near the side. The whole air was so drenched with moisture that there was scarcely any difference between the colour of what ought to have been purple and what ought to have been yellow. A grey Scots day could rob even a peacock's tail of its colour, and even a West Highland glen in midsummer can become as drab as a street in Glasgow on a Sunday morning. But I did not care for any of these things; for the trout, after days of starvation in the drought were in a happy, careless, and hungry mood. I think they would have taken my finger as a bait had I put it into the burn. At any rate, they took every worm that I offered them, and soon my pockets were bulging with little fish, not one of them quite a quarter of a pound, and many of them hardly longer than a grown man's finger. At last my pockets could hold no more, and so I cut off a bit of the line from my reel, and threaded through the gills the rest of the trout that I caught upon it. The night began to fall, and at last my bait began to give out. I became conscious of the fact that I was wet to the bone, and cold, and, I had to admit to myself, rather frightened by the approaching twilight.

It was a twilight not so much dark as dirty grey;

the white mist of the day began to be stained with the obscurity of night. I must be many miles from the road where I had left my bicycle, and I remembered the name of the glen which I was in. It was called Glen Scorrie, and with that memory I also recalled why it was called Glen Scorrie. Someone in the village had told me that there was a legend that many years ago there had been a sort of idiot giant who had inhabited this glen, and who used to worry and torment travellers on their way home from the market. Eventually, the people of the district had defeated this giant by standing in groups at either side of the glen. First one group would shout the word, 'Scorrie' (which in Gaelic is a highly insulting word); the giant would lumber up the hill to punish them, and just as he was on the point of reaching them, the people on the other side of the glen would shout out 'Scorrie.' The idiot would turn on his tracks, and run towards them; no sooner had he reached them than the process was repeated from the previous side, and so on throughout a whole day until the terror had exhausted itself and collapsed in the middle of the glen. Then the villagers rushed down from either side, with their dirks, and rid themselves of their pest.

It was a silly story, and I remember laughing when I had heard it, but somehow, in this deserted, wind- and mist-swept glen, with the twilight coming down from the sky, and the noise of the burn going on ceaselessly beside me, it didn't seem quite so silly. Perhaps there had been some truth in it. Legends like this did not grow out of nothing, and there was no smoke without fire. Perhaps the old idiot giant still lived. I hurried quickly down the glen, and learned for the first time in my life that lesson which I had not remembered—nor which any keen angler will ever succeed in remembering—the lesson that you may go fishing up a stream, and it will seem only to be half a mile, but when you retrace your steps you find you have to walk something like six miles.

When I reached my bicycle it was quite dark. I had no lamp, and where the road was not straight, and when the clouds covered the moon that had only just now risen, I had to walk. I did not reach home till nearly midnight. I was tired and cold, and there still hung about me the remnants of my fear. But when I gained the lamplit hall, and turned my pockets out on to a kitchen plate and unstrung my fish from the line, I knew that I had never been so happy in my life. My only regret then (so great was my reaction) was that my tin of worms had given out, and that I could not have gone on fishing all night.

The other scene that I remember took place only a year or two ago. It was also in the West Highlands—in Skye, to be exact. I was away on a fishing holiday in June, but this time I was armed with much more extensive and expensive tackle than on that day many years before in Argyll. I had a couple of trout rods and one sea-trout rod; I had books of flies, and plenty of made-up casts. I had two reels, waders, whisky flasks, patent lamps, to hang upon your button when you are putting on casts at night; sweet-smelling oils in bottles to keep off the midges, fishing-baskets, landing-nets, and, indeed, all the odds and ends that an angler collects about him during the successive summers when he practises his main obsession.

Once again, I had landed upon a drought. For days,

Skye looked as superb as only Skye can look, and though it was lovely wandering about the island, and marvelling at the almost impossible colours of the scene, it was a little trying to watch the streams and burns dwindling each day, and to try to fish on lochs on which there was no breath of wind, and on which the sun beat endlessly all day long. On Midsummer Eve, however, I determined to try to beat the weather at its own game, and stay up all night. Someone told me of a loch far up in the hills, where there were big trout which had the reputation of feeding well at night. I got my directions for it, and set out at eight o'clock. It took me two hours to get there, the going was heavy, and though the directions were easy, I had to take care with my way, for I had never been there before.

When I reached the loch—or lochan, as it ought to have been called—I found that it was scarcely any bigger than Trafalgar Square, and lay, not so much in a deep hollow of the hills as in a kind of cup on the top of a hill. From the shores of the loch I could command a huge view in almost every direction; the light had not yet gone from the sky, and I could see the great hills to the north of me, and to the east of me on the mainland, as clearly as if it had been midday. I sat down, and, with all the delicious leisure of one who knows that he has several hours fishing before him, adjusted my rod, and made up casts of night flies. I decided to wait till the twilight was more advanced, and it was nearly eleven o'clock (by summer-time) that I put out in the little boat on to the unbroken surface of this mountain pool. By eleven o'clock the trout were beginning to rise, and all round me I could hear the plop of their fat, lazy bodies, turning over as they sucked idly at their food on the surface of the water. I cast, and cast again, but even night did not seem to be my friend, and the flies landed with hideous splashes upon the still surface. By midnight I decided to rest a bit. My round, uncouth little boat lay almost as flat as a water-lily, utterly becalmed on the centre of the loch. I pulled in my rod, and looked round me. I must have been floating about a thousand feet above sea level, floating on a loch on a hill in the middle of the Atlantic Ocean. The mountain peaks on the mainland to the north were still visible, the sun was beginning to think of making his short and almost imperceptible retiral for the night. The scene was so astonishing that I do not fear being called sentimental when I say that it was painfully beautiful.

After resting a little, and having eaten a couple of sandwiches, I shook off my mood of Celtic twilight sleep, and decided to try one small light-coloured fly, which would float upon the surface of the water. At my second cast, I got a rise. With my fourth, I hooked a fish. Within three minutes he was in my net, a beautiful, fat, gasping pound-and-a-half trout, that in day time would have taken me five or six minutes to land. By the time the dawn was well up again, some time between three and four, I had landed another seven trout. There was a quick rush of a rise just after the dawn, but somehow they would not rise to my fly, and after floating a little more, and wondering what to try in the way of a lure, I eventually decided to pack up. I rowed the little boat into its crude stone harbour, tied it up, picked up my rod and fishing-things, and walked down the mountain-side, home again. The sun was beginning to be hot by the time I had reached the house. A large, steaming cup of coffee, a dish of bacon and eggs, and then bed. That, I think, is the second-happiest fishing memory of my life.

One of the more obvious pleasures of fishing for trout in the West Highlands of Scotland is the almost infinite variety which the sport offers you, or, to be more accurate, the infinite number of variations upon the same theme. To the casual tourist one part of the West Highlands (especially in misty weather) may seem very much like another, but to the angler who chooses the West Highlands as the background for his sport, every stream and loch, every burn and river, has its own peculiar attraction and its own particular appearance, and in that small piece of coast-line between, let us say, the Firth of Clyde, including Arran and the borders of Ross and Sutherland, with all the attendant islands on the way, you will get such an astonishing variety of scene, colour, atmosphere and of sport, that I think it would be impossible to believe anyone, however old and however truthful, if he told you that he had fished throughout every part of the West Highlands.

In the variety of this scene there is a great variety of pleasure—pleasure which finds a faint echo even in looking at a map of that fretted and tortuous coast. One thinks of the great hills and little tumbling streams of Arran, so charming to look at but full of such disappointingly small trout; of the green rolling hills between Crinan and Kilmelfort; of the green hills of Mull and the coast opposite it; of Lismore (so well deserving of its Gaelic name which means 'The Great Island') with its lochs swarming with fat little half-pound trout, as silver as sea trout but somehow mysteriously separated from the sea. The eye on its tour up the West Coast pauses enviously round about Ballachulish. Here the scenery is as beautiful as you could wish to find, but somehow the streams are too clear, and as they go rushing down through the great black heights of Glencoe they either get rid of, or never had, any peaty deposit, and if there are trout in this stream they are far too fly to be caught on ninety-nine days out of a hundred. Still there are lochs up in the lip of Glencoe where the glen widens out into the desolate spaces of Rannoch; lochs that are hardlymore than scattered pools of peaty water in this huge and coloured desert. The trout out of them are stained a dark colour. They fight like demons and they must have plenty of food. I have often wondered where they get it, for there are no trees hanging over the edge of the loch and the streams that feed it run dry quickly.

When one passes north of Ballachulish there is a large space of country, both by the sea-coast and further back, which brings you to the very heart of the Western Angling Highland country. Loch Arkaig, for instance, on which it is possible to hire a boat, is thirteen or fourteen miles long, but it is difficult to believe that there are ten yards in it where you can't catch fish. I have had some of the finest days' fishing in my life on this loch, and not even scenery could distract me from my pleasure. The trout run there, on a good day, to an average of about one pound, and you will be amazed when you net your first fish, for until you actually see it in the net you will believe (so strongly has it fought) that it is at least twice its own weight. Arkaig is the loch in which it is supposed the Prince's treasure was sunk after the '45, and it is an old joke of the boatman whenever you hook a big fish or get stuck in the bottom, that you have hooked the treasure.

The blue hills on either side of Arkaig always seem to remain blue, but they change their shade of that particular colour so often that between hooking and netting of trout the whole scene seems to have changed its atmosphere.

There is a little island at the east end of the loch which is a charming place to lunch. It is hardly more than thirty yards in diameter but it has the remains of a chapel on it and is thickly overgrown with trees. If you have had a good morning's fishing it is pleasant to draw in your boat there and lunch undisturbed on this small island—pleasant, that is to say, until the midges come across from the Mainland and drive you back on to the loch.

But it is in the further northern parts, in Wester Ross, and even further North than that, that memories come to this particular angler of his most successful days. They have been days which Southern fishermen would have found particularly difficult to have enjoyed. September mists and wind were coming in from the Atlantic—for on the West Coast you can actually have a mist and a wind at the same time—and the mist at times would become so thick and so quickly driving that it would be more like great buckets of rain flung in one's face; but with the mist from the West there came other and agreeable things; sea trout coming up from the sea, and with the rising stream brown trout coming out from their holes underneath the stones, bold and hungry. When the mists come down in a West Highland glen you will feel yourself more cut off from what is known as civilization than almost anywhere else I know in Europe. There is a silence that is oppressive and a coldness and a wetness that penetrates more keenly than in any other place. I can well imagine that if one was not fishing for trout one could easily become depressed and even appalled by this waste of loneliness. The whole thing, however, becomes transformed and delightful if one is fishing successfully. There are few things so vital and youthful in spirit as a freely-run sea trout or a fat three-quarter-pound brown trout in good condition, and if one is compelled by the mist and the rain, the half-hidden hills and the dying daylight, to forget such agreeable things as warm beds, fires, pleasant conversation and music, there is a compensation in the contrast between the wild loneliness of the scene and the kicking, struggling animation of your brown and silver victims as they seize your bait in a kind of wild greediness and pull out your line till the reel screeches.

The hills in Wester Ross are usually pretty black and precipitous, and are naturally suitable to the kind of weather which I have described, but if the scenery is particularly wild and the fishing particularly good, there is also hospitality which is worthy of the scenery and of the sport. There are other memories connected with fishing in this part of the world which are almost as happy as the memory of the first brown trout coming into the net or the first sea trout throwing himself out of the water in that peculiarly sea-trout manner. Memories of the arrival home at a small white-washed hotel at the head of the glen; home when the dusk had finally and irretrievably been lost in the night for at least an hour; when the oil-lamps were lit and one walked into the hall with cold and squelching feet and emptied a basket of shining, slithering, brown and silver fish into the great ashet provided by the hotel for the vanity of its clients. Memories of the luxuriously idle way in which one would remove big heavy boots that were soaked through with the rain and the streams; of how one would peel off two layers of stockings and throw them towards the kitchen door where a hand would mysteriously draw them in. But the best memory of all is when one had gone upstairs and bathed one's tired and cold muscles in a hot bath of peaty water; had at last got out, dried, dressed and gone down again; had poured out a whisky of such a noble size and such a fine flavouring that it seemed in its essence to sum up the whole day of mist, peat, heather, tumbling streams and fighting trout.

11. Glen Affric, Inverness

Robert M. Adam

Imported meal was very dear. It cost forty-five shillings the boll before the railway came in 1862. Afterwards it fell to fifteen shillings.

The times were bitter hard. My grandfather saw sheep lie dead in flocks, killed by famine during a bad spring. Any hay that reached the destitute farms was hauled in horse wagons from Perth. When summer came every fence in the country was loaded with skins. Twelve hundred in Biallid, a thousand at Ettridge, eight hundred in Crubenmore, hundreds upon hundreds in front of every croft and farm of upper Speyside. The people's food consisted chiefly of potatoes, milk, and meal. When these failed they had nothing. An old man said to me: 'I've seen when there wasn't a boll of meal between all the houses in Crathie at New Year's time. I remember it fine. No early ripening oats then, Ian. And all the men out playing shinty in the snow. There wasn't a doctor in the country either. What did they do when they were sick? Do what they do now, get better or die and be damned to them.' Wages were low, a shilling a day for casual labour, twelve to fifteen pounds a year for shepherds and gamekeepers. Nevertheless the country was gay. The folk had a gaiety which is almost gone to-day. Gaiety does not keep itself alive by its own warmth, but feeds on talk, and company, and the gaiety of others which our depopulated land cannot now supply.

Speyside was well-populated sixty years ago. You could count scores of reeking chimneys along the valley about Laggan where to-day there are scarcely even ruins. More than a hundred children came to school at Laggan Bridge when my father was a boy, each one carrying his peat, and a hundred more at Balgown. The two places scarcely muster twenty-five between them now, though boys do not leave school at eleven as they did then. And besides the crofters there were smearers and drovers who came crowding over Corrieyarrick each autumn. The droves halted at Garvamore. My grandmother often lodged as many as thirty drovers in a night and baked to feed them all, besides a dozen smearers and her own family and neighbours who came ceilidhing in the fashion of that hospitable time. There was no tea, except a quarter of a pound at the New Year, very little sugar, some flour, but they had braxy mutton, as black as coal with unlet blood, salmon, kippered for the winter, salt herring, oatcakes, milk, butter and cheese, venison killed with some ancient muzzle-loader. There was dancing on the turf before the house where Wade once drilled his troops, or they ran and jumped and tossed the caber and played quoits with horses' shoes there when the summer evenings were long. There was piping and fiddling and whisky ran like water. You could buy smuggled whisky or make it yourself. Suspicious plots of barley grew by the river. Affrays between smugglers and the Preventative Men furnished stuff for tales which led inevitably to other days in the past. The folk of the Central Highlands loved tales then as they do still. Poachers strove with the newly appointed water-baillies who dared to forbid a man to take a fish from the water as his fathers had done. The people of Carrbridge marched out with pipers at their head to empty the Dulnain of salmon while the water-baillies put their heads beneath the blankets and kept quiet. Laggan parish played Kingussie in a great shinty match once a year on New Year's Day for the prize of a barrel of whisky. A hundred or more players, boys and greybeards too, strove for the pride of their parish. Heads were broken, feuds fought themselves out in the general mêlée. They played and made merry as if they knew their time for making merry together was nearly spent, as if they were fated people fit only to adorn a tale.

And yet something of their spirit survives, though most of the old native families have died out or gone abroad so that you will find scarcely a Macpherson in the parish of Laggan where formerly men of other names were rare. Strangers have come in, giving the people the appearance of an altered character. But the character of the people of Badenoch has not really changed. They still would dance and play shinty like their fathers. An old traveller who passed through Speyside long ago described the people as sly, soft-tongued and deceitful. This in Highland opinion is more like the picture of a West-Coaster. The faults of the people of the Central Highlands are glaring enough but they are the reverse of mean. They are an ebullient folk, as easily depressed as exalted, like their forebears who could bewail their evicted fate one moment with the accents of despair, and snatch up a shinty stick the next. They have little dexterity in hiding their emotions. Gaelic-speaking people may seem reticent when they talk English, but at a word of Gaelic their appearance changes, they come to life, old men greet each other with smiles and gestures across a busy street as if they were alone in the moors. They are in fact of the type we commonly call Gallic; eloquent in talk but halting speakers; full of gestures and animation, vivid and unselfconscious, inaccurate lovers of the marvellous from whose observations of pike with hair on their necks and stags two hundred years old one might write a new text-book of natural history. They are not oppressed with religious doubts and fears and beliefs like their neighbours in Strathdearn and Strathnairn where the stern sect of Free Presbyterians predominates and makes money. They are in fact a gay, shallow, irreligious people who go to church because they meet each other there. Their ideal minister is typified in the famous Big Minister who once lived at Laggan Bridge. When he reproved his parishioners because they did not come to church they retorted that he did not join them at shinty. So it was arranged that if they came to hear him on Sunday mornings, he should play with them in the Sunday afternoons. But at heart the folk are with the old woman who longed for summer and the sheilings when she could go to 'Finglen, Finglen of my heart, where there is no Sunday.'

Tattered shreds of old gaiety still flaunt themselves in the emptying country so that to this day the people of Badenoch are namely in the Highlands for their love of dancing, fiddling, shinty, and gossip. They have a passion for dancing. No distance, no weather, can keep them from a dance. A few years ago before the inhabitants of the village of Dalwhinnie had anywhere else to dance they used to stretch tarpaulins across the platform of the railway station between the fiddler and the wind, and there they danced by the light of the moon.

There is no stern Calvinistic reprobation of moral defects in the Central Highlands such as one encounters in Ross-shire, but drinking is regarded with an almost complacent eye, and scarcely any stigma attaches to illegitimacy. I have heard a very quiet pleasant woman describe the annual Children's Christmas Tree of her village as 'Such a nice affair! Everybody had a droppie and nobody too much.' But even where more serious sins are concerned the countryside, though it gossips maliciously enough, does not practise malice towards the sinner. I do not know any other part of Scotland where illegitimacy is treated so casually. I do not mean that bastards are more plentiful in the Central Highlands than elsewhere. But the cruelty which the very children in Aberdeenshire and Banffshire and every other rural district of Scotland use towards children without parents is never seen in Speyside. The people there had a reputation for virtue in at least one respect. When the sheilings were closed a great band of men and women and young lads gathered on the height of the Monadhliahs to look their last on Badenoch from that familiar ground. They had lived their summers amongst these hills for a hundred years without an illegitimate child being got there. Tolerance is a lovely virtue which grows best where men avoid the faults they do not condemn.

Shallow and uncertain as they are in many ways, cowardly before authority with no love of freedom to uphold them, the spent people of the central north are not entirely lacking in a capacity for violence and depth of feeling. Sometimes love moves them out of the normal course of their natures. A shepherd who lived by Loch Rannoch swam the loch each night to visit the girl he loved, and give his name to a bay near her home. We have no poet to build a nobler memorial for this later Leander. But generally the passion which moves the folk to their deepest feeling is love of their country. That indeed is a thing which resides in all and cannot be destroyed by eviction nor overwhelmed by time. Rather it grows. Their stay is precarious, others have been driven out, they cling in despair to all that was ever permanent in their lives, the hills and the valley where the river flows.

I have often heard people marvel that men should be willing to suffer the poverty and the discomforts of our soil and our climate while all the world, endowed with fertility and pleasant weather, lies open to them. Indeed, liking for a place cannot be measured by its cause, or else there might be little love spent on Speyside. It is unlikely places which seize our hearts and make us slaves to them, never happy elsewhere. The bare bones of the world often clothe themselves with colours out-flaunting the flowers of rich ground, and passion for a place may root itself in barren wastes where every prospect is dreary to those who do not belong to that place.

If the country of the Spey is lovely it is by tiny chances; now in a summer dell beside the river with scented herbs and day-wasting wild roses and thyme a dusky red on the banks and gravelly shores of the stream; or else in a brief prospect of birch woods drifting like smoke along the valley's sides. It is seldom such jewelled glimpses offer themselves. The dark moors reach out to the hills which circle all, the colours of the country are dull, save when the sun at dawn or evening, or else snow, transforms the scene. Yet the dank cold moors, without sign of people, have such power that all other country seems unreal after them. The very green of fields in the south appears too bright to be real. And one is afflicted with a sort of claustrophobia. Woods close at hand, and many people near one, and the restraint of fences, make an unbearable prison. The south is not free as the great expanse of moor and sky and hill is free. People and things crowd in, overlooking, jostling, choking. To taste the wild pleasure of freedom is to be for ever bound.

Not ribbon development and overcrowding, but utter emptiness and desolation, seems to be the fate to which this country moves. The landlords are no better and no wiser to-day than they were a hundred years ago, though they have less power. Here, where houses are yearly falling down, and crofts are destroyed as soon as their occupants die, one cannot buy nor feu nor lease ground to build a house on save in the villages, and the people are moving perforce to the villages. I have seen many houses emptied and broken down; it is not difficult to foresee a day when there will be villages but nothing else to relieve the intervening miles of grouse-moor and forest. No doubt the country is being preserved from ribbon-development, and the game saved. This land alone could suffer bungalows and lines of houses along its roads without suffering, for here the house that is in bad taste and foolish does not spoil nor conflict with the scene. The scene is too great for spoiling. Even a red brick shooting lodge in a narrow glen merely makes a fool of itself, the country seems to stay apart from those execrable works of men's hands. Yet without men it lacks meaning. A picturesque wilderness is a wilderness still, no matter how many deer and grouse it harbours.

Behind their show of gaiety there is despair in the native people's hearts of which they are scarcely conscious. They are defeated, the country lost, they live like beggars in a land owned by strangers who hate them for what they represent, the past. And so the past is great in their hearts. The past is all they can possess of their own home. You can scarcely talk to any man belonging to Speyside without hearing him recall the old days. The old days form the burden of their thoughts, the old days when Cluny had land he sold to incomers. Then there were folk in the country. 'They're growing less every year, soon there won't be any at all any more, ah me, the old days!' Their essential pessimism reveals itself in those backward-looking glances. Their ancestors had the small ambition to live in their country. They were uprooted by force. Their children would stay too but they cannot live, crofts they would like to rent are broken up before their dead occupants are cold in their graves and the houses are torn down. Perhaps they might fall on a sheep or even a grouse, you see. So the walls come down. Sometimes you come on a man unawares to himself, hopeless and bewildered. A few years ago I visited the smiddy at Balgown. Lachie, the smith, flung open the door of his smiddy before me. It was dark and cold in spite of the sun. I said how cold it was. 'Smiddies are like that when there's little work,' he said. While he lighted the fire I looked round me at Balgown, Balgown, place of the smiths.

Its few crofts looked over the ruined Spey valley where great banks showed the work that had been done to keep the river from the fields; and ditches choked with water-weeds and water-loving plants, fields soggy even in the dry weather, reeds and rashes spreading from the ditches across the fields, showed how the river regained what was taken from it long ago when the meadows of the Spey were worth striving for. The Cluny woods came down to the east of the township, hiding the home of Badenoch chieftains.

I was never so lost from my fellows as to regret the passing of old fine things as if the world ended with their decay. I could not look on any country with men in it and see it only as the place of old battles, theme of old songs, or the home of ghosts more living than the living men who ploughed the battlefields. The day of chiefs and clans was gone; more than gone, for it betrayed its children without future, leaving no issue, and the place I saw was a country where men worked in the fields. A crofter's wife slaving her day down in a wilderness of rocks and winter sky has more value, because she lives and makes things become, than all the captains, than all the armies that ever strutted through this river valley. Yet even I felt in Balgown how dead the present was compared with what had been. Perhaps it seemed more lost because it clung to the protection of its Chief. And as his house waned, as his people clung more desperately to the past, because they had nothing else, so Balgown waned under the shadow of the past's memorial, Cluny's house. It grew under the shelter of a leader, it lay now in the gloom which surrounds decaying strength.

There were swords made in Balgown. The pack-horses which brought French wines, claret and brandy for the great men of Badenoch from the Western Seas, over Corrieyarrick, halted here.

A few fields stretched from the few houses to the road. Women sat knitting in the sun before their houses on the edge of their fields where busy children herded cows from the corn. Cars went by in clouds of dust which smirched the green of the fields, and thus, one felt, modern life went past this place and smirched its final treasure, the past, as it went by.

Lachie the smith lit his cold fire and while he rummaged in a heap of iron beside the door I blew the groaning bellows till the smiddy came to life as trees and grasses come to life when the sun grows warm in spring. It was at once a happy place. The smith too seemed happier since his fire was lit. He dropped an armful of iron beside the anvil.

'Lord knows,' he said, 'where all the trock gathers from. I'd have sworn there was no bit of spring iron in the place and look at that!'

He knelt on the floor, handling the leaves one by one. 'There's some been here almighty time,' he said, 'that the smith before me or the smith before him got God knows where but I often wonder because it's good spring. And this came out of the last dog-cart in Badenoch. What would Gaskbeg say to hear his fine dog-cart was knocked to bits and some of it put into a Yankee car? He didn't like America—a son went there you see.'

As he handled the iron and named it he looked up now and then and his sudden smile lit his face.

Then while the spring-leaves heated he talked in a quiet voice; and that was the way it was with blacksmiths now.

He counted farms that had been where reeds and water and thinning flocks of sheep were now. He said, from such a place came two pair of horse to the smiddy, and now the summer sun shone through their stable roof, and now winter winds went through the broken windows, through the wasted lands, through the skeleton that was a living countryside. He swept the valley with his hand, swept it clean of horses for smiths to shoe. Two pairs of horses were in that place, and now a puckle sheep; and sheep, you see, never needed the smith. Over the river Cattlodge had its crofts which sent horses to Balgown, but that was done with, for the sheep were in and sheep did not get shod, poor pity the blacksmith.

His quiet voice spoke sentence of death to himself and his craft and the country folk after them. There were no horses, soon there would be no smith, and when the smith was dead a country had come to decay. A neighbour came to borrow a stone to sharpen his scythe.

'That's my busiest job now,' Lachie smiled, 'lending.'

I asked him how the unlet shootings would affect him. 'They'll touch me like every other one,' he said. 'Here's Cluny and Cattlodge and Craigdhu unlet at my back door as you may say. There's be a dozen horses there alone, and shod maybe three times in the season—that's places at my very door you see. Ach, the shootings are only trade for a while at the best—oh well, the country's done.'

Motor-cars went past to Lochaber on their way through romantic Badenoch, where broken walls and holes in rocks were the only things worth a moment's attention. I left Lachie waiting for work to come, watching his craft die, his work done by botchers, his skill lose its reward, and the smiddy fire, glowing heart once of a country alive in all its members, burn more seldom and lie more often dark and cold.

We cannot put the blame for our state on recent years, though they have done little advantage to country-dwellers anywhere, and to the Central Highlands least of all. But the roots of our present distress are buried in the past when lairds and factors and men who should have united to help the country combined to exploit it. Their successors are reaping a bitter reward. Signs of neglect and decay and ill-guiding are everywhere patent, in deer-forests with broken fences and hundreds of switch-horned stags as well as in crofts where sorrel betrays the want of lime. No one has been heedful for this country's good. People would not unite to clear the channel of the Spey at the mouth of Loch Insh beneath Kingussie and now the river floods higher with every spate, while its exit from Loch Insh silts up. Sheep-grazings are losing their value every year because the ground is sheep-sick and will not support the flocks it fed with ease so recently as twenty years ago. The accumulated fertility of the land is used up but nothing is returned. Broken deer-fences let in droves of deer to raid the farms. You can see their tracks, broad swathes of dead torn-up heather, amongst the moors, and grouse suffer. A sort of justice befalls the exploiter, though his victim is most commonly involved in that settling day.

Hopelessness is coming on. The summer visitors for whose sake people built big houses with an inevitable shack behind them, for the owner of the house to occupy, are vacant in the summer.

I have heard people praise the country because it is unspoiled, rejoicing that there are deer-forests where no one can build, or persecute wild creatures. If we still see eagles sailing above the moors, and peregrines screaming from Loch Erichtside, and wild cats in the woods of Tulloch and Benalder, it is because they have escaped the stalker and the gamekeeper who will scarcely permit even owls to live. You need but visit a shooting lodge to see the vermin board with its wild cats and hawks hung up with a nail through their head to realize how and what wild creatures are being preserved. I have seen a stag shot through the guts run with his feet tripping in his entrails. I have seen a sportsman kill a hind and two calves and wound no one knows how many more while he blazed madly at a herd of deer less than a hundred yards away. I think I would rather see a slum in the loveliest glen that meets the Spey than know that the corries were occupied by paunchy beer-barons using telescopic sights.

The woods are slowly coming down. Before the sheep came, birch woods and fir woods renewed themselves, but now the saplings are eaten by sheep or killed by heather burning. It is a country which requires woods. The crests of the hills surge magnificently from forests without whose covering the hills look bleak, base-heavy, lacking in grace and proportion.

And still there's something in the country which contents one. I know an old man who comes up from Morayshire every year to view a certain hill in Badenoch. When he has seen it, renewing his memory, he can go away happy. There are no places of which one can say, They will look like this, or, You must see them from a certain point, for the appearance of the land changes with the moods of the weather. I have seen the sun break through at the close of a drab day when the mountains had lowered and the moors were sullen. Then all at once an empyrean light shone amongst the topmost corries of the Cairngorms, as if these bleak heights were the courts of evening, and the scarp of the Monadhliahs, a line of rock and boulder and rough broken ground, stood against the sky like a delicate filigree of black. Or when the clouds lift from a slushy winter day and wind springs up, drift smokes from the peaks of the hills, and the driven snow is as black as night against the clouds beyond. But the country is most dear when summer burns the marshes dry. We do but endure winter, waiting for summer to come. The level moors, the trickling streams amongst their stony beds, hot sun and wind from the west, exhilarate the mind. Then it is time to cut peats or win them, to make the meadow hay, to swim in silky pools, and enjoy for a little the long-sloping sun. And night is brief with the sun's course plain where it sinks a little way beneath the horizon. And the sheep come newly clipped with their lambs round the doors of isolated houses. And old men remember the sheilings where they never were. Frost on May mornings, burning heat at noon, the peaks a hand's reach off and low like little hills of sand under the sun, cattle lowing to be milked when women go out calling 'Proo-yae! Proo-yae!' make us happy enough to forget that we are few who now enjoy what many lost.

12. Dunscaith Castle, Isle of Skye

Robert M. Adam

SKYE

by

GEORGE SCOTT MONCRIEFF

SKYE lies, a ragged bird, in the sea, its tail a few hundred yards from the Scottish mainland; measuring fifty miles from talon to crest, yet nowhere five miles from the encircling water, so deeply do the sea lochs bite the land.

The Cuillins lie with outlines rapidly familiar, never long from sight. They are the embossed stamp of Skye, they become her emblem, so that, apart from such tourist trophies as Flora MacDonald's tomb and the fairy flag of Dunvegan, other features tend to be ignored or quickly forgotten. These less remarked facets are many and varied, they include a coast of ancient conglomerate rock, heaved, scarred, worn; flower-deep gorges of hill burns; lochans of great loneliness: they include even the problems of the people and the persisting legacy of a crazed Genevan.

Here is a peninsular of Bracadale. Fine cliffs drop with varied feature to the sea. The folded and flawed rock takes forms continually surprising beneath the flogging or the seeping waves. The tide withdraws itself and leaves a long ledge at the base of the cliff: a platform pitted with pools, slashed by gullies, and here bridged by a tremendous arch at the far end of which the receding waves flap, and echo carries and magnifies their patter, playing it round the fistula that utters it again, a megaphone of rock. The rock floor is rough with barnacles. Some of the pools are shallow pans, pink or white, with blood-red anemones at the brim. Another is a deep cup turned by the round pebbles which now, the waves gone, lie tranquil in the bottom. A larger pool on a promontory with a steady outlet pouring waters to the tide is as dense with foliage as an Amazonian jungle, no rock showing between the growth; hair- or sword-like, sacs or fronded, smoothly moving if the water is disturbed.

Here in the sun the rock gets hot and the shallow pools warm. The sea that coils and twists a foot below the ledge is cold, but not so intimidating to the bather as that pool whose weeds are so dense that any horror framed of fact or the imagination might lurk there. And there is always awe in the solitude of a cliff-foot, although beyond the water is gleaming blue in the sunshine: above it only gulls float, sea-swallows dip-dive, gannets plunge. Always the sea rustles in the fretted rocks and gurgles in the pot-holes. Behind, the cliff rises, its crumbling rock supporting rare tufts of grass, patches of small white flowers, and ledges brilliant with briars.

I have lowered my body into the weed-deep pool and swum violently across it, feeling like a tingle each touch of the groping weed, and reached the other side, glad with achievement.

In canvas shoes to protect me from the barnacles I have walked far along the rock ledge, swimming the intervening gullies, and have gone into the black cave mouths, where the sunlight ends abruptly and sluggish water trickles through the roof. The black cold within and the muttering of the sea behind chasten all ardour of exploring with a splendid fear, making me return to the warm sun and the sunlit rock floor; the sun welcoming my nudity, the cave-mouth alone sombre against its ubiquitous light which reflects and reflects again from sea and rock floor.

Elsewhere there are shores of sand, of piled smooth pebbles of all sizes, or deep with fragments of coral, white or coloured a blue-pink, broken from long dead coral reefs that thrived perhaps when the Quirang was an active volcano, before its fury burst it and the cooling of the earth sloked it. But this coral is brittle stuff, it snaps between the fingers, it is too dead to be worked. Below the Storr Rock there is a shore that resembles the worn bricks of a baby giant, left huck-ster-muckster, slab on slab or sloping from slab: a rounded cliff rising steep above it and a waterfall plunging down to it.

I have lain on the hot moss of burns that run through gorges which earlier were densely flowered with bluebells and with enormous lush primroses, and to dry myself run on banks of grass and heather. I have swum in lochans whose water is dark with peat that leaves a faint sweetness on the lips and motes the body seen beneath it with the colour of wine: and walked back in the long evening that prefaces no night.

A summer evening in a boat fishing for lithe or mackerel, or, more tranquilly, for haddies, while the haze of the northern night faintly occludes the slopes of the fiord, has a sharp tranquillity that sharply dis-tinguishes it from a more southern twilight. Mackerel are a thrilling fish, breaking the sea's surface as they chase the herring-fry: and when you have rowed your boat amongst them, where the water boils with their urgency, they keenly fight at the end of your line. Within the boat there is cheerful conversation, and the floor is deep with silver writhing fish. And in late September when the phosphorescence is on the water, sea-fishing is transformed to the fantastic, when you lower your haddie line over the side and see it meticulously lit up, so that it is visible far into the black depths, as though it were a trident of neon tubing. At every stroke the oars strike pools of fire, that linger behind and slowly fade. In the shallow water the small fish scudding before your landing cut flaming arrow-heads.

The patches of wood in Skye, rare and, save at Dunvegan, small, have the bearing of armies recently come from battle. Tree limbs are twisted. Even the most healthy trunk supports boughs broken and dead. Rotted branches lie on the ground. These trees have lately fought with the wind, you feel: they have repelled him once more, but not without losses. And it is the winds of Skye, rising from the open sea, breaking the waves, bowing the plants, that shape and describe the island. The small woods lie in sheltered folds of the hills. The traveller finds them unexpectedly. On the hills' flanks twisted thorn-trees caricature the grimness with which they cling to pockets of soil in the loose rock: grappling with their gnarled roots, contorting their few branches, arms bent in defiance of space. They seem always near enough to death, dried and sapless, and when they pass the border line they are no more than white bones on the hillside.

The common hills of Skye are steep enough to provide invigorating walks with their reward of views of great diversity. The deep-cutting sea lochs strike inland at contrasting angles: some with cliffs, some with soft slopes. The small islands off the coast, the familiar horizon of the Outer Isles, the mountains of the mainland, are the terrestrial limits. A cliff face may be scarred with the white line of a waterfall falling five hundred feet to the sea, or, if there is a high wind, may be crested with a white plume—the waterfall is flowing upwards, only reaching the sea in the form of drops invisible in the distance. Dykes, always in the act of tumbling, stone desperately supporting stone, run up the hills, or neatly flank the dusty grey road: or wire fences flaunt the Board of Agriculture subsidies in steel-supported parallels. The cultured patches round the crofts stick out, curiously shaped, distinctive from the surrounding boscage, the coarse grass, the heather, the bog-myrtle. An old croft house has whitewashed walls, its grey slate roof is ridged with red tiles: its steading clusters on the nearest available flat surface with stable, byre, a roofless building, and an enclosure of multi-coloured sheets of corrugated iron, whose red and grey neatly match the roofs and whose rust echoes colour of the seaweed ridge left by the tide. A new croft stands starker: its walls still black stone, with corner pieces of grey concrete. Motley hens eternally busy scrape and search: stirks still too young to be bored watch their master and frisk away when he approaches. A queerly crossed cow, the colour of a mouse, searches tender grasses.

To many Kyleakin is the stepping-on ground to Skye. Nor is it easy to forget that first sight. For me it was a day of rain and sunshine. A shower had just passed, wetting the grass and the roads: the sun lit the green setting to Kyleakin and the darker background of the moorland, and gave the sea a green translucency that I had never known before. The white houses by the slip shone, the castle ruin had a muter glow: overhead snatches of cloud flecked the very blue sky.

The road from Kyleakin coils and doubles, clings to the land and seems at points to overhang the sea. It has been re-made, and in places is a terrace with white concrete balustrades on the seaward side. At one point the route itself is new: the old road can be seen striking more boldly across the hills.

Broadford is the first township after Kyleakin, a string of houses along the seaboard, often ugly, but with an active appearance rare in Skye where ruins are the rule. Beyond Broadford we come to the Red Hills, and double deeply round Loch Ainort, where the sea is often dead calm, with many gulls and a few duck sitting on its surface, strangely tranquil. We round the vast slag-heap of Glamaig, run down Loch Sligachan, and see from the bridge the splendid view up the glen, between the soft hills and the hard Cuillins. From here on the country is lower, up to Portree, the town of Skye. It is a half street town that never looks urban, even on a day at the season's height when that grand natural harbour is full of craft: half a dozen yachts of various sizes, the daily steamer, and an excursion boat from Glasgow. The excursionists climb the brae, each with his camera and looking inexplicably silly, probably feeling it. The natives idly watch them. The shopkeepers' eyes light. Or it rains and only the hearty come ashore, saying they like the rain. The half-street is grey, and the rain hisses in the dust, turning it to hard mud.

The roads of Skye are remarkable things in themselves, with the way they twist, and come into sight far ahead, and lose themselves again, interminably rise and fall. Often they make wearying walking, when fragments of the road to come are visible ahead, either round a loch or up a brae, when the dust or the rain is thick, and worst if one is herding a drove of disgruntled cattle. Everywhere along them there are places bearing satisfying names. Sometimes a bare patch of hillside has its own name, and one wonders why, until one recalls that this must once have been a village whose very ruins are now indiscernible. Talisker, Portnanlong, Tayinlone, Vaternish, Fiskavaig, Fernilea, Skeabost, Totardor, Sulishaderbeg, Oronsay, Armishader, Skerinish, Edinbain, Camasunary, Varragill, Tarskavaig, Tormore, Inver Dalavil, Armadale, Flodigarry, Kilmaluag, Coillor, Staffin: they require the Gaelic for their full savour, as indeed does all Skye.

Winter comes to Skye with November. The glory of red bracken is dimmed by the damp of the streaming rain. The grasses die to draggled brown blades. We dig the potatoes below their dead foliage: finding more stones than potatoes. We pull the turnips, shaw them, toss them into the waiting cart. To-day it is frosty and the white crofts gleam like blocks of ice: the sea slides greyly.

There is no feeding for the beasts. Many sheep are sent to the Black Isle for winter grazing, and those kept at home require quantities of cake, and when that is not forthcoming they die.

Snow early comes to the Cuillins and cloaks Sgurr nan Gillean. Days of rain wash them black again, but always in some deep corrie a white seam remains until at length a further fall refreshes the whole range. Elsewhere snow is rare, and the frost is inconsiderable, though I have seen a small limb of a sea loch frozen over for a week when the tides were neap and there was little wind. The yellow ice alternately rose and subsided with the tides; it crackled and rustled, splintering round the rocks. The tides increased, and one night a high wind came. The ice broke up, sinking a ferry-boat anchored in mid-loch, cutting its bows as with an axe, and in the morning lay piled in jagged fragments along the shore. Day after day the winter winds blow; cold from the east, wet from the west, storming the landskip and flattening the dead vegetation, pressing against the houses so that in the small crofts one is never away from the wind. In the daytime it either sweeps one along with hectic gait, or relentlessly holds one back. In the evening by the fireside it is still present, clamorously leaning against the wall. At night one goes to sleep to its howl and rattle. The days are very short. Little work can be done: everyone is waiting for the spring.

The coming of spring is slow, long drawn-out. Although snowdrops and croci flower early the new grass is tardy in appearing. Gradually the slopes engreen, anxiously watched by those who await the bustle of the spring work. Then at last it is time to sow, and the furrows manured with seaweed and dung have grain flung across them or potatoes turned in. The peats are cut. Each man gives a day's work to his neighbour. The peats are brought home and stacked by the crofts, set to dry in the wind and the welcome sun.

Stirks come out to grass. The sheep return. The

burns are bridged by the yellow flowers of the flags. Life hastens towards the profusion of summer, when the wild orchids flower everywhere, with heavy perfume: when the bracken is green and shady and the few trees have their fullness. Cuckoos become tiresome with their cry, uttering it into the early hours of the morning in defiance of the darkness that never comes. The herons also make use of the long light, and feed and call by the waterside. Corncrakes are still, though less commonly, vociferous in the small fields.

The harvesting of the hay and corn are anxious periods. At best the crop is small. Wind and rain are hard on it. One year, shortly after the European War, a gale of immense force literally swept away a whole season's crop of hay as it lay drying in the fields, carrying it in a night off the face of Skye.

Once again the bracken darkens on the hillsides, the leaves yellow and drop from the trees: winter returns in her starkness.

In Skye few people swim or play games: cookery is a dead art: even piping that, in the MacCrimmons, presented Skye with one of the most remarkable families of artists in the history of the world, has come to be a thing proscribed and an object for pompous patronage. Calvin survives in all his monstrosity in Skye. You will hear the tourist who has attended a two-hour service in a hideous and acutely uncomfortable church saying with a sigh of relief as he comes away: 'A hard religion, but it has bred a splendid type.' And this is sheer bunkum. It is a hard religion, and it has taken a splendid type to withstand it as well as the Skyeman has: he has done so by endowing it with a certain, howsoever baneful, dignity, such as is lacking in, for instance, the Welsh Nonconformist communities. None the less, it detracts from him, and looks like being the end of his kind. True, there are houses where ceilidhs are frequent and free: where you may sing, and where there is no moral objection to playing cards, parlour games, or the gramophone. These are predominantly the homes of those who have been away from the island and who have in consequence a wider culture than the all-powerful kirks allow within their reach. There are many homes where, the work for the day finished, there is nothing to be done but sit by the fire; where the old man actually utters the despairing *Ochone*, *ochone*, until it is time for prayers and bed. An occasional visitor brings sober talk. The atmosphere is heartbreaking. And, while recipes for delightful foods surviving in a few places tell of a one-time respect for the palate, the predominating dietary of Skye is inimical to tongue and stomach alike. In these days even the fish is harder to get, and laws passed without consideration for such outlying parts of Britain present the anomaly of sheep on the hill but tinned meats from the Argentine on the table. Undernourishment promotes tuberculosis, and many young people leave Skye to spend years in some hospital in Glasgow. Stewed tea, potatoes, brose, oatcakes like cardboard, eternal tin-tasted meats, these present a decent humiliation of the flesh for the glorification of the grim God of Calvin. Dancing, sports, and piping are actively condemned by the seceding ministries; and by far the greater part of the population belong to the various secession churches. One is glad to see the young people revolting, but their revolt is handicapped. For example, the regular reading matter in many houses consists of no more than the Bible, the lives of a couple of self-tortured seceding ministers, and the church magazine. These magazines of secession churches are incredible productions. Month by month they resurrect the corpse of Montrose and with elaborate untruths and a stately nineteenth-century prose proceed to savage that noble body. Again and again the Lords of Argyle are vindicated with cold fury for want of fact. Other articles underline the sins of reading novels, of having trams on the Sabbath; the heresy of using the word *Sunday;* the monstrous iniquity of *Rome;* the sole righteousness of this particular sect, with its handful of a congregation standing out in scorn against the hundreds of millions of heretics. Biblical reference is almost completely confined to the Old Testament, to Paul in his confusions with the Law, and to the well-loved obscurantism of Revelations. Into this home comes a penny paper, fresh from Glasgow, with its trumpery opinions, and presents the only printed alternative. The popular press has nothing to offer the young man who is trying to get away from the horrid fallacies of his Church. There is, in short, for many Skyemen no vehicle for thought other than that of fallacious theology. If Skye does produce great men nowadays it is only in the rather shameful ranks of the industrialists. For, although you may not spend your money in delight, West Highland Calvinism does not forbid you pleasure in amassing it: indeed, it encourages you, for it has a strong respect for Mammon, and making money may keep man from carnal mischief. Let him bully his employees, manufacture trash: these may be justified, especially if he remembers his Church and her needs for the further spreading of the One Word. The ministers incorporate, besides the perverts to be expected, many pathetic creatures, pompous and nervous. I know only one who has a fine quality, who could inculcate life into the drivel he had to promulgate, and who would certainly have been a poet in a happier community; who remained, moreover, humane, intelligent, a good companion: but he, it should be added, had not gone through the requisite training for full qualification, and was only a 'missionary.'

The Skye Sabbath must be spent in the proper company to be believed: no shaving, no laughter, no reading—save in the Bible, no walking—save to church. The hatred and the misery of the churches constitute a refinement of barbarism. That the people can yet be human stands to their great honour. But such a background is hard to overcome. It breeds a hopelessness, a barrenness of effort, and a distrust of happiness and passion that must inevitably baulk. Since the formation of the Land League of half a century ago Calvinism has been strengthened by the secession of the Free Presbyterians (the stricter the sect the more strongly they stress their freedom). The Land League, formed to combat rotten landlords, created such alarm at Westminster, where they seem never to have forgotten the '45, that warships were sent to the Skye lochs in a stupid and vain effort to intimidate the people. The Land League achieved something. But to-day there is no collaboration amongst Skyemen to fight for their existence, although that existence is more perilous than it has ever been.

There is no history of Skye, or of the North-west, or, for that matter, of Scotland, that deals adequately with the last two hundred years. It would make an ugly story. Johnson, on his tour, was horrified at the privations forced upon the islanders, and spoke in strong terms of the work of Westminster. No attention was paid to him. Since then there have been the unforgettable Clearances and ultimately a steady depopulation produced by the inevitable neglect and sacrifice of an outlying district. After the late War the Government in alarm purchased most of Skye through the Board of Agriculture and set on foot schemes for stabilizing, even for re-settling, the population. New houses, new marches and fences, even a pier and a slip here and there, are the work of the Board. On the other side of the picture the Board is widely unpopular and the population has continued steadily to decrease. It has gone down to below ten thousand, a decrease of almost two thousand since the Board took control. No doubt the Board deserves some of the opprobium it receives: it has made many obvious mistakes. But it never had the remotest chance of succeeding. Its powers were too small and the Government's attitude too superficial. Firstly, since the days of the big farms instituted in the nineteenth century the croft had been only an auxiliary occupation for almost all the crofters. It provided them with part of their food and a small income: for the rest they were either fishermen or they worked on the farms. Now the farms have been broken up and the fish have been systematically over-fished and poached by high-powered combine-owned trawlers from elsewhere. It would seem that by any moral law the fish at his door were firstly the property of the Skyeman; but to-day he cannot catch enough for himself, let alone to sell.

In 1934 I heard that the Government were again alarmed at the state of Skye: that an inquiry was to be made, but at the same time that it had been decided that the crofter-fisherman must go. To all intents and purposes he has gone. What one would like to know is how the Government imagines that the people of Skye can live on their crofts alone, as crofting stands to-day. Not a single ordinary crofter in Skye can do it (I exclude some whose crofts are tantamount to small sheep farms). His only realizable asset is the two or three stirks he can rear, worth about five pounds apiece, and the dividend from the sheep club stock—if any of the disastrously inaugurated clubs have yet paid a dividend. It is possible that he may sell a sack of potatoes on a fortunate year. Every crofter is dependent upon some outside income: it may be work as a carpenter, on the roads, as a postman, on a ferry, rarely the boarding of summer visitors; it is very often a pension, or a remittance from a relative abroad. Scarcely a secure existence or one conducive to a fine fearless independence. Empty crofts, many of them new, with their late owners perhaps on Poor Law Relief in Glasgow, stand, tombstones to those who had faith in the Board and had no other support.

Unless the Government is prepared to take radical steps for the future of Skye, it should at once set about a methodical evacuation of the island, leaving it for the summer vultures and their parasites. Yet, as the Government knows, for all its pleas of having magnanimously subsidized the crofter, whom it has already robbed beyond compensation, the crofter finally disinherited would require the larger subsidy of relief.

No doubt the communist and the internationalist æsthete, the efficiency expert and the centralization crank, is likely to deem the evacuation of Skye fundamentally desirable and in accordance with that hallucinatory World Progress. But Skye has suffered enough already from romanticism: one hopes that realities may prevail. Although its state is now so feeble, Skye's desertion would still be a loss to the world. Even, to judge by discountenanced standards, if only that your city man of three or four generations, now sterile, needs wide breeding grounds for his heritors.

I for one am certain that Skye, given proper consideration, could support a good population. Firstly she must be allowed her own fish. The potentialities of her soil, poor though it often is, have yet to be given due consideration. Early vegetables have been shown to be marketable from other parts of the Western Highlands. Skye raspberries are magnificent and profuse. One attempt made to market them failed, owing to their being too damp for a long journey by boat. Therefore canneries and jam factories should be installed on the island. Less scientific adaptation of other vegetables than has been required to make the North of Canada a productive region would provide Skye with new possibilities. The encroaching bracken must be driven back: such diverse comestibles as bacon, lobsters, honey, must take its place as emblematic of the island.

Genuine consideration of Skye would save her. Unfortunately she is unlikely to get it, with less than ten thousand of a population, from an overwrought Government endeavouring to provide for over forty million. Unfortunately, again, Skyemen are unlikely to-day to demand consideration. Calvinism is a bulwark against insurrection, and an invisible government does not provide the inspiration of a resident landlord. There is a sense of gloom and defeat in this island whose natural development has been aborted. Historians tell us that Scotland is an unconquered country: actuality disagrees. Nothing is surer proof of defeat than the abject surrender of a culture, and the acceptance in its place of a defeatist religion is only better than complete degeneration. To speak to a Skyeman is to sense his latent and subtle culture: he is, in the true sense, a man of honour. And he who has turned from the iniquity of Calvinism, and in doing so has escaped the pitfall at the doorway, that of a joyless atheism, is a splendid man, with the added virtues of smeddum and enjoyment of life. But escape for most is too difficult. The Brahan Seer prophesied the evacuation of the Islands: St. Kilda first. . . . Does Skye only move to fulfil this fate?

13. The River Tay, Perth

Robert M. Adam

PERTHSHIRE

by

CAMPBELL NAIRNE

I

It would be shortly before the outbreak of war in 1914 that my father conceived the idea of attaching a carrier to his Rudge-Whitworth so that I could go with him on his cycle runs.

Where he took me I had not the faintest idea, for his schoolhouse was then my world, and the last cottage along the road stood on the edge of the uncharted. I feel pretty certain, however, that we must have gone bowling through a large part of Strathmore, down such roads as the Roman track which hurries with arrowy straightness from Gask into the sleek valley below Crieff. The country there has a flatness and suavity that would commend it to a patient pedaller. On various occasions I must have been wheeled up the weary incline of the Necessity Brae outside Perth, so-called because in a less temperate age it was thought imperative that the traveller should snatch a quick one before he essayed its ardours. (There was a convenient inn.) At other times, mahout-like on the handlebars, I must have penetrated to the upper reaches of the Tay and its tributaries.

Certain changes have come about within the last twenty years. Of that more anon. But it takes the white agony of an Ice Age to bring new expression to a land whose features are so deeply graven as Perthshire's. Festoon the bases of Schiehallion with pylons, and the traveller coming over from Rannoch or up the valley of the Tay will still see its exquisite point cleaving the sky, plum-blue or ivory or apple-green in accordance with the weather and season. Though the Tummel must now find its way past a concrete dam—a monstrous one at that—nothing has been lost to the snapshotters who train their Kodaks on the crashing plumes of black and white water under the Queen's View. So that I do not think I shall err if I fill out my babyish recollection of the country as it appeared to me on those bicycle runs with the sharper impressions I acquired later.

For me the core of the universe was Perth. A Mr. Willis who took coach through our barbaric land about the end of the eighteenth century paused for a moment in his appraisal of 'gentlemen's seats' to remark that Perth is the most elegantly built of any town in Scotland, and that 'the light and beautiful bridge which throws itself like a rainbow over the Tay is deservedly admired.' Lord Cockburn, who joggled from Edinburgh a few decades later to hold court in Perth, wrote of it as 'this rose of country towns'—a compliment inspired, one fancies, by the smooth workings of his Lordship's digestion, for there is evidence that we dined him well.

Ignorant of these tributes, but already a stout local patriot, I used to conclude essays with the pronouncement that Perth is rightly known as the Fair City. It is the strangest of titles. By 'city' we do not usually understand a town which has fewer inhabitants than a metropolitan housing scheme—I mean one of those red bungaloid rashes which it pleases the perpetrators to call garden suburbs. And 'fair' is not perhaps a just epithet now that we can boast of a disproportionately-sized railway station, a slum or two, and even, here and there, a hulk of windowless factory, with a stalk dribbling smoke towards the steep of Kinnoull Hill.

On the other hand there is still a bleating of sheep across the road from Dewar's red-brick warehouses, the collies go 'way wide' under the panache of smoke thrown up by the London express, red-faced men in tweeds climb down stiffly out of the brakes and gigs that come *clip-clop clip-clop* into town on market days behind the swift-sliding motor-cars, and Lord Cockburn's perfumed phrase is not yet without meaning. It may actually reacquire its old aptness. In recent years the octopus of industrialism has begun to drop back from Perth, and it looks as though we shall soon be left with nothing but its putrescent tentacle about our vitals.

Perth was, as I say, the core of my universe. We lived outside it and were yet of it. North-east and south-west, broken by short swells of heather upland or fir wood, stretched the quilted floor of the great strath which runs from Alyth to Auchterarder, for the most part sweet arable country that in autumn had a melting and swaying motion as the wind shivered across it and set the ears of the oats rustling. Netted in the loops of its small roads one discovered the hamlets and the 'farm towns,' the hamlets mostly of one street, with a kirk propped over the dove-grey sandstone cottages, the farm buildings clustered around a square-set house of two storeys, grey-slated and trellised, the central porch like a jutting nose between the peaked windows of the bedrooms. A much-tilled country, this, yielding its crops to unnumbered generations of settlers. Everywhere there was evidence of long occupation—lonely monoliths, green burial mounds, the ridges of Roman road—and the finger-posts with their clusters of names bore witness to the continued fertility of its sandstones.

Rides east by the Tay flats revealed country that now seems to me a miracle only less astounding than the white challenge of orchards in Lanarkshire within an arrow's flight of pitheads and blast-furnaces. Here, under the bleak Sidlaws, and not thirty miles from the dash of the North Sea, we came out upon gardens that rustled down to the river in falls and swirls of fruit blossom. The frothing flow of it would hurt the eyes; it had the white glitter of light refracted from snow-fields. The road gave rather a distant view, and it was better, leaving the cycle propped at the lane-end, to wander down the steep little paths towards the river and railway. Then one saw how crooked old trunks stood in rows under the white flood. There was a murmur of bees, sometimes a train shattered through a cutting, and the blue stillness received into its quiet the creak of winches that came up over the beds of marsh marigolds from a salmon fishery round the neighbouring bend of the Tay. My mother's kinsfolk farmed in the Carse, so I knew it well.

The boundary fault which geographically divides Perthshire (and Scotland) into Lowlands and Highlands—its ethnological significance is now small—crosses the Tay about fifteen miles north of Perth. At

Dunkeld the country had unmistakably a Highland look, even if it was not 'totally different'—as the guide-books would have us believe—from the land over towards Perth. Here were sharp-rising slopes, hung with firs and birches, and through that screen could be glimpsed miniature precipices—sheer drops of the naked schist—over which slid ropes of white waterfall. Up in the wooded cleft of Strathbraan there were more outcrops of rock and a constant brawling of churned water. You heard the roar of it through the trees. The fields hereabout climbed steeply, there was much pasturage and little ploughland, the farm-houses with their distinctive white-harled walls lay cupped in the hills and looked at each other across wide gaps. Above the trees there was a sense of bareness and spaciousness, an intimation of the heather-smell and peat-smell of the deer forests in Rannoch and Atholl.

I acquired in due course a bicycle of my own. It was no shining roadster, and to cover its deficiencies (or to save myself the trouble of applying emery paper to its rims) I painted over the metalwork in sober black. Then I christened it Black Bess and fancied myself a swaggering Turpin.

From that moment the range of my explorations extended, and I began to realize Perthshire as an entity. I was astonished then (as I am now) by the variety of its aspect. It is relatively so small a land—its greatest length about seventy miles and its greatest breadth about fifty-six—yet it comprehends almost every distinctive feature of the Scottish scene. It is Scotland in little, with Highlands and Lowlands proportionately represented on a reduced scale. Up in remote parts of Breadalbane I would hear the farmers greet each other in Gaelic—'It's the fine day that's in it'—and over the strath in the Ochils they would be saying, 'Aye, man, it's a braw day, this.' I was never conscious of the racial dichotomy which is said to bear so hard upon a land rooted in two traditions.

Wherever Black Bess carried me there were hills. Mild hills, some of them, like the sweetly dimpled green shoulders of the Ochils; others of a picture-postcard prettiness, white or blue cones that one saw framed in a network of birch twigs from roads winding in and out along the northern shores of lochs; others again that always preserved a majestic aloofness, not that they were of great height or insuperable obstacles to climbers. I was encouraged to identify the tops. 'What's that yonder?' 'Ben Ledi.' 'And that?' 'Ben Vorlich.' 'And that?' 'Ben More.' 'And that?' 'Ben-y-gloe.' The names, horribly Englished as they were, rang a carillon in my mind, and so did the names of the townships and villages I linked with them—Aberfeldy and Ardvorlich and Amulree, Killin and Callander and Kenmore, Fortingal and Struan and Dalnacardoch.

What intrigued me most about those hills was the mutability of their mood. It is, I think, the secret of their appeal, for they are not high, and only in certain weathers do they achieve beauty. One evening I would see the Beinn a' Ghlo peaks in clear sunlight, striated with snow, perhaps, blue shadow in all the corries, and the crags pasturing white flocks of clouds. Next morning I would wonder where Beinn a' Ghlo had hidden herself. For the black mists would be down on Glen Tilt, rain falling in sheets, the birches crashing their tops together, and the Garry making a great to-do among its wet boulders. That afternoon, however, the rain would stop, the lower slopes of the mountain would reappear, spotlights would travel up its green bulk, mists would smoke from its rocks, and by evening the sky would be clear enough to mirror the sunset.

Perhaps the moors and hills made a stronger impression on my mind than the lochs and rivers, for Black Bess was not a three-speed machine, and we have some pretty gradients within our boundaries; but the noise of water—the slap of waves on reeds, the thunder of white falls, the indefinable soft gurgle of runs trapped in heather—is of course as quintessential in Perthshire as the lift of hilltops against the horizon.

In my possession is an illustrated textbook on rocks which (so runs the label) was awarded to me by the Perthshire Society of Natural Science. What I did to deserve this I know not; I have a dark suspicion that I once perpetrated a prize-winning essay on (God save us all) the fertilization of primroses. It serves anyhow as a reminder that in my childhood I was an ardent botanist. The amiable hobby of collecting wild flowers can certainly be as well indulged in Perthshire as in any other part of these islands. The commoner species grow abundantly in the river valleys. The woods of Strathtay are enamelled in March with carpets of lesser celandines, in April come the violets and anemones, and a month later the glens smoke with wild hyacinths. If you are a real naturalist you will labour up the schistose corries of Ben Lawers in search of such rarities as the *saxifraga cernua*, which is not found elsewhere in Britain. It is also a grand country for the bird watcher. Fishing in the Tay or the Tummel you are bound to see the oyster-catcher go past, orange-billed and pink-shanked; out of the black pines of Rannoch beat the capercailzies; and always on the moors there is a calling of curlews—two notes repeated and prolonged into deep trills, a wild plaint that may appear to you (if you come primed with notions about Prince Charlie) an evocation of the sadness of our 'lost causes.' A very meagre percentage of the thousand odd species of flowers and plants known to Perthshire found its way between the leaves of my blotters, and of its 127 nesting birds I never could spot more than a round dozen. But at least I made contact with the living face of the land in my pursuit of them.

Then, of course, there were holidays. I do not think I ever plowtered with pails or spades, and such toy craft as I owned took the water on the linns of the Tay and the Garry. Once or twice we would venture over the northern border into Inverness, but for the most part we holidayed in our own country. So that all my exploits had the Perthshire scene for background. I can remember joggling over the moors to hill bothies, and how we rounded up the black-faced lambs with much whistling of collies and bleating of bereaved ewes; ahead of us, through the cool summer dusk, the flock glimmered down the heather track on its way to the station and entrainment for Perth mart. There were long days on the hills when we lay cushioned in hot heather and ate sandwiches and watched the blue sail of the cloud shadows across the moor, and sometimes bestirred ourselves to take up a rod and bring startingly big trout out of the little peat-stained pools that lay open to the sky between the dash of orange cascades. Another autumn there was harvesting in Atholl. The sun blazed all week out of a clear sky, and each afternoon the mown straw of the oats was burning hot as we gathered it from the ground.

II

The monied folk who descend upon our big houses in August, heavily disguised in our kilts and tweeds, and withal so 'foreign,' so deliciously and quaintly English, must take it for granted that the country which furnishes the grouse for their expensive slaughterings had always the look of desolation it wears now. (August is incidentally one of our worst months for weather.) They can hardly be expected to know that at the end of the eighteenth century there were crowded communities along both shores of Loch Tay and Loch Rannoch, and that there was actually a danger of over-population in some of the glens which have since been abandoned to sheep and deer. I myself left school without having been told what fate overtook the crofters of Rannoch and Breadalbane when their chiefs discovered that there was a good thing to be made out of black-faced sheep. The aforementioned Mr. Willis was much vexed by these 'clearances.' He observes pointedly of the depopulation he found in progress: 'How cruel it is, is obvious, but I am inclined to think it will eventually prove impolitic and disadvantageous. The present race extinct, who will ever inhabit these barren regions, unless from *Kamtschatka*?'

But the greed of landlords was not the only agent at work. With the agricultural improvements after the Forty-five came the break-up of the old infield and outfield system of cultivation, under which intermixed strips of land were held by groups of small tenants, and the collapse of the clan system hastened the end of the sub-division of land among the chief's kin—*dhuine uasail* and tacksman and cottar. It is not so long since Perthshire had its pendiclers, who held pieces of land belonging to a large farm, and its portioners, younger sons among whom was sub-divided the land owned by a family, but for the last hundred years, outwith the areas that suffered at the time of the clearances, there has been a tendency to consolidate small holdings into big farms. It all loosened the bonds that tied rural communities to the soil. Before the War the order which exists at present—landowner, tenant farmer, and labourer—was already established, and the final emptying of the whole countryside, Highland and Lowland, had begun.

Rural life in Perthshire has since been withered by the desiccating influences at work on scores of other hitherto 'unspoilt' parts of the country. Not all has been loss, though. The isolation of the glens before the coming of wireless and the petrol-engine was a safeguard against inroads on their primitive culture, but it also tended to fetter the thought of the people and restrict their outlook. The standard of living has been raised, and shorter hours of work have led to the development of new interests. Tam will be getting a book whiles out of the County Library—the van comes round from Perth—and two nights a week Jean will be down at the Institute rehearsing her part in a Joe Corrie play which the local W.R.I. intend to enter for the next community drama festival. If farm work leaves no residuum of time and energy for intellectual pursuits it can be just as deleterious to the good life as pen-pushing and machine-minding in the big cities. There is not such a great deal to choose between the monotony of pushing over a lever and the monotony of thinning turnips.

It looks as though the exodus to the towns has reached its peak. The countryman is not so green now about cities. Glasgow can offer him League football and greyhound racing and big cinemas, but the radio and the newspapers keep before him the sobering fact that its total of unemployed runs into six figures. Besides, a man is less likely to feel the restraints of a rural environment irksome when he has a motor-bike and can be in to town of an evening to see Marlene Dietrich and Mae West.

The heart of the country still throbs, though its pulsations grow fainter. You can ausculate it most conveniently at the spring ploughing matches; at the summer flower show (but Lady Dum-Dum from the Big House declares it open and Major-General Sir Blank Cartridge is lessee of the gardens to which go most of the red tickets); at the sheep shearings; at the autumn games (but here again the alien aristocracy are patrons, and a goodly share of the prize money is taken south by hulking policemen and bemedalled dancers from distressed areas).

Wandering through Perthshire to-day you will discover some very curious phenomena, and you will not be wrong if you see in them evidence of profound changes in the social structure of the country. Standing about on good sites near villages are a number of small schools, well built of enduring stone, and most of them with an adequate schoolhouse attached. Their chimneys are smokeless; no youngsters chant multiplication tables behind their windows. It is partly that the population of school children has dwindled, but that is not the whole reason why they stand abandoned. We are all for centralization these days, and rather than spend a little money on ensuring the continuance of the 'village dominie' system, which gave Scottish education its unique character, we charter buses and pack the children off to the instructional factories in the towns. It is one of the means by which we drain life from our countryside.

In other counties the land is sapped by the fungoid excrescences of bungalow-builders. Our parasites are the Big Houses. Some of them, one has to admit, are not architecturally objectionable, and those that can boast of crow-stepped gables and corner turrets in the baronial style add something to the dignity of the land without warring against its native character. But there are others—stately homes of England in a Scottish setting—and it is not to be expected that the country should take them quietly to its bosom. Reared above clipped parks their presence as the dominating feature of a landscape has exquisite rightness. When perched against the rough steeps of hills they look utterly *dépaysés* and (let us whisper it) rather vulgar.

There has long been a cry that the millions of gallons of water running to waste in the Highlands should be converted into electrical power. We have echoed it, and we ought to be pleased now that the hydro-electric enterprises and their frightful works are realities. It had to be, and one accepts the spoliation of the country about Loch Tummel and Loch Rannoch as the toll levied for progress. But it is difficult, when you have come down through the singing Tummel birchwoods, not to feel numb with horror at your first sight of the black pipes that lance the loins of Schiehallion. Nor is that all. There is the power-station across the river, dwarfing the pitiful span of the Wade Bridge below it, a glass-fronted hulk galvanized by the soundless shudder of its transformers. Far and wide over the hills deploy the armies of pylons. It is the same a dozen miles farther west. And here one could wish that uniformity of design had not been so diligently studied in the creation of a village for the workers. The miners' row has a queer look in Rannoch.

That note of contrast must constantly be sounding for those of our visitors who spare a moment from their guns and golf clubs to consider the character of their environment. Over towards the Sidlaws toil men whose lives are salted by the east winds that swing in upon them from the coast. A grim and typically northern sense of humour is one of their qualities. 'Aye, aye,' they will say of a miser, 'he'll find nae pooches in his winding-sheet.' Or used to say—for of late 'cineamerican' has been creeping in, and it is now possible to hear a lad warn his sweetheart, 'See here, Jean, you lay off that guy.' Yet the native wit survives. You will be cracking at the road-end with John Ferguson, and the talk will be rather dull, confined to mart prices and the state of the ploughing, whether it is or is not 'weel forrit'; and without warning his humour will dart across the longeurs of the conversation and light it up. Afterwards you will think back to the remark, 'What was that John Ferguson said?'—and realize with admiration how felicitous and illuminating it was. It is a cold country hereabout, and there is no time for a man to stand and stare if he would keep the chill out of his bones. So the natives are hardworking, with few graces. *Dour*, as the Scots tongue has it.

It might be said that the core of the country, which is tough-fibred and tight-packed on the east side of Crieff, tends as you step westward to shred out. Or that the vitality breaking from the land appears first as a white jet, steadily burning, and later grows wavy and fitful, until the incandescence of Strathearn has paled by imperceptible gradations to the luminosity of Strathfillan.

The inertia of the Gael on his own land is puzzling when you consider what a hard struggle he had always had to wrest a living from it. That inertia, strangely, is not evident when he goes furth of Scotland. Men with Gaelic names are numbered among the hustling '100 per cent. efficients' of the U.S. It is not that he is a past-haunted dreamer or idealist. His high-cheekboned face is not set in expressions of unrelieved gloom, and he is devil a bit more 'poetic' than his neighbours. But on the western border of Perthshire you get the idea that here are people who do not care very much how the world wags. They stand about talking; they are the great ones for the cracks. If the travelling concert party bills its show in the hall for seven it need not begin making-up till eight, for it will be that hour at least before the villagers begin to gather. All the time, of course, they had been meaning to come, but there was no need to hurry, surely. Life is long. It is with the same disinclination to take time by the forelock that on other occasions they wash up the visitor's dishes in the back-kitchen, pump Summer

Shell, and look out loch flies for the Colonel. Explain this fatalism as you will. There are those who hold that they are aware of themselves as the last representatives of a race that has got left behind, and is now too spiritless to catch up. Perhaps it is a secret-smiling wisdom that underlies all the apparent lassitude, a realization that a lifetime of ploughing and scything will not move the hills one inch from their bases, and that, though a man labour at his bit of ground till his heart bursts, the heather and the bracken will still be up over it the moment he has turned his back.

The stranger may sometimes be made to feel that he is not welcome in Perthshire, for the reserve which proceeds from shyness lends itself to misinterpretation. The warm vulgarity which makes Glasgow the friendliest town in Britain is here to seek. Once the outworks are toppled, however, there is no distrustful retreat to an inner line of defences. It is part of the basic quality of the Scot that he does not do things by halves, and the men of Perthshire are representative Scots. If their manner is rugged and austere it is for the very good reason that they must have a safeguard against the dangerous fervour of their emotions.

It is true that the tradition of Highland hospitality is moribund. Circumstances have killed it. The custom of open house derived in part from the native kindliness of the people and in part from the conditions they lived under. A man had need to leave his door unsnecked when he did not know how soon he himself might be dependent on a neighbour for his night's lodging. Our hospitality is apt nowadays to manifest itself in the shape of boards hung out to advertise 'Bed and Breakfast' and 'Accommodation for Tourists.'

A year or two ago I was in Rannoch and thought to stop the night at the old inn which for years had marked the junction of the Pitlochry and Aberfeldy roads at Tummelbridge. It was still indicated on the map, but when I came down past the hydro-electric dam I found that it had become the headquarters of constructional engineers. The hotel at Balnabodach was on the heights overlooking Loch Tummel, and I had been afoot since daybreak. So I knocked at the door of the first cottage I saw and asked the *bean-an-tighe* if she could put me up. She shook her head. I do not know that I have ever felt so hurt and insulted. My own country, my own people! But I was dusty and tired, and perhaps my normally mild aspect had acquired an air of villainy; or perhaps, since I was wearing a kilt, she would be taking me for an Englishman, poor woman.

A hundred odd years ago Sir Walter Scott wrote of us: 'Amid all the provinces in Scotland if an intelligent stranger were asked to describe the most varied and the most beautiful it is probable he would name the county of Perth.' A pretty compliment, though the men of, say, Wester Ross might dispute its truth. Since then the gush of guide-books has nearly persuaded us that we live in an earthly paradise. But it has to be admitted that the county is not all beautiful. I would like to hale some of the rhapsodisers to Rannoch Moor and bid them contemplate the shuddering desolation of its peat hags under a March downpour. If the coarse moors stretching from Struan into Badenoch are not downright ugly at least their beauty is difficult, and not of the sort understood by charabanc tourists. In times of drought there is not much charm about our hills. The monotony of greens and greys and browns can be wearisome to the eye, and the *fuaradh-froise* or rain-breeze must sweep in from the North Sea or the Atlantic before the flow of colour and cloud-shadow is restored.

Paradisal scenery can in any case be just a wee bit dull if one is not in the right mood to appreciate it. The people matter most, after all. It is not by recollecting the aspect of its beauty spots that I can most easily evoke in my mind the spirit of the land. I think rather of a dusky road between hills, the lights of lamps burning in cottages, and two figures posed awkwardly around the gate of a field. The lad chews a straw and leans over the top bar. The girl has her back to the gate, one knee raised, and her print frock shows white in the darkness. They talk in low tones. He turns to her, and suddenly in petulant protest she breaks from him—'Och, don't, Jock, you're crushing my good blouse, and there's folk looking.' They come up the road, side by side, kicking at small stones. 'Fine night,' a man greets them from the inn door, and the lad answers absently, 'Aye, fine night.' Past the last of the low cottages the girl draws close to him and takes his arm.

When there is an end of that it will be small consolation to know that a sunset looks mighty fine from Lawers.

14. Ewes Water, Dumfries

Robert M. Adam

THE BORDER

by

COLIN WALKINSHAW

THE traveller into Scotland from the South may know the Border country by name and anticipation better than any other Scottish countryside. Certainly he would have so known it a couple of generations ago if he were a literary-minded tourist. But, paradoxically, he was (and is) unlikely to get more than a very distant glimpse of it as he crosses the Border.

Over the plain of the Tweed, as his car or his train carries him into Berwick, he may watch for a moment or two the purple peak of the Eildons or the slopes that drop from the Cheviot to the Kale Water. (They say, though I have never been able to believe it, that ships making Berwick harbour used to set their course by Smailholm Tower, solitary on its crag twenty miles away to the west.) Or if the traveller is making for Glasgow by Carlisle, he will look to the east up the long trench of Liddesdale before he has left English ground. To be sure he must traverse a borderland either way, but that Border country which is so individual a province of Scotland will have escaped him. The wide plain, the low hills of Berwickshire, belong by nature to the historic eastern province of the Lowlands, Lothian. Dumfriesshire is of the west, a sort of half-way house between Clydesdale and Galloway, as Galloway itself is a half-way house between Scotland and Ireland. The Border of tradition and of modern economic fact is the old Middle March, stretching from the Carham Burn to Kershopefoot on the Liddel and embracing the three shires of Roxburgh, Peebles and Selkirk.

The Middle March is just the country of the Tweed and its tributaries so far as Tweed is a wholly Scottish river. This simple description needs, indeed, one or two qualifications. The valley of the Gala Water, Wedale, *Vallis Dolorum*, a place of legends and sanctuaries from beyond the beginnings of history, belongs properly to the Border, but some political accident has placed the greater part of it in Midlothian, just as Lauderdale, with Dryburgh Abbey and the house of the Haigs, has been pushed into Berwickshire. And to the south-west lies the valley of Liddesdale—once the home of the wildest and most enterprising of Border reivers but now, in spite of its railway, almost as empty and remote from the main life of the Border as it was when the young Walter Scott entered it in the first wheeled carriage to pass beneath those big green hills. The waters of Liddesdale run to the Solway, but the thoroughly illogical and inconvenient twists of the borderline cut it off from the neighbouring valleys of Dumfriesshire, so it remains a sort of remote dependency of Roxburghshire, to which it is connected by roads that rise above the thousand-foot line.

Each of the three counties is built upon a particular river valley. Peeblesshire is simply Upper Tweeddale, following the river northward and then east till it begins to turn south again towards the fine gateway of the hills at Caddonfoot. The shire has more of a Highland look than most of the Border country. The hills above Peebles town are sometimes abrupter and more Grampian-like than the great, rolling, green downs or isolated, stormy peaks of the true Border. Along the river stretch the deep, warm, narrow haughlands, with here and there a castle upon a knoll, reflected in the smooth-flowing brown water, here and there (less happily) the wool mill and the half-emptied burn, slimed with dyes and waste, of a little town. The true villages of Peeblesshire lie small and little seen in the glens of the burns, in countrysides almost as empty of men as if this were indeed the Highlands and the 'sporting interest' were king ruling through clan chiefs who no longer have any use for clans-people except at some annual 'swarry' in the cities.

The modern wealth and activity of Selkirkshire are concentrated on its eastern border in the town of Galashiels, not so long ago (so we are told) a new and slightly sordid place, but now rather a handsome one as Scottish towns go, with Mr. Clapperton's carved horseman standing guard between the perpetual lights of the second best War memorial in Scotland, and a market-cross that rises above spurting streams. The true Selkirkshire lies to the west, an endearing little backwater of a county, almost railway-less, even almost bus-less, and yet not dead. It is the country of the Ettrick, and that water's chief tributary, the Yarrow—a stream immensely sung about by poets from Wordsworth back to that too-ingenious rimer who first discovered that the appallingly convenient phrase 'winsome marrow' could be applied to a young woman rather than to some distinguished product of the market garden.

But Yarrow, in spite of the poets, retains its charm, a charm of remoteness and simplicity, of light and shade upon hills that are neither overpowering nor fantastic, but have just enough that is odd in their shape to distinguish the place from other dales. In no valley of the Border does the romance of the more tragic or melancholy of the ballads lie so thickly.

> Oh gentle wind that bloweth south,
> From where my love repaireth,
> Convey a kiss from his dear mouth
> And tell me how he fareth. . . .
>
> She sought him east, she sought him west,
> She sought him braid and narrow,
> Syne, in the clifting of a craig,
> She found him drowned in Yarrow.

It was here, on the Dowie Dens, that there was fought, so long ago that it is scarcely a memory, that battle which has left behind it almost the oldest native words in Scottish history, the tombstone record of the Sons of Liberalis. It was from Blackhouse Tower in one of the glens that fall to Yarrow Water, that the lovers of 'The Double Tragedy' set out on their ride to death.

> 'Hold up, hold up, Lord William,' she says,
> 'For I fear that you are slain.'
> 'It is but the shadow of my scarlet cloak
> That shines in the water so plain.'

It was on the haugh where Yarrow and Ettrick meet that tradition, or an unknown romancer, set the scene of the fairy ballad of Tam lane, which inspired

Walter Scott (or 'some ingenious gentleman residing near Langholm') to four of the most magical lines in Border poetry:

> About the dead hour of the night
> She heard their bridles ring:
> And Janet was as glad of that
> As any earthly thing.

And it was on the opposite bank of the river that the most brilliant (and careless) of Scottish soldiers met the defeat that ended a miraculous year of victory, and that his men surrendered—to be butchered in cold blood to please the ministers on Slain Men's Lee.

Teviot is the central river of Roxburghshire, a stream almost as big and notable as Tweed, which it joins just above Kelso, neatest and most satisfying of Border towns. Teviotdale has nothing of the half-Highland quality of Upper Tweeddale. It is a typical hill strath of the Scottish south country on a scale (so to speak) rather larger than life. Its crags, its woods, its meadows, its quick running tributary burns, checking a little as they issue from steep green valleys, its pasture lands and moorlands rolling away to the bare hills—all these things could be paralleled in a dozen Scottish counties whose dales are nearly unknown to history, romance, or the tourist. But the Teviot is a hill water magnified. There was room in its valley, even four hundred years ago, for the one hundred and forty-eight 'monasteries and friar houses, castles, towers and peels, market towns, villages, mills and hospitals' burned by Hertford in the course of one of those statesmanline raids designed by Henry VIII to persuade the Scots to give him their Queen. There is room in it now for one largeish burgh, Hawick, which, lying high among its moors, seems closer to its countryside than any other centre of industrialism of its size in Scotland; for Jedburgh, climbing its hillside above the lovely but defiled Jed Water, a little town reeking of history and of a sort of violent liveliness which time and cloth factories have not destroyed; for a whole succession of villages, from Denholm, which looks like a place in a hunting print, to the sad little railway settlement of Roxburgh Junction. And between the lower reaches of Teviot and the Tweed lies the plain strewn with woods, battlefields, unexpected little hills, and relics of the Roman armies, over which the triple Eildon stands guard and which is closed to the west by the lacy red ruins of Melrose Abbey.

In these last paragraphs I have tried to make it plain that the Borderland owes its fame and its character not to nature but to men. The visitor from other parts of Scotland who comes to the Border in search of the beauties of scenery which Scott and the poets have praised so loudly, is apt to feel rather disappointed. Tweed and its valley, though pleasant enough, he finds nothing like so magnificent as Tay or Spey. Even the Forth basin with its string of parent lochs, its guardian mountains, its hidden, hollow land of Mentieth, and the rock of Stirling to mark the limits of its tidal flow, is noticeably finer. As for Yarrow, Ettrick, and Teviotdale, has not the stranger something quite as good (though smaller) at his own back door?

It is only when he has spent a little time on the Border that he begins to understand what it is that sets it apart from other Scottish countrysides. The great rivers of the North may be more beautiful than Tweed, but their valleys, for the most part, are dead or dying. Except at their mouths, the active movement of the modern world has passed them by. At the best they are no more than highways from coast to coast. And never since the Dark Ages have they had that unity of spirit and of practical working life which is the mark of the Tweed country from Peebles to Kelso.

Men have made the Border counties, by what they have done and left undone. Essentially it is a 'human interest' which gives them their place in the world's eye, though it does not seem, as yet, to have endeared them to the penny papers. Nature has very evidently made Tweeddale to be a prosperous, quiet, and rather sleepy country, the Scottish Wessex, to compare small, poor and cold things with greater, richer and warmer ones; or at least the Dorset and Somerset of the northern kingdom. The sheltered, welcoming air of the Border country is emphasized by its surroundings. Moving directly from the south upon Teviotdale, one must cross a sort of wilderness. The bare, windy slopes of the Northumbrian moorlands sweep down into England for a long day's march, making, even in modern times (and much more in the beginnings of history), a barrier to travel or to settled comfort and prosperity. And then one descends almost suddenly by Jed Water or Kale into the lowland of Roxburghshire, the finest and richest river valley in all South Scotland. Here is a country obviously made for tillage, with fine, grassy hills about it for pasture, the stretch of deep haughlands north and west by Tweed and Leader, and a mountain wall all round to protect it.

Here, before modern industry came to shift the centres of wealth and population to coalfields and iron-mines, was a natural home of prosperous security, the nucleus and stronghold of a kingdom or a great province. Here should rise the fine towns, great churches and castles of a pre-industrial age and a country where the proper sites for such prosperity were few.

And this, in fact, is what did happen. In the early Middle Ages, after the close of centuries of confusion and devastation that had lasted in the Scottish Lowlands since Roman times, the Tweed Valley contained two of the four chief burghs of Scotland. Perhaps they were actually the two biggest and richest towns in the whole kingdom. There grew up in it, with the first true glow of mediæval civilization, four great and lovely abbeys, the favourite churches of kings, one of whom came to Jedburgh for his wedding, while another made Kelso the chief monastery of his realm. Along the Tweed and Teviot farmers and lairds grew rich. The forests, where deer ran in their hundreds, were favourite hunting-grounds of the court. The two greatest names of Scottish mediæval learning belonged to this country of the Tweed: Duns Scotus, the rival of Aquinas for theological supremacy; and Michael Scot, the 'Wizard' who helped to bring Greek and Oriental knowledge to the Western World. The whole region must have seemed more clearly marked than any in Scotland for a long and easy prosperity.

And then, almost at the climax of the great age of mediævalism, the English wars began. What this meant to the Borders can be suggested by a single fact. There are three Scottish counties named after towns which no longer exist on Scottish ground, and of these two lie on the Tweed. Before the end of the Border wars, the two big burghs of southern Scotland had disappeared. One of them, Berwick, had become an outpost of Northumberland, condemned to dwindle into insignificance since it was isolated from the shire that should have fed it. The other, Roxburgh, was no more than a name, a fair, a tiny hamlet, and that enormous green mound under the trees between Tweed and Teviot which still looks across the river to the impressive scene-painter's Gothic of the ducal palace of Floors.

The final destruction of Roxburgh (by the Scots, determined that England should never hold it again) makes perhaps the central date in Border history. Before that moment in the mid-fifteenth century, the Borders had been very thoroughly raided, wrecked and fought over for something like six generations. The peaceful farmers of earlier days had learned that they could never count in safety on reaping where they had sown. Their descendants had taken to the glens, to the little peel towers or bastel houses which stood in groups for mutual protection, or to caves in the river banks. They had become shepherds, hunters, cattle-men, but most notably horsemen and fighters. But, however violent fate might have taught them to be, their main object was still the expulsion of the English from what yet remained of their conquests in Scotland. When Roxburgh, the last great English stronghold on the Middle March, fell, their legal and national purpose in life was finished. And yet peace did not return. Agreements with England were no more than truces. The authority of the Kings of Scots had been fatally weakened by the impoverishment of the long wars and a series of royal minorities. And so began the great age of Border reiving, when moonlight brought the thieves out of Liddesdale on their tough little horses to harry Scots and English cattle alike; when the great families of the Marches, Scotts and Kerrs, Elliots, Armstrongs, Turnbulls, Murrays, Douglases, Graemes, were continually at feud; when the very idea of normal justice and police came to seem an outrage—

> There came a man by middle day,
> He spied his sport and went away,
> He brought the King that very night,
> Who broke my bower and slew my knight.
>
> He slew my knight, to me sae dear,
> He slew my knight and poined his gear;
> My servants all for life did flee
> And left me in extremitie.
>
> I took his body on my back,
> And whiles I gaed and whiles I sat;
> I digged a grave and laid him in
> And happed him wi' the sod sae green.
>
> But think na ye my heart was sair,
> When I laid the moul' on his yellow hair?
> Oh, think na ye my heart was wae
> When I turned about awa' to gae?
>
> Nae living man I'll love again,
> Since that my lovely knight is slain;
> With ae lock of his yellow hair
> I'll chain my heart for evermair.

It is a lament for a man who, in cold and legal fact was a thief, a murderer and a traitor. But there is no mistaking where the sympathies of those who sang it lay. That is as plain here as in the magnificent ballad of 'Johnnie Armstrong,' whose hero was, also, in life a notorious and ruthless reiver:

'To seek het water beneath cauld ice
Surely it is a great follie—
I have asked grace at a graceless face,
But there is nane for my men and me!

'But had I kenn'd ere I cam' frae hame,
How unkind thou wadst been to me!
I wad hae keepit the Border side,
In spite of all thy force and thee.

'Farewell! my bonny Gilnock Hall,
Where on Esk thou standest stout!
Gif I had lived but seven years mair,
I wad hae gilt thee round about.'

John murdered was at Carlinrigg,
And all his gallant companie;
But Scotland's heart was ne'er sae wae,
To see sae mony brave men die.

The 'murder' was, of course, an entirely justifiable execution.

It was these generations of violence and crime, varied by English raids whose atrocity increased under the enlightened and reforming rule of the Tudors, which made the poetry and tragedy of the Border a magnificent inheritance that can be equalled in no other region of Britain. They also made, or helped to make, the Border character. Local patriotism was, quite literally, burnt into the people. Not a single town of the Marches but has its favourite legend of resistance to invasion; even Galashiels, new as it is, delights to display the sour plums and the rather apocryphal fourteenth-century date which are said to commemorate a successful encounter with the English, and the older burghs preserve for peaceful modern occasions their battle-cries and their songs, and banners which are believed to be the spoils of war. And with such patriotism went (and goes) an intense individual independence and pride in the past. The Borderer was forced to rely on himself and at the same time to be ready at any moment to strike a blow with or for his neighbours. He was familiar, even if he was a townsman, with lonely hills and their legends. And the impression of these things was too deep to die when wars ended with the Union of the Scots and English Crowns and reiving was at last put down with the strong hand.

But other hill countries of Scotland, after all, have had their traditions and legends which are either forgotten except by antiquarians and the makers of guide-books, or have a pitiful survival among people whose countrysides have been emptied and who live as caretakers of the playgrounds of strangers, or are precariously supported by the bounties of an unwilling State. It is true that these have not had a Walter Scott to spread the fame of their past abroad in the world or to strengthen their pride at home. But the writing up of tradition in the Scott manner can, after all, be a rather dangerous business for the countryside concerned. Scott made the Border the first great 'show district' of British tourism. And the fate of the show district is apt to be deadly.

It was the Borderers themselves who saved their land alive. Tourism should have made it a period piece, one of those museum-like regions, sometimes charming on a first visit, but always depressing in the end, where the exterior of the past has been zealously preserved (and polished) while its spirit and inner meaning are wholly dead. The Border of Scott preserved a century beyond its time would have been a land of thatched cottages and 'picturesque' tea-shops, of country houses self-consciously harking back to the peel tower, of salmon speared out of season in the name of old custom and of little towers in a carefully arrested condition of decay. For in Scott's day decay was in the air for the Borders, in spite of their energy and local pride. The great days of farming were not to last, the towns were remote from the new routes of trade, there was no coal or iron to maintain new industries. The whole region ought to have become a picturesque backwater with its only future in the exploitation of its past.

The Border has made a good deal of its past, certainly. I am told that in summer the string of cars and buses lying in the country road that leads down to Dryburgh is a mile long. Tourists troop through the extraordinary mock-Gothic galleries of Abbotsford, which prove how hard it is for literary imagination to translate itself into stone. At Darnick you may find an extremely well-preserved Border tower transformed to the show-place of a tea-garden, and carrying off the situation remarkably well. Moreover, it is true that the modern Border is a period piece. But the period it preserves is not that of Scott's youth or of the moss-troopers. It is, on the contrary, the period which was just coming to its strength elsewhere in Scotland during the last years of Sir Walter, the period when industrialism had already enriched the towns but had not yet changed the character of their people or blackened and laid waste the countrysides. In the Scottish towns of the early nineteenth century, industrialism did, of course, produce the most appalling squalor behind the new façade of prosperity, and on the modern Border as elsewhere the worst of that has been duly tidied away. But for the rest, the country is like a survival from the earlier and more hopeful industrial age, matured, polished and even given a touch of historic quaintness by the passing years.

Nature's greatest gift to the three counties was a negative one which did not display its full value till the nineteenth century. It was the denial of coal and iron. If those things had been present, the vigour of the Borderers would certainly have hastened to make the fullest possible use of them, and tradition or no tradition, Tweed and Teviot would have become the central streams of a Black Country. But since the fatal endowment was lacking, that vigour took a turn which was almost wholly beneficent. Though they had none of the appropriate resources, not even the resources of transport (for their rivers are not navigable, and the railways were long in coming to their country), the Borderers refused to be left out of the Machine Age's race for wealth. Their sole possessions were water-power and wool from the hill pastures. They combined the two so successfully that, in face of all disadvantages, they succeeded in establishing a great industry well divided between the towns and prosperous enough to revivify the countrysides in which they stood.

No one will pretend, of course, that there was or is

anything idyllic about a wool mill. The evil side of industrialism was seen on the Border as elsewhere, in crowded, bad housing, polluted streams, hideous buildings, trade cycles, and social degradation. But without industrialism there could be no life in Victorian Scotland. And life flowed back into the Border towns. Their business could not extend beyond a certain point, and so the little ancient burghs did not lose themselves in uncontrolled expansion. Even Hawick and Galashiels which industrialism swelled most noticeably, did not grow beyond the limits of neighbourliness. So far from being destroyed, the sense of the past and of local patriotism was invigorated. The cornet of the Common Riding still led out his troop of horsemen on a morning of early summer to sweep the hills round Selkirk, Peebles, or Hawick. The Hawick Callants still ceremoniously repeated in song the ancient war cry which is said (I do not know how truly) to enshrine the memories of paganism in the names of Odin and Thor. The Selkirk Suters (shoemakers no longer) still ritually denounced the treasons of the Earl of Home. Jedburgh plunged through cold February waters in the handba' game. New ceremonies of the same local sort have grown up quite spontaneously elsewhere. Galashiels has acquired a Braw Lad (and also, disarming note of modernity, a Braw Lass) who ride out annually to bring back a stone from the ancient tower of Torwoodlee or to pay homage to the descendants of Sir Walter Scott. Innerleithen, which can seldom have heard of St. Ronan before Scott published one of his less successful novels, has begun to produce, each July, its Boy Bishop. Peebles crowns its Beltane Queen—though not at Beltane.

For each town and its district these festivities, designed with no eye on the tourist, colour the year.

And outside the towns the life of the Borders has continued vigorously upon a model which still seems to belong to the spacious half-traditional days of Victorian prosperity. No doubt there have been changes on the Borders as elsewhere. There has been impoverishment, farmers have suffered from the bad years, estates have changed hands, the historic families in whose names Scott delighted have grown fewer. But Border farming is still notable. Border mansions look trim. The sports of the country are carried on for the enjoyment of people who live there and not, in the main, for rich men from the cities or from America. Only Peeblesshire, and particularly its little capital, have taken on a slightly suburban air which suggests that their real life comes rather from Edinburgh than from their own land and people.

Can it last? Can the Borders remain lively relics of what was best in Mid-Victorianism or develop, in this very different age, a new life of their own? The collapse of the last few years has hit them hard, for their main business had become international, depending on imports of wool and exports of knit-wear and of the cloth which was once called twill, but is now tweed. One may doubt how far the full prosperity of that sort of trade is ever likely to return.

And yet there is a vitality and a genuine toughness about the Border spirit, scarcely touched by the influence either of Socialism or of Big Business, which has something about it that should be promising for the future. And even the Border townsman is still close to his land. A newspaper 'investigator' noticed the other day that the Borderer out of work can (and often does) spend his time fishing hill streams, roaming the moors, or digging his garden instead of hanging about street corners like less fortunate people.

At any rate, I think the Borderers will make a fight for it when the chance offers. This is a region where even despair can go gaily. The verses of the condemned reiver which begin, 'This night is my departing night,' run in one's head, with their defiance, their resolution, and their hint of menace:

> What I have done through lack of wit
> I never, never can recall;
> I hope we're all good friends as yet,
> Good night, and joy be wi' you all.

15. RATHILLET, FIFE

Valentine

FIFE

by

J. H. WHYTE

THERE are whole English counties that have the same character throughout, and where the chief difference between this or that village or farm or pond, stream, road, spinney or meadow is one of name. There are parts of Scotland of which this is also true, but Fife, too often and inadequately described as King James's 'grey cloak,' is not one of them.

As many travellers see it, it is not a particularly attractive county. From the train there is not much which causes one to raise one's eyes from the newspaper until one emerges from dreary cuttings to front the noble estuary of the Tay, encircled by the Ochils and the Sidlaws, or, on the south side, until the train skirts the rocky coast from which Arthur's Seat can be seen rising above the reek of Edinburgh. Yet the county contains within its marches almost as great a variety of scenery as any county in Scotland. In a day's motoring one can encounter hill pastures and fishing villages, fertile straths and coal mines, the oldest University town in Scotland, and the mills which manufacture the finest damask in Europe. It is not for nothing that Fife is still as often called the 'Kingdom' as it is the County.

Even if road bridges are built across the firths of

Forth and Tay, as certainly would have been done long ago had not Westminster been so remote, Fife will still be the 'Kingdom,' smaller than in historical times, but still a peninsula. From the air it appears almost as cut off as the Black Isle from the rest of the country. Dr. Johnson voted it dull when he journeyed through it, but the trees which had been cut down in the sixteenth century to build the 'Great Michael' had not yet been replaced, and it was to be some years before long-headed landlords set about planting beeches, oaks, pines, chestnuts, planes, elms and much more excellent timber which is to-day one of the county's glories. And Johnson never saw Fife from the Lomonds, in all its present-day variety. The highest of the Lomonds—and the highest hill in Fife—is less than two thousand feet, but from its summit the thirty-odd miles from Loch Leven to St. Andrews lie stretched out like a geography lesson—hill, moor, valley, corn belt, woodland, cliffs and dunes.

Two ranges of hills, the Ochils and the Lomonds, run almost parallel and divide the county into three parts. The Ochils, skirting the northern border, drop down gently sloping braes into the Tay; the finely wooded valley of the Eden, where the river is relatively little polluted and fat worms still feed fat trout, separates them from the Lomonds. The Lomonds, on a clear day to be seen petering out in the Moors of Fife and eventually the East Neuk, are set back from the Forth, and the intervening ground is a broad, uneven surface watered by the Leven and the Ore, and rich in minerals. Fife, if the farmers of the western districts had not so strenuously resisted the encroachments of the North, would be a microcosm of Scotland. Gaelic names, such as Glencraig and Lochgelly, are to be found, as in any part of Scotland, but the language itself has not been heard in the county for many a decade.

I had hoped to master the diversity of Fife in a generalization, and from the greenstone and amygdaloid summit of the Lomonds to see its heterogeneity take on some uniformity. But no—its only uniformity is that of a peninsula, that of a land uniformly dry and practically surrounded by water. The east, topographically, does not resemble the west, nor the north the south. There is a world of difference between the small rocky bays and projecting headlands of the Forth and the flat dunes of Tentsmuir, for instance. A dangerous and mostly bleak coast fringes the Forth, right round to where the extraordinary sandstone dykes run into St. Andrews Bay—

'Tween the Isle o' May
And the links o' Tay,
Mony a ship's been cast away—

and then north of St. Andrews it becomes first sandy, then green and charmingly wooded where the Dundee business men have their houses in Newport. There is no uniformity of coastline, and when it comes to the towns, villages, farm holdings and manufacturing centres there is nothing which one could call typically 'Fife' without reservations. True, the red-tiled houses, a relic of the Flemings who came over in the Middle Ages, leap to mind whenever one hears the very name of Fife, but they and the familiar crow-stepped gables rising from, say, the harbour of Crail, to the dignified Tolbooth above, are a far cry from Auchtermuchty. From the West Law I can look beyond Falkland, at my feet, towards the towers of St. Andrews, the smoky horrors of Cowdenbeath and Lochgelly, the fringe of decaying fishing-towns in the East Neuk, the rich farmlands of the Howe, and the Cleish Hills, hiding from sight Dunfermline, where rest the bones of the Bruce.

Every phase of Scottish history is represented somewhere in the county, for prosperity has not ebbed from one part to another without leaving behind its memorials. Falkland, with its lovely Franco-Scottish palace, retains tokens of a former importance in such street-names as College Close and Parliament Square, while the phrase 'Falkland manners' recalls the genlility associated with the courts of the last three Jameses. For upwards of three centuries Falkland has lain in a backwater, and so has the once equally famous Culross, though the mines of that burgh, when they belonged to the Cistercians, used to turn out a hundred tons of salt a week. That was before the Union, when as many as 170 foreign vessels were sometimes seen in the roads. A whole string of coast towns has lost prestige almost as completely: after a long and slow struggle they succumbed to the divorce of Scotland from the Continent following the Reformation, and to the jealousy of the English merchants, which culminated in the Darien scandal, after the Union. Fife has thirteen royal burghs, as against the five of Angus, and half of them are in decay. Pennant, when he visited the 'golden fringe,' said he had never seen so many prosperous and crowded towns so close together; in the interval they have grown mushroomlike with the industrial revolution and then caught the full force of the economic blizzard, or declined from fishing-ports into quiet holiday resorts. They were places of real importance when Knox set out upon his preaching tour in 1559. He helped to destroy their beauty, as the Reformation did their importance. His hearers in the collegiate church of Crail smashed the altars, images and decorations, and made havoc of everything Popish in Anstruther; there was a large Augustinian priory belonging to the priory of St. Andrews for them to destroy at Pittenweem; and after they had gutted the parish church of St. Monance, the largest cathedral in Scotland—the only one, except for Elgin, built on an English scale—awaited them at St. Andrews. St. Andrews, however, has advanced beyond religion; and the grisly head of Patrick Hamilton that appeared in the stonework of the College Chapel tower—surely the only authenticated Protestant miracle!—is now a mere holiday-makers' raree show.

In spite of its long historical importance St. Andrews has never been the county town of Fife. But Cupar, situated right at the centre of the Eden valley, is no microcosm of the county. It is a legal and administrative capital, and serves as a rallying-place for the farming community—four-fifths of Fife is arable—but the miners of Methil, say, are seldom seen there. The country people, indeed, regard the miners, like the fishermen, as a race apart—as a proletariat whose affinities are with Lancashire or South Wales rather than with Monimail or Cults. And 'The Red Flag' is certainly as familiar a tune in the drab streets of Methil Cowdenbeath, Lochore and Lochgelly and the miserable one-storey houses around the pit-heads as 'The

Cooper o' Fife' or 'The Carles o' Dysart.' Nevertheless, among the men up from the back-shift, in the 'Gothenburgs,' at the 'whuppets,' or at one of the muddy corners where they play quoits, one finds a breath of the East Coast in the speech and all the shrewdness and warmth of feeling that ensure rural Fife a place in any collection of Scottish proverbs. These men are of the salt of the earth. The world they look out on may be over-simplified; but it is a larger place than that of the peasant. They are skilled technicians, they are several degrees more intelligent than the farm workers, and they have a spirit of fellowship, such as Lawrence found in Derbyshire, that is tending to disappear in a countryside of which the traditional economy is in decay. Agriculture survives, but its servants have lost their old way of life and have not yet entered fully into a new, as have the colliers: in Cupar one cannot look for the contemporary awareness that expresses itself, for instance, in the miners' eager questions to the W.E.A. lecturer. The yokels' tradition is slipping from them, although they cling to it—especially to its profligacy.

Some four-fifths of the population of Fife lives in towns, and the rural dwellers continue to dwindle in ratio to the urban. The spread of economic nationalism may make a difference: otherwise the tendency of the young men to make for the towns will continue. The county's future, like that of Scotland, is vague, though one thing is fairly certain: Fife will never be exploited as a tourist centre to the extent that the Highlands and the Borders have been. It has no Dunvegan, no Abbotsford, few renowned 'beauty spots'; even the multitudes of Dundee hikers who cross the Tay on summer Sundays have left little trace upon the south shore of the river, from Wormit to the ruins of Balmerino Abbey. The entire Howe is what the garden-city countryman would call 'unspoiled.' There are as many people who go to look for the fossil ganoid fish enshrined in the yellow sandstone of Dura Den as there are who picnic among its trees—a mere handful. Leslie Hunter, who painted only a few miles away, was described to me as '*the* man who painted. . . .' The literary associations, too, are chiefly fifteenth-, sixteenth- and seventeenth-century, and not nineteenth, as in the Highlands and the Borders. Lindsay is still one of the best known names in the 'Kingdom': the home of Sir David, whose 'Satire of the Three Estates' was performed before the court of James V, stood at the Mount, near Cupar, while Pitscottie, three miles west of the town, calls to mind the best-written history of Scotland. A few miles away stands Scotstarvit Tower, the home of worthy Sir John Scott, the author of *The Staggering State of Scottish Statesmen*, who was known to continental scholars as a munificent patron of literature; there also Drummond of Hawthornden wrote the *Midden-Fecht*. . . . We are strong on history, for Scotland is a backward-looking country.

I had not stood for five minutes on the old bridge at Ceres before being told that the men of the village had marched across it on their way to Bannockburn, and that Archbishop Sharp's coach lumbered over it on his way to Magus Moor. Also, that Ceres is named after the goddess of fertility, and in the next instant—for Fifers are a contradictory lot—that it is named after no Greek goddess, but after St. Cyr, the patron saint of pre-Reformation days. But one can forgive the 'buddies' their long tales when recompensed by the beauties of the Ceres landscape, which Leslie Hunter recorded with the force of genius. The lyrical quality in him at its strongest, his eyes opened by the triumphs of the post-impressionists, Hunter turned from Provençe to the roofs of Ceres parish, its lush green fields and rich foliage for the subjects of some of his finest works. The crow-stepped gables of Pittenweem and Anstruther are the most charming features of Fife only if one does not know the tiled roofs of Ceres and its neighbouring parishes. Ceres itself lies right in the heart of Fife, encircled by low hills, protected from the winds, sleepy and comfortable. There are parts of Fife, almost within sight where crops are snatched from the teeth of the elements—

> Laddedie, Radernie, Lathockar and Lathone,
> Ye may saw wi' gloves off and shear wi' gloves on—

but here the land undulates from a mere hundred to two hundred feet. As luck would have it, there were enough limestone quarries in the parish to facilitate the reclamation of moss and moor; if, after a rainstorm, the burn rises with surprising suddenness, that is because the surrounding deep cold earth is so well drained. The visitor who has taken his ideas of central Fife from the *Journey to the Hebrides* would be surprised by the ample woods around Ceres and the magnificent beech avenues in the parks of the Howe.

In spite of the many buses which pass through the Howe, it is still fairly self-contained; there is little coming and going between it and the fishing towns of the Forth, and Cupar and St. Andrews are still the destination of most of the youths on a Saturday night. The Fifers' St. Andrews has almost disappeared in the fashionable St. Andrews of the golfers. The three main streets of the town, built seventy feet wide to allow of ecclesiastical processions, run to the gates of the Cathedral, but in the summer the crowds are all making in the opposite direction to the links, and the voices are alien. There is a path, worn through the grass in the cathedral graveyard leading to the memorial stone of Tom Morris; the tombstones of Professor Adam Ferguson, with its grandiose inscription and the memorable epitaph to Dr. Samuel Rutherford have yet to be discovered. How many of the thousands of visitors to St. Andrews know of Samuel Rutherford's achievements?

> Most orthodox he was and sound
> And many errors did confound.
> For Scotland's King and Scotland's cause
> And Zion's covenanted laws
> Most earnestly he did contend
> Until his time was at an end
> And then he won to the full fruition
> Of that which he had seen in vision.

St. Andrews is a unique town. It contains not only a University, but the R. and A., and St. Leonard's School as well, within the ancient city walls; it is a dwindling fishing port, a miniature Bath, and the largest seaside resort in Fife. After being as quiet as the grave for the greater part of the year, it teems in summer with people bent on nothing but enjoyment. Suddenly one is made aware of brown legs and arms and bright frocks and a general air of gaiety, instead of the tweeds and dogs and the old-fashioned hats and the bicycles with shopping-baskets which greet one during the rest of the year. By July most of the citizens, except for the caddies, boatmen, shopkeepers and landladies, have disappeared. The University is 'down,' and the girls of St. Leonard's are looking forward to playing cricket with their brothers instead of with each other. A warm, dry summer—and most summers in St. Andrews are like that—brings cart-loads of light-hearted people, who have little thought for the ghosts who frequent Andrew Lang's 'cold, grey city by the sea.' The St. Andrews of the Kate Kennedy Procession is pushed into the background. And yet for a few days the traditional St. Andrews re-asserts itself, in the middle of the holiday season, at the time of the Lammas Fair. The April and November fairs are no more, but in the second week of August booths and merry-go-rounds are crowded together in Market Street and South Street, and the town is given up to noise and hilarity, as in the past. The push-penny merchants are more numerous, perhaps; the merry-go-rounds, more alarmingly efficient, go round to jazz tunes; the large bilious-looking pink sugar hearts are scarcely so much to the fore; the fair, however, is still a great occasion, a great outing for the country folk, who swarm into the town on buses and bicycles, shy at aunt-sallies and coco-nuts with a skill and savagery which amaze the gentler holiday-makers, get roaring drunk, dance reels to a pipe band behind the town kirk, make violent love, and are disgustingly sick—very much in the manner of a century ago.

Traditionally, the Scot of the East Coast is racy of the soil. Lewis Grassic Gibbon in his novels did not hesitate to show this. This lusty vigour is commonly assumed to be due to hard living in a boisterous, rude climate; but racial and religious history surely plays its part. In any case, Fife has not so harsh a climate as to produce a race of Berserks. The luscious green landscape one finds in Galloway is confined to a few districts, such as Ceres; nor are there the soft, birch-clad slopes of southern Perthshire; still less the warm air that enables palms to flourish in the peninsulas of Argyllshire; but we enjoy spring weather before the gowk storm marks the coming of the cuckoo in the middle of April, and, with a little luck, we are sun-bathing by June. Although winter lingers along the northern slopes of the Lomonds and people are curling at Cupar when there is a thaw in Glasgow, the North Sea exercises a moderating influence on the county as a whole. In its numberless small dens carrying streams down to the sea—every other one known as Spinkie Den—the spinks can be gathered weeks before Easter, even in a hard year. In the Howe, just after the Coos' Quak' in May—the cold spell about the turn of the month which makes the cows shiver—I have found watercress already showing white along the Eden's bank, and lady's smock and ragged robin, marsh marigold, comfrey, and the cheerful blue of brooklime. They appeared in England only a week or two earlier.

That day, a company of field naturalists, from Dundee most probably, was busy among the flowers. I have seen them, too, on Tentsmuir—where the Danes are said to have settled, but which is now given over to heath and Forestry Commission plantations—poking at the strange 'shell mounds,' peering at bog pimpernel and Baltic rushes, happy as schoolboys, in the harmless company of terns and eider ducks. They are pleasant creatures—and very Scottish, painstaking and pedantic, studying nature scientifically and looking to it neither for a religion nor a philosophy. Scotland is fortunately free of those pestilential post-Wordsworthians whom one finds in the Lake District, in the New Forest, in all the more favoured parts of England where two or three hikers are gathered together. The Scotsman's attachment to the country is patriotic rather than pantheistic, and Scotland has yet to throw up a Jefferies or a Hudson. Fife is practically virgin soil for the writer doing his purple prose for the morning paper.

Yet I can recall one by no means humble emulator of Jefferies who had strayed into Fife, and whom I found sitting beside me on the top of Drumcarro Craig—the Craig is a jagged little hill, over seven hundred feet in height, four miles inland from St. Andrews. From its top we saw the Bell Rock lighthouse, just on the horizon; surf breaking on the banks of Tay was a reminder of how treacherous an estuary it is; north beyond Dundee were the Sidlaws and behind them the Grampians, with Lochnagar visible almost fifty miles away, and to the west, Ben-y-Ghlo, Ben Vrackie, Schiehallion, Ben Lawers, Ben Vorlich and Ben Ledi—in no part of Scotland is one far from the hills. The young man at my side was sucking in the scene in such a state of exaltation that we might have been on a peak in Darien; during the tense silence I stole a glance at the book which lay with his sandwiches. He handed it to me, and where it fell open my eyes lit on this: 'Every blade of grass, each leaf, each separate floret and petal, is an inscription speaking of *hope*. Consider the grasses and the oaks, the swallows, the sweet blue butterfly—they are one and all a sign and token shewing before our eyes earth made into life, so that my hope becomes as broad as the horizon afar, reiterated by every leaf, sung on every bough.' Fascinated by this extraordinary stuff, I read on. But the slim volume's owner was by this time telling me how well Mr. Jefferies wrote and how impressive was Nature and how particularly fine was the hill. It was impossible to resist telling him in return what good road metal the Craig made, and that, if he were walking far, he would no doubt come across some of it; it was basaltic; the columns were pentagonal; there they were, down there, at an angle of thirty degrees. . . . Before I was left in peace I had shown him what was Dactylis glomerata and Phalaris arundinacea, I had told him about ground rents and the law of trespass, how the old dykes which he had been admiring were too low when black-faced sheep were introduced and what a damned nuisance the barbed wire is to the Hunt. . . . Facts, hard, dry facts are the best protection from the mystagogue.

It was enough for me that the day was fine, with only a light brown haze above Dundee—the smoke from which Dundee business men wisely flee to Fife. Someone was throwing turnips into an empty cart; there was the pleasant smell of burning green twigs; a dog barked, but not so insistently as to make one wonder why; instead, I asked myself what they were to plant next year instead of the oats yonder. The links of St. Andrews, separated from the bluest of seas by a faint, straw-coloured strip of sand, where I hoped to bathe later in the afternoon, struck me as an excellent improvement on the nature in which my unwanted companion was content merely to wallow. An aeroplane rose from Leuchars, a silvery blur so long as the sun caught its wings, and then set off towards Largo Law. Fife was looking its best. To think that on the other side of the Lomonds, unemployed miners were lounging about the street corners of Lochore and Lochgelly, awaiting the results of the three o'clock; erstwhile fishermen in St. Andrews Bay were eking out a living by taking children for sixpenny motor-boat runs to the Spindle Rock; and the crop at my feet, I had just been told, would be sold at a loss. . . . If we were to pull through, it would need the firmest resolve to exploit to the full all our human resources, all the wealth of land and sea. My unwanted nature-worshipper, as he told me how he loved 'getting away from things,' seemed even more unreal than most of his kind.

Country people themselves are not given to such 'nature baths,' and the Fifers are certainly no exception. A garden is more to them than Nature, and they prefer their own humanized landscape to the homeless wastes of the Highlands. They are a renownedly hard-headed people, as a host of anecdotes testifies. The decay of the once prosperous coast towns has not dulled the native wit of the people; certain qualities of shrewdness characterize the whole peninsula. The county is not one 'natural region,' but a dozen, yet the worker from the heavy rolling farmlands, mine- and mill-worker, the fisherman living on parish relief in one of the lovely old houses with rosy pantiles and an outside stone staircase—all are Fifers. They all look at both sides of a penny, speak in voices that rise at the end of each phrase, work hard when they get the chance, and have that quick homely kindliness that redeems the otherwise too harsh Scottish temperament. Their independence is a byword. For although Fife is famous for its fine mansions and owes much of its beauty to their parks, it has always had a remarkable number of small lairds, and small farms are dotted across practically the entire county—a state of affairs which developed in the countrymen those qualities of self-reliance found in the burghers. They drive a hard bargain, but they give good value. And perhaps some day they will restore the 'Kingdom' to its old position in the cultural and economic life of Scotland. There is at least hope for them. Kirkcaldy is less proud than it once was of having produced Adam Smith.